The Reader
the Text
the Poem

THE TRANSACTIONAL

THEORY

OF THE LITERARY WORK

Louise M. Rosenblatt

·

Southern Illinois University Press

Carbondale and Edwardsville

Feffer & Simons, Inc.

London and Amsterdam

Library of Congress Cataloging in Publication Data

Rosenblatt, Louise Michelle.
  The reader, the text, the poem.

  Includes bibliographical references and index.
  1. Literature—Philosophy. 2. Criticism.
3. Reading.   I. Title.
PN45.R587   801'.95   78-16335
ISBN 0-8093-0883-5

To Sidney Ratner

CONTENTS

PREFACE

*T*HE premise of this book is that a text, once it leaves its author's hands, is simply paper and ink until a reader evokes from it a literary work—sometimes, even, a literary work of art. It might seem, therefore, that I should allow this text to shift for itself. If it were being offered as a work of art, I should indeed honor that inference. But since the following pages call for what I shall later define as "efferent" reading, I believe it not inconsistent to offer the customary preface, with the suggestion, however, that some may prefer to read it after the final chapter.

This book centers, then, on the reader's contribution in the two-way, "transactional" relationship with the text. Critics and literary theorists, who have traditionally lavished attention on authors and texts, have only recently begun to recognize the reader. A few have reacted to the point of insisting on the predominance of the reader's personality. Others focus on the reader's response—but to the literary work of art still assumed to exist "out there" in the text. What in fact does the reader respond to? What does he interpret? Such questions lead me in the following pages to discriminate between the reader's activities in "efferent" and in "aesthetic reading."

This cardinal distinction generates new light on the multidimensional process of evoking a poem and on the dynamic "mode of existence" of the literary work of art. Analysis of both the openness and the constraint offered by the text clarifies its complex role in the transaction with the reader. The theoretical foundation is thus laid for dealing with such persistent and controversial problems as validity in interpretation, criteria of evaluation, and the relation between literary criticism and other disciplines.

The views set forth here have been tested and tempered by over forty years of observing and reflecting on readers' involvements with texts ranging from Chaucer and Shakespeare to Joyce and Wallace Stevens. For two decades, in a course on "Criticism and the Literary Experience," I was able to pursue the study systematically. I presented texts—many of them repeated year after year—to graduate and undergraduate students, who were often helped to develop a measure of self-criticism before their study of the critical canon from Plato to Eliot and beyond. A by-product for me was the opportunity, through various techniques, to gather evidence of what went on during their reading. I was able to discover continuities and differences in response with changing student populations and changing mores, and to analyze the processes and patterns that manifested themselves in the actual movement toward an interpretation. My aim was to immerse myself in a rich source of insights, not merely to accumulate a body of codified data. What follows, therefore, is a distillation of my observations, reflections, and reading.

As contemporary philosophers remind us, the observer inevitably enters into his observations: although I stress the inductive groundwork, obviously I brought to these inquiries various assumptions and hypotheses to be either supported or discarded. Further, strict training in the historical and critical disciplines of literary scholarship had established in me habits of thought from some of which I needed to be liberated. Perhaps this book can perform a similar service for others, not merely by articulating a particular set of intellectual theses but by inducing a new way of thinking about literary works of art.

With one exception already alluded to, I have avoided the current tendency to create new terminology. Citations also have been kept to a minimum; a list of the works consulted over the years, or even those to which I am in some way indebted, beyond the ones mentioned in the notes, would be excessively long. I shall try simply to suggest the intellectual matrix within which the transactional theory of the literary work has evolved.

As I look back on a long scholarly career, I become aware of a continuing need to affirm and to reconcile two often opposed positions, phrased, in earliest terms, as a Keatsian sense of the unique values of art, on the one hand, and, on the other, a Shelleyan feeling for its social origins and social impact. My first book, *L'Idée de l'art pour l'art dans la littérature anglaise* (Paris, 1931), written for the doctorate in comparative literature at the Sorbonne, was a study of the theories of art for art's sake developed by nineteenth-century English and French writers to combat the pressures of an uncomprehending or hostile society. In the concluding pages, I stated the need for a public of readers able "to participate fully in the poetic experience"—readers able to provide a nurturing, free environment for poets and other artists of the word. Their texts possess, I believed, the highest potentialities for bringing the whole human personality, as Coleridge had said, "into activity." Here already was the germ of an increasingly intense preoccupation with the importance, to the arts and to society, of the education of readers of literature.

My second book, *Literature as Exploration* (1938), confronted this problem directly, setting forth a philosophy of the teaching of literature—the outgrowth mainly of my experience in teaching English and comparative literature at Barnard College. The book also reflected work with Franz Boas and Ruth Benedict in the graduate department of anthropology at Columbia University. By that time, the writings of William James, C. S. Peirce, George Santayana, and John Dewey had provided a philosophic base for reconciling my aesthetic and social commitments. Dewey's *Art as Experience* especially left its mark, perhaps more through its vision of aesthetic values woven into the texture of the daily life of human beings than its specific treatment of the literary arts.

Hence, in *Literature as Exploration* I sketched a theory of the literary experience as the springboard for a philosophy of teaching. As early as 1938, I wrote: "There is no such thing as a generic reader or a generic literary work. . . . The reading of any work of literature is, of necessity, an individual and unique occurrence involving the mind and emotions of a particular reader." Alan C. Purves and Richard Beach, in *Literature and the Reader* (1972), begin with I. A. Richards's seminal work, *Practical Criticism*, which I had cited in 1931. They write: "Rosenblatt added to Richards' concentration on analyses of readers' comments an emphasis both on the process by which what the reader brings to the text interacts with its special character . . . and on the teaching process. This provided the theoretical frameworks or hypotheses for a number of studies of response, bibliotherapy, and teaching methods." The studies of readers' responses, they report, "tend to support the transactional theory." Space permits mention here only of James R. Squire's early analysis of adolescent readers' responses during their reading of short stories. These citations may show the relationship between the earlier book (a second edition of which was published in 1968—1970 in London— and a third, in 1976) and the present one. Eschewing further educational themes, I concentrate on presenting a matured and more fully developed theory of the literary work of art and the implications for criticism.

The transactional approach has withstood the challenges and has incorporated the sustenance brought by the intervening years. During World War II, for example, when I found myself associate chief of the Western European Section of the Bureau of Overseas Intelligence (OWI), the problem of eliciting meaning from texts took the form of propaganda analysis and the derivation of economic, social, and political information from the Nazi-dominated media. As a result, I became keenly aware of the differences between "intuitive reading" and such techniques as content analysis; this contrast had repercussions in my later thinking about critical method and critical theory.

After the initially favorable response to my approach, postwar, post-Sputnik intellectualism fostered the extraordinary dominance of the New Critics in university and critical circles. My research on their aesthetic forebears had prepared me to sympathize with their concern for formal values and to admire their analytic skills. Their practice was always better than their theories. I rejected the notion of the poem-as-object, and the neglect of both author and reader, bred by their point of view. I continued to espouse the transactional view, as a member of various educational commissions, in my classes and in articles. Allies peristed, mainly among those facing the educational needs of a democracy in the schools and in the preparation of teachers. Since I had often seemed a lone voice acclaiming the reader, the second edition of *Literature as Exploration* in 1968 was interpreted by some as evidence of the end of the hegemony of the New Criticism and as a sign of the rediscovery of the reader. Ironically, since I was not caught in the pendulum-swing disillusionment with the New Critics, the transactional theory expounded here repudiates recent efforts to make the reader all-important.

When the structural and transformational schools of linguistics emerged, my work in linguistics with Franz Boas had prepared me to be receptive, though it became apparent that they offered less than had been expected for those concerned with the actual practice of the arts of language. Semantics, from Ogden and Richards's *The Meaning of Meaning* on, has seemed more relevant, although not very successful in treatment of the aesthetic manifestations of language. As I indicate later, psycholinguistics, sociolinguistics, and a broadly conceived semiology offer new possibilities.

Concern with education enforced continuing attention to work in the social sciences and especially to those in psychology, such as Piaget and Bruner, who were studying the developmental process. Traces of various influences—often in highly selective form—must be apparent in the following pages: the Gestaltists, especially Wertheimer on productive thinking; the topologists, especially Kurt Lewin; and certainly Freud, despite his too-rigid codification of personality structure and symbolic expression, in contrast to the more congenial approaches, say, of Gordon Allport or Floyd Allport.

The eclecticism suggested by these remarks underlines the fact that I am not presenting a psychology of literature, nor am I applying a particular set of psychological doctrines—such as the psychoanalytic formulae—to reading. At this point when fundamental questions, from the acquisition of language, to the relations of the hemispheres of the brain, are still so controversial, the exclusive application of a set of psychological doctrines may become reductive. The transactional psychology based on the Ames-Cantril experiments on perception seems valuable to some extent precisely because of its openness. The criterion is whether concepts of this, or any other,

Preface

discipline provide tools for creating a model of the individual man and woman's lived-through evocation of literary works.

It is difficult to assess the residue of successive waves of philosophical thought. An important source of enlightenment has been the interdisciplinary Conference on Methods in Philosophy and the Sciences; I was a member of its executive committee for some years, and its secretary the year of the William James centenary program. I recall the clarifying effect of a negative reaction to logical positivism, and my excitement over the works of thinkers as diverse as Whitehead, Russell, Wittgenstein and the ordinary language philosophers, especially Gilbert Ryle, John Austin, and John Searle. The phenomenologists did not arouse my interest, perhaps because Peirce, Dewey, and James (to whom Husserl owed inspiration) had already anticipated for me whatever seemed pertinent to the literary experience—and without the uncongenial idealist framework. Existentialism strengthened certain of my emphases, though mainly through the early literary works of Malraux and Sartre. From an early point on, the selective process has been guided by a Deweyan anti-dualism, a sense of the human being in a reciprocal relationship with the natural and social environment. When the philosophical correspondence of John Dewey and Arthur F. Bentley was published, I was amused to discover that in a letter of April 20, 1950, Bentley had told Dewey that I was "all excited about application of *Knowing and the Known* to literature." Their book provided my transactional teminology.

Some of the ideas developed more fully here have appeared in "The Poem as Event," in *College English* (Nov. 1964); "A Way of Happening," in the *Educational Record* (Summer 1968); and "Toward a Transactional Theory of Reading," in the *Journal of Reading Behavior* (Winter 1969).

My gratitude goes out to the hundreds—more accurately, thousands—of readers who have shared with me their evocations of literary works from texts. My hearty thanks, too, to Mitchell A. Leaska, of New York University, James R. Squire, former executive secretary of the National Council of Teachers of English, Erwin Steinberg, of Carnegie Mellon University, and James E. Miller, Jr., of the University of Chicago, all of whom kindly read the manuscript. Responsibility for its lacks remains, of course, my own. The dedication to my husband, Sidney Ratner, historian and philosopher, inadequately symbolizes a most important transactional relationship.

L.M.R.

Princeton, New Jersey
March 1978

The Reader, the Text, the Poem

1

THE

INVISIBLE

READER

*T*HE long history of the theory of literature, from Plato to the present, records certain well-known shifts of emphasis. In surveying these changes, I find it helpful to visualize a little scene: on a darkened stage I see the figures of the author and the reader, with the book—the text of the poem or play or novel—between them. The spotlight focuses on one of them so brightly that the others fade into practical invisibility. Throughout the centuries, it becomes apparent, usually either the book or the author has received major illumination. The reader has tended to remain in shadow, taken for granted, to all intents and purposes invisible. Like Ralph Ellison's hero, the reader might say, "I am invisible, understand, simply because people refuse to see me."[1] Here or there a theoretician may start to take him seriously, and the spotlight may seem from time to time to hover over him, but actually he has never for long held the center of attention.

Of course, both author and reader were mainly taken for granted, relegated to the periphery of vision, during the many centuries when classical and neoclassical ideas prevailed in one or another form. The poet's personality, his motives for writing, the process by which he produced his work, the conditions under which it was written, were given little attention. The focus was on the literary work as a mirroring of "reality": the primary concern was the relation between the work and that universe of orderly and permanent forms of which it was to some (debated) degree an imitation or reflection.

Then, toward the end of the eighteenth century, the poet, the author, emerges into effulgent visibility. In the post-Lockean philosophic climate, with the waning of confidence in an ordered reality behind the world of appearances, the emphasis shifts to the poet and the poet's sensibility. Both Wordsworth and Coleridge, for example, find the question, What is poetry? practically interchangeable with the question, What is a poet? The traditional formulation is that the mimetic view gave way to the view of art as expression. The relationship between the poet and his work was primary. Hence the literary work, viewed as embodying the personality and life of the author, came often to be treated mainly as a document in the biography and times of the author, or as a document in the history of literary movements. Even those who seemed to continue the concern for reality admitted ultimately the preeminence of the author. Did not even the naturalist, Zola, persist in phrasing the work of art as "un coin de la création vu à travers un tempérament"?[2]

Thus the reader was left to play the role of invisible eavesdropper. John Stuart Mill, for example, carried the expressive theory to its logical conclusion, freeing the poet from even the duty of seeking to communicate to a reader: Mill declared poetry to be "of the nature of soliloquy," a soliloquy "overheard."[3] We need think only of Yeats's personal system of symbols or the recent poets who often merit the rubric, "poets talking to themselves," to see how prophetic was Mill's dictum. When an emerging industrial society placed unwelcome social and moral limitations on the writer, this view of the primacy of poetic creation and its implicit disregard of the reader permitted recourse to the battle cry of "art for art's sake."[4]

Some readers found their escape from this limbo by taking over the prerogatives of the poet. Seeking to express his own personality through "the adventures of [his] soul among masterpieces,"[5] the impressionist critic's role as a reader became blurred, merged into that of the artist.

The twentieth-century reaction against the obsession with the poet and his emotions brought no aid—on the contrary, even more unrelenting invisibility—to the reader. I. A. Richards, drawing on both scientific and literary sources of inspiration in his seminal works, had indeed studied the performance of readers.[6] The formalist critics, who set the dominant critical tone in the midcentury, rejected this interest and followed Richards mainly in developing their method of close literary analysis. But they insisted on "the work itself" as a self-contained pattern of words, an autonomous structure of literary devices. The art-for-art's-sake claim for the autonomy of the artist was translated into the autonomy of the work of art itself. The critics' ideal was to analyze the work apart from "extrinsic" concerns, and that meant apart from both poet and reader. To the more doctrinaire, concern with the reader seemed to be linked with brash betrayals of the integrity of the work.[7]

But surely, it will be objected—and I have already conceded—the reader was not totally ignored during all those centuries. Is he not indeed recognized from the very beginning? When Plato graciously but firmly excluded poets from his ideal Republic, was it not because he feared the morally deleterious effect of poetry on the audience? Did not Aristotle implicitly counter this by making a positive cathartic effect on the audience one of the criteria of tragedy—"through pity and fear effecting the proper purgation of these emotions"? Did not Horace provide the doctrine that has been echoed through the centuries—that the aim of poetry should be "to teach and to delight" the reader? Was not this a continuing view of many even during the flowering of Romanticism, as Shelley's "Defence of Poetry" so eloquently demonstrates? Was it not the didactic, moralistic concern of the Victorians for the reader that produced the art-for-art's-sake reaction? Have not all the efforts at censorship through the ages testified to anxiety about the reader? To all such questions, the answer is, of course, yes. But these do not invalidate my contention that the reader was mainly invisible.

Although the reader is sometimes glimpsed, the spotlight does not focus on him in an active role. The theoretical discussion turns quickly—as in Aristotle's *Poetics* or Horace's *Epistles*—away from the reader to the means of producing the required effects; that is, to

3

what aspects of life the text must or must not treat, what technical strategems the author should employ, or what qualities of vision he should possess.

Emphasis on feeling and creativity might especially have been expected to establish a unique role for the reader. Edward Gibbon was delighted to learn from Longinus "a new kind of criticism"—he told his own feelings on reading Homer so vividly as to communicate them![8] But even Longinus focuses mainly on analysis of the elements in a text that might produce a noble or "sublime" style. The Romantics' preoccupation with "the overflow of powerful feeling" did lead to some awareness of the reader—as in various statements of, for example, Wordsworth, Coleridge, and Poe. Here, too, as I have already suggested, attention soon moved back to the poet or to the text he produced. And the romantic ethos led ultimately to the kind of impressionistic effort usually associated with Walter Pater, whose critical writings themselves aspire to be works of art.

As we survey the field of literary theory, then, the reader is often mentioned, but is not given the center of the stage. The reason is simple; the reader is usually cast as a passive recipient, whether for good or ill, of the impact of the work. He is still, in a sense, invisible, even when he is treated as a member of something referred to under such collective rubrics as "the audience" or "the reading public." Thus readers are viewed mainly en masse, as in studies of Shakespeare's audience, or accounts of the emergence of the middle-class reading public in the eighteenth century, or analyses of categories of fiction and their respective types of readers in the twentieth century. The individual reader has seldom been acknowledged as carrying on his own special and peculiar activities. There is a great difference between the concept of the reader as a passive "audience" and the kind of visibility that I claim for the reader.

Within the past few years, the spotlight has started to move in the direction of the reader. Sometimes the reaction has been more against the social-political implications of the New Criticism than against its aesthetic theory. Sometimes the rehabilitation of the reader takes the form of a rather extreme subjectivism or Freudianism. Thus, some, preoccupied with the author's text, have seen the reader as a tabula rasa, receiving the imprint of "the poem." Others, in reaction, see the text as empty, awaiting the content brought by the reader. Rejecting both of these extremes, the discussion that follows begins with readers encountering a text and pro-

4

ceeds to meet the basic questions that flow from this event. The purpose will be to admit into the limelight the whole scene—author, text, and reader. We shall be especially concerned with the member of the cast who has hitherto been neglected—the reader.

2

THE POEM

AS EVENT

$\mathscr{T}$HE nature of the reader's role may best be approached inductively, by looking at readers as they encounter an unfamiliar text. I shall draw on one of the hundreds of instances in which, during the past twenty-five years, I have studied the process by which readers arrive at an interpretation. A group of men and women, graduate students in English, were handed a text. They were told that they were to remain anonymous, and that they should start writing as soon as possible after beginning to read. They were not asked to introspect *about* what they were doing, but simply to jot down whatever came to them.

This differed from the procedure reported in I. A. Richards's pioneer study, *Practical Criticism*, in which readers' comments represent the end results of repeated readings and reflections on a text over the course of a week. My aim was rather to discover the paths by which these students approached even a tentative first interpretation. The text had no author's name or other identification. Knowing the author and prior acquaintance with his work may speed up the process, but I was interested in what happens when the reader has to start from scratch with the text on the page.

Although the readers did not note their very first responses, they indicated at least some of the early ones. Their notes turned out to be reports of various stages in a developing process. I shall cite some of the kinds of responses and stages manifested as they moved toward an interpretation of the following quatrain by Robert Frost.

It Bids Pretty Fair

> The play seems out for an almost infinite run.
> Don't mind a little thing like the actors fighting.
> The only thing I worry about is the sun.
> We'll be all right if nothing goes wrong with the lighting.[1]

Two examples of the opening remarks in the commentaries reflect an initial confusion. One writes, "Upon reading . . . the first time, I couldn't make any sense out of it." Another comments, "I am torn between trying to put these sentences together in order to evoke one impression, and taking each as an individual entity, or perhaps even taking each as a number of word pictures and allowing myself to be borne away on whatever current each of them chooses to take me."

Other readers evidently waited until they had passed this stage before jotting down such typical notes as the following: "This seems to me to be bits of conversation between people who are interested in movie-making or a legitimate play." "Sounds as if it could be producer of a play giving encouragement to backers." "Perhaps the director is writing to the producer."

These notes reflect, one might say, a rudimentary literary response, yet they already represent a very high level of organization. There had clearly been added a groping toward a framework into which to fit the meanings of the individual words and sentences. Who is speaking? Under what circumstances? To whom? are questions already assumed in these first tentative comments.

The following reader reveals another step or kind of awareness; it starts like the others, but quickly makes articulate the realization that this text is to be read as a poem: "This seems to be bits of conversation between people who are interested in movie making or a

7

legitimate play. On second thought, the rhymes show it is a poem." This led to a rereading of the text for the purpose of paying attention to rhythm; the lines had evidently first been read as simply conversation, or an interchange between two speakers, and hence with no effort to sense a rhythmic pattern or a structure.

One reader focused initially on the second line: "At first, it seemed a somewhat cynical statement about the nature of the theatre (my own experiences somehow forcing me mainly to envision the squabbling)." This reader later explained that he was leading man in an amateur play then in rehearsal and that he had been having trouble with a temperamental leading lady.

Some of the readers became involved with ideas called up by the first two lines, and neglected the rest: "These brief thoughts might have been culled from a conversation in which an apprehensive director is trying to placate an indifferent producer. . . . [And then the reader goes off on a chain of associations drawn, evidently, from knowledge about the theatre]: During the last rehearsal before the play has its tryout in Philadelphia or New Haven, at this point nerves are raw, and the persons that were once ingratiating now seem to own ferocious tempers."

But for most readers, the third line, with its reference to the sun, created the necessity for a revision of the tentative response to the first two lines. In comment after comment, there occurs a phrase such as "on second thought," "a second look," "another idea." One reader spells out the problem: "The third line seems most confusing. If I stick to my theory of producer talking to backers it really makes no sense."

Many of the readers, having called up such a vivid notion of a director or producer talking about a play, immediately attempted to adapt this to a situation in which there might reasonably be a concern about the sun: "I am reminded of the Elizabethan theatre open to the skies, which indeed was dependent upon the sun (good weather)." "Seems to be about life in a summer stock theatre. Is it a summer theatre? But then there would be worry about the rain, rather than the sun."

Within the brief time given for reading and comment, a number of the readers never freed themselves from the problem of finding such a practical explanation for a play's success being dependent on the sun. One comment ends on this realization: "I'm afraid this is a very literal reading."

8

Others more quickly became aware of the need for another approach: "However, after a moment or two, the implied stage begins clearly to represent the world, and the actors, the world's population." "On second thought, play metaphor—'all the world's a stage'—Life goes on in spite of quarreling, but it won't if the 'lighting' (moral? spiritual?) fails—what does the 'sun' mean? Outside performance? Technical term for stage light? Anyway, war, disagreement, etc., don't matter so much—so long as we still have the 'light' (sun—source of light—nature? God?)."

Several readers were alerted, evidently, by the contrast between the word "infinite" and the colloquial tone of the rest of the line. When they were led to wonder about the kind of play for which the sun provides lighting, the notion of infinity evidently had prepared them to think of the great drama being played out through the ages by mankind on this planet. Some, in addition, felt it necessary to pack in as much symbolism as possible and tried to find another level of meaning for "the sun" as well.

A few readers sensed the Olympian remoteness of the "I" who could find it possible to view man's life on this planet in the light, almost, of eternity, and who was thus able to see as "little things" such momentous episodes as wars.

The following illustrates the range covered in one commentary: "Sounds as if it could be producer of a play giving encouragement to backers. . . . I just got another idea: First line—the world will always be here. Second line—there will always be fighting. We shouldn't worry too much about it. Third line—worries about H bomb." Here we see also how the reader's latent fears of an atomic catastrophe were activated by the reference to "worry" about the sun. Others had a similar association, but thought in more general terms, about "the work of scientists" and its dangers.

For another reader, the reference to something happening to the sun awakened a recollection of Burns's "Till a' the seas gang dry" as an image of boundless time. This led to a feeling that the person's "worry" was ironic, a belittling of human conflicts when viewed against the background of the life of the sun.

Recall that we are not here concerned with evaluating the responses to this text, since these commentaries were not presented as finished interpretations. The reports quoted are rather to be considered notations of points in the ongoing process during which the reader sought to arrive at an interpretation of the quatrain. The readers had been invited to make articulate the very stages that are often ignored or forgotten by the time a satisfactory reading has been completed. The poem was selected because it did not yield too readily to such automatic assimilation. The author's name was omitted for the same reason. The interest of these notes (and of other such studies of readers' responses that I have carried on for decades) lies in the fact that they do give us some clues as to what goes on during the active relationship between reader and text. It is as though we are reconstructing a slow-motion picture from "stills" of various moments in the film. The notes indicate where the readers are at that stage. For our present purposes, we need not worry about how completely the complex process has been revealed. Enough emerges from even these few responses to Frost's quatrain to give concreteness to some general comments on the reading process.[2]

First of all, each reader was active. He was not a blank tape registering a ready-made message. He was actively involved in building up a poem for himself out of his responses to the text. He had to draw on his past experiences with the verbal symbols. He had to select from the various alternative referents that occurred to him. To do this, he had to find some context within which these referents could be related. He sometimes found it necessary to reinterpret earlier parts of the text in the light of later parts. Actually, he had not fully read the first line until he had read the last, and interrelated them. There was a kind of shuttling back and forth as one or another synthesizing element—a context, a persona, a level of meaning—suggested itself to him.

Moreover, we see that the reader was not only paying attention to what the words pointed to in the external world, to their referents; he was also paying attention to the images, feelings, attitudes, associations, and ideas that the words and their referents evoked in him. The effort to fix on a kind of play that would depend on the sun seems to have generated what looks like a certain amount of reasoning. Actually, the notes show that this was usually an aspect of the effort to fuse both ideas and feelings, associations and attitudes that had been called forth. For example, the sense of the play as metaphoric for the life of mankind, and the sun as suggesting the backdrop of space and time against which to view it, seems to have been arrived at largely by paying attention to qualities of feeling due to such things as the images or the qualities of tone created by the diction. Notions of mankind as a whole, of war, or of astronomical time, were part of the readers' contribution to the "meaning" that evidently arose in this way.

The reader's attention to the text activates certain elements in his past experience—external reference, internal response—that have become linked with the verbal symbols. Meaning will emerge from a network of relationships among the things symbolized *as he senses them*. The symbols point to these sensations, images, objects, ideas, relationships, with the particular associations or feeling-tones created by his past experiences with them in actual life or in literature. The selection and organization of responses to some degree hinge on the assumptions, the expectations, or sense of possible structures, that he brings out of the stream of his life. Thus built into the raw material of the literary process itself is the particular world of the reader.

But the text may also lead him to be critical of those prior assumptions and associations—as was the reader with too vivid a recollection of an actor's quarrel. He may discover that he had projected on the text elements of his past experience not relevant to it, and which are not susceptible of coherent incorporation into it. Or he may have failed for various reasons to respond at all to some of the stimuli offered by the text. Most important at this point in our discussion, however, is the fact that the reader's creation of a poem out of a text must be an active, self-ordering and self-corrective process. We have seen how the interpretation even of a brief quatrain did not proceed in a purely linear fashion, phrase by phrase, line by line, but consisted in a subtle adjustment and readjustment of meaning and tone, an effort to achieve a unified and coherent synthesis. The text itself leads the reader toward this self-corrective process.

Even these rudimentary responses to Frost's quatrain enable us to see clearly the two major functions of the unique pattern of words which constitutes the text. First, the text is a stimulus* activating elements of the reader's past experience—his experience both with literature and with life. Second, the text serves as a blueprint, a guide for the selecting, rejecting, and ordering of what is being called forth; the text regulates* what shall be held in the forefront of the reader's attention.

Much confusion in current critical theory would be eliminated by a

---

*These terms are used to suggest two aspects of the reading process and are not derived from the traditional stimulus-response model. Note that the reader seeks out the text (see below).

11

semantic distinction between "the poem" and "the text," terms often used interchangeably. Teachers tell students to "read the poem"; contemporary critics write indiscriminately of the poem, the work, and the text. Perhaps it is utopian to hope to change such entrenched confusions in critical terminology, but at least the present discussion will observe the following distinctions:

"Text" designates a set or series of signs interpretable as linguistic symbols. I use this rather roundabout phrasing to make it clear that the text is not simply the inked marks on the page or even the uttered vibrations in the air. The visual or auditory signs become verbal symbols, become words, by virtue of their being potentially recognizable as pointing to something beyond themselves. Thus in a reading situation "the text" may be thought of as the printed signs in their capacity to serve as symbols.

"Poem" presupposes a reader actively involved with a text and refers to what he makes of his responses to the particular set of verbal symbols. "Poem" stands here for the whole category, "literary work of art," and for terms such as "novel," "play," or "short story." This substitution is often justified by the assertion that poems are the most concentrated form of the category, the others being usually more extended in time, more loosely integrated. Especially in this century, with the novels of a Woolf or a Joyce, or the confessional poets, it is necessary to abjure such a distinction. I shall use the term "poem" to refer to the whole category of aesthetic transactions between readers and texts without implying the greater or lesser "poeticity" of any specific genre.

The poem, then, must be thought of as an event in time. It is not an object or an ideal entity. It happens during a coming-together, a compenetration, of a reader and a text. The reader brings to the text his past experience and present personality. Under the magnetism of the ordered symbols of the text, he marshals his resources and crystallizes out from the stuff of memory, thought, and feeling a new order, a new experience, which he sees as the poem. This becomes part of the ongoing stream of his life experience, to be reflected on from any angle important to him as a human being.

The concept of the poem as the experience shaped by the reader under the guidance of the text shocks those who succumb to the tendency to assume that a name, a title, must point to a thing, an entity, an object. But when we try to think of what a title—*Hamlet*, say, or *Moby Dick*—might refer to apart from a reader, whether the author himself or another, "the work" disappears. The title then refers simply to a set of black marks on ordered pages or to a set of sounds vibrating in the air, waiting for some reader or listener to interpret them as verbal symbols and, under their guidance, to make a work of art, the poem or novel or play.

We speak of Barrymore's Hamlet, Gielgud's Hamlet, Nicholson's Hamlet. We accept the fact that the actor infuses his own voice, his own body, his own gestures—in short his own interpretation—into the words of the text. Is he not simply carrying to its ultimate manifestation what each of us as readers of the text must do, even if, like the reader in Wallace Stevens's poem, we remain entirely silent and motionless?

> The house was quiet and the world was calm.
> The reader became the book; and summer night
>
> Was like the conscious being of the book.
> The house was quiet and the world was calm.
>
> The words were spoken as if there was no book,
> Except that the reader leaned above the page.[3]

Does not the reader leaning above the page of Shakespeare's script have to respond to the symbols by hearing in his inner ear the sounds of the words and the rhythms of the verse? Does he not have to call up what these sounds point to, in idea and action, so that he may create the play? Does not the reader, like a director, have to supply the tempo, the gestures, the actions not only of Hamlet but of the whole cast? And must he not perform similar acts of evocation from any text, be it poem, novel, or play?

To illustrate the reading process, I shall sometimes refer to the texts of plays. The complaint "Plays are to be acted, not read" may suggest itself. Without rejecting the idea that plays are usually written to be ultimately acted, I still insist that *before they are acted they must be read*—first by the author evoking his intended work and, second, by the director and the actors, who before they interpret must go through the process that I hope to illuminate further in coming chapters.

Perhaps an even better analogy for the reenactment of the text is the musical performance. The text of a poem or of a novel or a drama is like a musical score. The artist who created the score—composer or poet—has set down notations for others, to guide them in the production of a work of art. Some might say that the performer, whether musical or literary, has only to be transparent, to obediently hit the exact notes decreed by the author of the work, but a contemporary composer reminds us of "the preponderant role of the personality of the performer": "honesty compels me to admit that the written page is only an approximation; it's only an indication of how close the composer was able to come in transcribing his exact thoughts on paper. Beyond that point the interpreter is on his own."[4] Moreover, in the literary reading, even the keyboard on which the performer plays is—himself. From the linkage of his own experiences with words, from his own store of memories, he must draw the appropriate elements symbolized by the score or text, to structure a new experience, the work of art.

John Fowles, the novelist, speaking of "the response from individual visual memory," acknowledges the reader's contribution: "A sentence or a paragraph in a novel will evoke a different image in each reader. This necessary co-operation between writer and reader, the one to suggest, the other to make concrete, is a privilege of *verbal form*."[5]

"The poem" comes into being in the live circuit set up between the reader and "the text." As with the elements of an electric circuit, each component of the reading process functions by virtue of the presence of the others. A specific reader and a specific text at a specific time and place: change any of these, and there occurs a different circuit, a different event—a different poem. The reader focuses his attention on the symbols and on what they help to crystallize out into awareness. Not the words, as uttered sounds or inked marks on a page, constitute the poem, but the structured responses to them. For the reader, the poem is lived-through during his intercourse with the text.

The popular phrasing is: the reader "finds" the meanings in the text. This has at least the merit of rejecting the imposition of irrelevant meanings: the reader should not project ideas or attitudes that have no defensible linkage with the text. But one can with equal justice say that one "finds" the meanings for the verbal symbols in himself. Actually, both formulations are false: to find the meanings solely in the text or to find them solely in the reader's mind. The finding of meanings involves both the author's text and what the reader brings to it.

We cannot simply look at the text and predict the poem. For this, a reader or readers with particular attributes must be postulated: for example, the author-as-reader as he is creating the text; the author as he reads it years later; contemporaries of the author with similar backgrounds of education and experience; contemporaries with different backgrounds; other individuals living in specific places, times, and milieus. Thus both text and reader are essential aspects or components, one might say, of that which is manifested in each reading as the poem. The text, we have seen, patterns and delimits, but it ultimately functions like a chemical element: it itself is merged in the synthesis with the other elements to produce a particular event—a poem, a novel, a play.

We post-Romantics are used to seeing behind the text the figure of the author. Nothing that I have said or shall say denies that the text is the outward and visible result of an author's creative activity. Nor does it deny the importance of the author's text. One can understand and appreciate the great interest in textual analysis in recent years, since the author has selected these words and no others as the cues that will guide the reader's performance. Perhaps because of preoccupation with the tie between the author and his creation, or the fixation on the text itself, there has been resistance to, and suspicion of, the idea of the reader's creativity. Yet we must remember that once the creative activity of the author has ended, what remains for others—for even the author himself—is a text. To again bring a poem into being requires always a reader, if only the author himself.

Critical theory and practice both suffer from failure to recognize that the reader carries on a dynamic, personal, and unique activity. Many contemporary critics and teachers evidently think that they are being "objective" when they discuss identifiable elements of the text. They do not include in their theoretical assumptions recognition of the fact that even the most objective analysis of "the poem" is an analysis of the work as they themselves have called it forth. The critics' analyses must then be tested by each of their readers on his own pulses through his own evocation of the work from the text. Even T. S. Eliot found it necessary in 1956 to remind contemporary critics of the personal nature of literary interpretation: "I suspect, in fact, that a good deal of the value of an interpretation is—that it should be my own interpretation. There are many things, perhaps, to know about this poem, or that, many facts about which scholars can instruct me which will help me to avoid definite misunderstandings; *but a valid interpretation, I believe, must be at the same time an interpretation of my own feeling when I read it.*"[6] (Italics added.)

"The poem" seen as an event in the life of a reader, as embodied in a process resulting from the confluence of reader and text, should be central to a systematic theory of literature. Keeping the live process of the literary event before us, I shall attempt to look more deeply into the nature of the literary experience, and to explore implications for problems of literary theory and critical practice.

The questions that I am raising about literature have their roots and analogues in much broader philosophic and theoretical fields—for example, theory of knowledge, theory and philosophy of language, linguistic (or ordinary language) philosophy. My theory of literature necessarily has such broader underpinnings, and especially links with a theory of language and a view of how man relates to the natural world. The past half century has seen an increasing gap between the intellectual schools like logical positivism and behaviorism that try to eliminate the human factor and concentrate on what can be construed as "objective" facts, and the various movements like pragmatism, phenomenology, existentialism, and psychoanalysis that seek in one way or another to incorporate the human consciousness. Throughout a long career, I have consistently been in the latter camp. Having made the reader and the text the point of departure, I shall introduce discussions of the conceptual framework as specific problems require it. The following explanation of my use of the term "transaction" follows that pattern and will serve to indicate some of the broader theoretical issues as they relate to the reading act.

In discussion of the reading process, as in other disciplines undergoing revision, we need to free ourselves from unscrutinized assumptions implicit in the usual terminology and in the very structure of our language. The usual phrasing makes it difficult to attempt to do justice to the nature of the actual reading event. The reader, we can say, interprets the text. (The reader acts on the text.) Or we can say, the text produces a response in the reader. (The text acts on the reader.) Each of these phrasings, because it implies a single line of action by one separate element on another separate element, distorts the actual reading process. The relation between reader and text is not linear. It is a situation, an event at a particular time and place in which each element conditions the other.

The "transactional" terminology developed by John Dewey and Arthur F. Bentley seems most appropriate for the view of the dynamics of the reading process that I have attempted to suggest. This philosophic approach, which has its roots in William James and Charles Sanders Peirce, and for which Dewey used various phrasings during his long career, has had repercussions in many areas of twentieth-century thought. Dewey and Bentley sought to counteract the dualistic phrasing of phenomena as an "interaction" between different factors, because it implies separate, self-contained, and already defined entities acting on one another—in the manner, if one may use a homely example, of billiard balls colliding.

Dewey and Bentley offered the transactional formulation, "in which is asserted the right to see together, extensionally and durationally, much that is talked about conventionally as if it were composed of irreconcilable separates."[7] Thus, a "known" assumes a "knower;" a "knowing" is the transaction between a particular individual and a particular environment. Bentley, finding the roots for this view in William James's thinking, spelled it out this way:

> For further study we differentiate between organism and environment, taking them in mutual interaction.
> We do not, however, take the organism and environment as if we could know about them separately in advance of our special inquiry, but we take their interaction itself as subjectmatter of study. We name this *transaction* to differentiate it from interaction. We inspect the thing-seen not as the operation of an organism upon an environment nor as the operation of an environment upon organism, but as itself an event.[8]

"Transaction" designates, then, an ongoing process in which the elements or factors are, one might say, aspects of a total situation, each conditioned by and conditioning the other.

John Dewey very early (1896) rejected the simple stimulus-response model, and pointed out that in a sense the living organism selects from its environment the stimuli to which it will respond, a concept central to the transactional view that he developed. "Something, not yet a stimulus, . . . *becomes* a stimulus by virtue of the relations it sustains to what is going on in this continuing activity. . . . It *becomes* the stimulus in virtue of what the organism is already preoccupied with."[9]

What the organism selects out and seeks to organize according to already acquired habits, assumptions, and expectations becomes the environment to which it also responds. Jean Piaget draws a similarly transactional picture of "the process or activity common to all forms of life," the process "whereby the organism in each of its interactions

17

with the bodies or energies of its environment fits these in some manner to the requirements of its own physico-chemical structures while at the same time accommodating itself to them."[10]

A group of psychologists have found Dewey's formulation so appropriate to their research on perception that they call themselves "transactional psychologists." Their experiments were based on the optical studies of Adelbert Ames, developed further by Hadley Cantril. For example, in one of the Ames-Cantril experiments the viewer "sees" a room as rectangular although it is actually trapezoidal or otherwise distorted. The observer is confronted with a definitely structured stimulus, but he selects, organizes, and interprets the cues according to his past experience of a room. The observer hits walls which he interprets as being elsewhere; he flails about with a stick at walls that are not there. Sometimes a disturbing period of readjustment is required. Such experiments demonstrate how much perception depends on the selection and organization of cues according to past experience and expectations. The perception may be revised, but it will be through an extension of the transactional process to which both perceiver and the environment contribute.[11]

The current interest in ecology also illuminates the value of the transactional formulation. To see man as separate from his environment, being affected by it, or affecting it, does not do justice to the ecological process, in which man and his environment are part of a total situation, to use Dewey's earlier term, each conditioned by and conditioning the other.

In ecological terms, the text becomes the element of the environment to which the individual responds. Or more accurately, each forms an environment for the other during the reading event. Sharp demarcation between objective and subjective becomes irrelevant, since they are, rather, aspects of the same transaction—the reader looks to the text, and the text is activated by the reader. A "subjective" response assumes an "object" at the other transactional pole; it is better to avoid the use of either in characterizing the reading and criticism of the literary work.

The transactional phrasing of the reading process underlines the essential importance of both elements, reader and text, in any reading event. A person becomes a reader by virtue of his activity in relationship to a text, which he organizes as a set of verbal symbols. A physical text, a set of marks on a page, becomes the text of a poem or of a scientific formula by virtue of its relationship with a reader who can thus interpret it and reach through it to the world of the work.

The transactional view is especially reinforced by the frequent observation of psychologists that interest, expectations, anxieties, and other factors based on past experience affect what an individual perceives. This is not limited to situations in which, for example, the perceiver projects his interpretation upon a formless or "unstructured" stimulus such as the inkblots of the Rorschach Test. As the transactional psychologists have demonstrated, the perceiver sees even a structured object or environment in the way that his past experience and habits determine. In short, what is perceived involves both the perceiver's contribution and the stimulus.

Contemporary linguistic philosophy has also been moving in the direction of transactional emphasis, in, for example, developing the distinction between an utterance and a "speech act."[12] A sentence—that is, a set of words that meet all the syntactic requirements—is still only "a string of words," "a string of noises," "an utterance." It can mean different things in different contexts. The utterance becomes a speech act when there is a speaker and a listener sharing the same language and rules of communication in a particular context under particular conditions. This coincides with Dewey's and Bentley's transactional formulation; it also reinforces my distinction between the text (an utterance) and the poem (a speech act).

The fact that language is rule-governed carries with it the trait of possessing formal features which admit of independent study. "But a study purely of those formal features, without study of their role in speech acts, would be like a formal study of the currency and credit systems of economies without a study of the role of currency and credit in economic transactions."[13] This analogy applies also to the formal analysis of a literary text without concern for the relationship of that text to readers in particular reading acts.

Although the linguistic philosophers seem to limit themselves mainly to the spoken word, their concept of the speech act can be related to the reading act. The familiar basic formula used in information theory summarizes the usual view of the speaker-listener relationship: "Speaker—encoding—message—decoding—listener."[14] The speaker encodes, that is, selects the verbal symbols (confusingly termed "the message") to be decoded by the listener. In reading, the message would be represented by the author's written or printed symbols, which constitute what I term "the text." The temptation is simply to adapt the formula and substitute "author" for "speaker," "reader" for "listener." This masks the fact that in any actual reading act, the author has dropped out. Only his text and the reader remain.

To speak of any reading event in isolation is, of course, to set up a useful fiction for analysis. Actually, as the analogy with the speech act indicates, any reading act is the result of a complex social nexus. Language is a socially generated and socially generative phenomenon. Obviously, no one would become an author (whether of an oral or written text) without the possession of the social medium of a language system. And literary art is in itself a social institution. Despite the tale of the inspired cowherd Caedmon and other such myths of literary autogenesis, authors have usually been readers (or listeners to oral literature) first, absorbing the linguistic and literary conventions of their culture.

But part of the magic—and indeed of the essence—of language is the fact that it must be internalized by each individual human being, with all the special overtones that each unique person and unique situation entail. Hence language is at once basically social and intensely individual. In other words, the transactional view of human life applies here with all its force, and the transactional view of the reading act is simply an exemplification, with highly rarified complications, of the basic transactional character of all human activity, and especially linguistic activity.[15]

The speaker, it is often pointed out, offers many nonverbal cues to the listener, for example, through emphasis, pitch, inflection, rhythm, and, if face-to-face, facial expression and gesture. The writer thus must seek verbal substitutes for these. Hence the reader, in contrast to the listener, finds it necessary to construct the speaker, the author—the voice, the tone, the rhythms and inflections, the persona—*as part of what he decodes from the text.* The relation with the author in actuality becomes a transaction between the reader and the author's text.

The reading of a text is an event occurring at a particular time in a particular environment at a particular moment in the life history of the reader. The transaction will involve not only the past experience but also the present state and present interests or preoccupations of the reader. This suggests the possibility that printed marks on a page may even become different linguistic symbols by virtue of transactions with different readers. Just as a knowing is the process linking a knower and a known, so a poem should not be thought of as an object, an entity, but rather as an active process lived through during the relationship between a reader and a text. This experience may be the object of thought, like any other experience in life, but it should not be confused with an object in the sense of an entity existing apart from author or reader.

The danger is that the transactional view may be misunderstood as focusing too narrowly on "the mind" of the reader isolated from anything outside himself. Recall that the text is more than mere paper and ink. The transaction is basically between the reader and what he senses the words as pointing to.* The paradox is that he must call forth from memory of his world what the visual or auditory stimuli symbolize for him, yet he feels the ensuing work as part of the world outside himself. The physical signs of the text enable him to reach through himself and the verbal symbols to something sensed as outside and beyond his own personal world. The boundary between inner and outer world breaks down, and the literary work of art, as so often remarked, leads us into a new world. It becomes part of the experience which we bring to our future encounters in literature and in life.

This has perforce been a very sketchy initial presentation of only the broadest view of the reading of a poem. Many aspects of the reading process and many problems of critical theory remain to be treated. The following chapters will offer answers to such questions, among others, as the following: How do we distinguish the reading event that yields a poem from other kinds of reading? (chap. 3). What are the reader's activities during the process of evoking a poem from a text? (chap. 4). How does the text function in the transaction? (chap. 5). If literary works are events in time, how can we agree on something called *Hamlet* or *The Waste Land*? (chap. 6). How does the reader produce an interpretation of the work? What are the implications of the transactional nature of the poem for evaluation? for literary criticism, literary analysis, literary history? (chap. 7). The complexity of these questions is such that the transactional theory of the reading process will not be fully developed until the final chapter.

*In discussing "The Fiction of 'Retinal Image' " (see n. 8), Bentley says: "What we get is not a seeing, plus a percept, plus an object, but the seeing-effect; and this not as sensation but as thing-seen, seeing-experience, this-seeing-effect." This applies also to the visual aspects of the reading process. What we get is not a seeing-of-the-verbal-signs, plus meanings, but the reading-experience, this-reading-effect.

3

EFFERENT

AND AESTHETIC

READING

*T*HE preceding chapter simply assumed that "the event" of the encounter between a reader and Frost's quatrain involved a poem. The reader, it was pointed out, was highly active in evoking that poem from the page. But, it is time to ask, is not *any* reader of *any* text active? Does not any reader, whether of a newspaper, scientific text, or cookbook, have to evoke the work from the page? The answer, of course, is that the reader of any text must actively draw upon past experience and call forth the "meaning" from the coded symbols. Wherein, then, lies the difference between a poem and a scientific work, between a play and a newspaper article? Differentiation of the literary work of art* from

---

*Aristotle's complaint that he had no single term for all the kinds of literary works of art still holds. The English term "literature" is notoriously fluid. Sometimes it simply

the other types of verbal expression or communication has been a perennial theoretical problem. The task of this chapter will be largely to answer that question by developing further the view of the reader's activity set forth thus far, and by showing how the event that produces the reading of a poem differs from other reading-events.

The tendency in the past has been to seek the answer to this question entirely in the text. If there is a different result from reading a book on biology and Yeats's "Byzantium," the explanation, it is commonly felt, lies entirely in the texts—the "content," the sentence structure, the syntax, the presence or absence of metaphor. Needless to say, the text is an essential element of any reading act. We have already seen, however, that, to borrow the logician's phrasing, the text is a necessary condition, but it is not a sufficient condition, for the re-creation of a particular work. The text is merely an object of paper and ink until some reader responds to the marks on the page as verbal symbols. That is why those who seek in the texts alone the elements that differentiate between the aesthetic and the nonaesthetic arrive at only partial or arbitrary answers. They assume the very thing that should be highlighted—the character of the reader's relationship to the text during these various kinds of reading events.

We must rephrase our question and ask, "What does the reader *do* in these different kinds of reading?" Only when this is answered does it become realistic to ask what manner of texts may be especially conducive to aesthetic activities. Although ultimately we shall be able to deal with the complexities of a continuum, it is first necessary to make clear the distinction between the two kinds of reading.

The reader performs very different activities during aesthetic and nonaesthetic readings. The contrast derives primarily from the difference in the reader's focus of attention during the reading-event.

In nonaesthetic reading, the reader's attention is focused primarily on what will remain as the residue *after* the reading—the information to be acquired, the logical solution to a problem, the actions to be carried out. An extreme instance is the mother whose child has just

---

refers to anything printed, sometimes it indicates that the writing is of high quality, and only sometimes does it designate a work of art. I find it necessary to fall back on the rather cumbersome phrase "the literary work of art." For the sake of brevity, in the following pages "the poem" will often be used as representative of literary works of art in general.

swallowed poisonous liquid and who is frantically reading the label on the bottle to discover the antidote to be administered. She wants to get through the reading as quickly as possible and to retain the information that will serve her practical purpose. She is interested only in what the words point to—the objects, ideas, and actions designated. Her own responses to these concepts or to the rhythm, sound, or associations of the words are of no importance to her, and indeed, the more she ignores these, the more she makes herself impersonal and transparent, the more efficiently she reads. Her attention will be concentrated on what is to be assimilated for use after she has finished reading.

Much less powerfully motivated than the mother's reading of the label, yet of the same nature, is the reading of a history book, a cooking recipe, a newspaper article, an algebraic equation or a chemical formula. As the reader responds to the printed words or symbols, his attention is directed outward, so to speak, toward concepts to be retained, ideas to be tested, actions to be performed after the reading.

To designate this type of reading, in which the primary concern of the reader is with what he will carry away from the reading, I have chosen the term "efferent," derived from the Latin, "efferre," "to carry away."* This term seems to be freer of misleading implications than "instrumental," which would in most instances seem appropriately to contrast with "aesthetic." Yet instrumental implies a toollike usefulness that does not fit some kinds of nonaesthetic reading. The mathematician reading his equations, the physicist pondering his formulae, may have no practical purpose in mind, yet their attention is focused on the concepts, the solutions, to be "carried away" from their reading. Moreover, I am not sure that all aesthetic reading excludes or is diametrically opposed to an awareness of possible later usefulness or application. For such reasons, the more neutral term "efferent" seems to be more unambiguously applicable to the reader's nonaesthetic activity.

In aesthetic reading, in contrast, the reader's primary concern is with what happens *during* the actual reading event. Though, like the efferent reader of a law text, say, the reader of Frost's "Birches" must decipher the images or concepts or assertions that the words

*ef'fer ent "*adj.* Directed away from a central organ or section. . . . [Fench *effér-ent*, from Latin *efferens*, present participle of *efferre*, to carry away . . .]" *American Heritage Dictionary of the English Language.*

point to, he also pays attention to the associations, feelings, attitudes, and ideas that these words and their referents arouse within him. "Listening to" himself, he synthesizes these elements into a meaningful structure. *In aesthetic reading, the reader's attention is centered directly on what he is living through during his relationship with that particular text.*

Implicit in this distinction between the two stances of the reader, the two directions in which he focuses his attention, is recognition that the same text may be read either efferently or aesthetically. To take a popular example: the mathematician turns from his efferent, abstract manipulations of his symbols to focus his attention on, and to aesthetically savor, the "elegance" of his solution. Again, we may focus our attention on the qualitative living-through of what we derive from the text of "Ode on a Grecian Urn," or we may turn our attention to efferent analysis of its syntax.

Recent psycholinguistic work on reading confirms my contention concerning the difference between the reader's activities in the two kinds of reading.[1] The experimenters happened to be interested in testing the idea that in reading there must be "decoding to sound," a translation first from the verbal symbol to the sound of the word and then to its meaning. Reading, they claim, can bypass the sound of the word and depend on a direct linkage between the visual symbol and meaning. The factor of speed of reading enters, and incidental references to speedreading make it clear that these discussions consider only efferent reading. Whatever further experimental evidence may reveal about the process of deciphering from the visual symbol, the distinction that I insist on between efferent and aesthetic reading is confirmed; because only the kind of reading directed entirely toward the end result of a residue of information would benefit from extreme speed and complete disregard of the sound of the words.

Hence the absurdity of the advertisements for speedreading that claim that a novel can be read in minutes. This would be only efferent reading. The text would simply not have been read as a novel, as a literary work of art; a brief summary of the "plot" would have served the reader just as well as the complete text.

If in ordinary reading good readers indeed can or do tend to ignore the sound of the words symbolized, then all the more reason to become aware of how different are the demands of aesthetic reading. In some texts—a novel by Dreiser or a clumsy translation of Tolstoy—the reader may not find much reward in turning his attention to the sound of the words in his inner ear (a metaphor, of course, for whatever the sensing of the sound equivalents may be). In most texts from which the reader is seeking to shape an aesthetic experience, however, attention to the sound element will probably play a part—differing in degree of attention from cursory sensing of the "voice" of the persona to full-scale awareness of, say, the symphonic harmonies of Milton's verse. And if this matter of selective attention applies to even the sound of the words, how much more obviously does it apply to all the other evocations from the text that make up the lived-through work of art!

The readers of the quatrain discussed in chapter 2 illustrate this characteristic of aesthetic reading. Ability to assign lexicographical meaning to each of the verbal symbols, and ability even to paraphrase each of the separate lines, did not guarantee the production of a poem. Some of the readings were of this efferent or nonaesthetic character. To produce a poem, the reader had to pay attention to the broader gamut of what these particular words in this particular order were calling forth within him: attention to the sound and rhythm of the words in the inner ear, attention to the imprints of past encounters with these words and their referents in differing life and literary contexts, attention to the overtones of feeling, the chiming of sound, sense, idea, and association. Sensing, feeling, imagining, thinking under the stimulus of the words, the reader who adopts the aesthetic attitude feels no compulsion other than to apprehend what goes on during this process, to concentrate on the complex structure of experience that he is shaping and that becomes for him the poem, the story, the play symbolized by the text.

Perhaps the reading of a Shakespearean lyric—say, "Under the Greenwood Tree"—illustrates most clearly the need for the reader to center his attention on the content of consciousness itself as he evokes the poem. In such a poem, there is little that can be summed up or retained for future use; hence there is little to support an efferent stance. The special character of the aesthetic stance, essential to all literary art, is unmistakable here. The benefit to be derived lies in the reader's moment-to-moment alertness to what is being activated in his consciousness by this particular pattern of words during the period of actual reading.

Keats, in his sonnet "On Sitting Down to Read *King Lear* Once Again," writes:

Efferent and Aesthetic Reading

> . . . once again, the fierce dispute
> Betwixt damnation and impassion'd clay,
> Must I burn through.[2]

The special mark of the literary work of art is indeed that it is "burned through," lived through, by a reader. At the end of the sonnet, the persona speaks of being "consumed in the fire," completely absorbed in the reliving of the play. He utters, too, the paradox that undergoing this intense experience would leave him renewed for actual life, that he would gain "new Phoenix-wings to fly at [his] desire." Seeing the work of art as a special kind of lived-through experience and formulating the aesthetic experience in terms of the inner-oriented focus of attention save us from the untenable opposition of art and life.

Absorption in the quality and structure of the experience engendered by the text can happen whether the reader is enthralled by the adventures of the Hardy Boys or by the anguish of *King Lear*. In either case, in my view, the text has given rise to a literary work of art. How to decide whether it is good, bad, or indifferent art is another question, to be faced later. Moreover, different aesthetic transactions with the same text may also produce different kinds or levels of experience, depending on the nature, state of mind, or past experience of the reader. (We are not always "enthralled.") Very important questions derive from these diversities of texts and of readers, and we shall later deal with them directly. They do not, however, negate the aesthetic stance as essential to the evocation of a work of art.

The distinction between aesthetic and nonaesthetic reading, then, derives ultimately from what the reader does, the stance that he adopts and the activities he carries out in relation to the text. At the extreme efferent end of the spectrum, the reader disengages his attention as much as possible from the personal and qualitative elements in his response to the verbal symbols; he concentrates on what the symbols designate, what they may be contributing to the end result that he seeks—the information, the concepts, the guides to action, that will be left with him when the reading is over.

At the aesthetic end of the spectrum, in contrast, the reader's primary purpose is fulfilled *during* the reading event, as he fixes his attention on the actual experience he is living through. This permits the whole range of responses generated by the text to enter into the

27

center of awareness, and out of these materials he selects and weaves what he sees as the literary work of art.

Most discussions of the literary experience are concerned with what one might call the substance of the experience—the intensities of feeling in the lyric, the world of characters and events in the novel, the tensions of dialogue and action in the play. I do not in any way seek to minimize the importance of these concerns, but on the contrary, to enhance it. I wish only to insist on the essential prerequisite for them—that the reader attend not to the concept of emotion but to the actual experiences that the text signals, as the way of sensing the inner reverberations of Keats's "Ode on Melancholy"; not to analytic classification of the types of character or intricacies of plot that might be outlined but to the actual qualities of the world of *The Ambassadors;* not to broad abstractions about jealousy and guilt and human tenderness that might be enunciated but to the actual moment-to-moment participation in *Othello*.

What, after all, is the reader describing as he talks about a literary work of art? Has he not drawn on his own inner resources to create the experience designated as the poem or novel or play? If he cannot feel on his own pulses the impact of Keats's words, and if he cannot out of his own past experiences with life and language, no matter how paltry they may seem to him, find the substance for responding to the great structures of Shakespeare's texts and what they point to, there will be for him no ode, no *Othello*. If a literary work of art is to ensue, the reader must turn his attention as fully as possible toward the transaction between himself and the text.

The central importance of this factor of the reader's focus of attention is assumed in Coleridge's famous statement about poetry: "The reader should be carried forward, not merely or chiefly by the mechanical impulse of curiosity, or by a restless desire to arrive at the final solution; but by *the pleasurable activity of mind excited by the attractions of the journey itself.*"[3] (Italics added.) Only if the reader turns his attention inward to his experience of "the journey itself," will a poem happen.

The reader of a text who evokes a literary work of art is, above all, a performer, in the same sense that a pianist performs a sonata, reading it from the text before him. Viewed from the vantage point of the performer, Pater's oft-quoted dictum, "All art aspires to the condition of music,"[4] takes on new significance. The effort to interpret this as the complete merging of "form" and "content" has led seekers after "pure poetry," such as George Moore or Mallarmé, to try to eliminate meaning from verbal art and to prize the poetry in which sound dominates sense, or in which the sense plays a minimal role, as in Shakespeare's songs. This seems both to diminish musical art and to negate the essential trait of literary art, namely, that its medium, language, consists of symbols that point to something outside themselves, their referents or their meaning. In my view of the aesthetic process, the semantic component need not be sacrificed. All art aspires to the condition of music, not in the sense of banishing all ideas or referents, but in the sense that the primary concern is with the musical event itself, that the performer's attention is absorbed in what he is producing *as he plays*. Once he stops playing, we are left with only the black and white score. Is this not "the condition of music" to which the reader of the literary work of art should aspire: a complete absorption in the process of evoking a work from the text, and in sensing, clarifying, structuring, savoring, that experience as it unfolds. Perhaps, as Pater suggests, this is easiest to achieve in music. But in the literary work of art, as well, what the words point to cannot be dissociated from the total lived-through experience in all its immediacy.

The aesthetic stance, as I have described it, should not be confused with a simple revery or train of free associations. Perusal of a text merely leading to free fantasy would not be a reading at all in the transactional sense. The concept of transaction emphasizes the relationship with, *and continuing awareness of*, the text. During the literary experience, concentration on the words of the text is perhaps even more keen than in an efferent reading. The reader must pay attention to all that these words, and no others, these words, moreover, in a particular sequence, summon up for him. When a fire breaks out, the man reading the directions for use of a fire extinguisher will pay no attention to whether the word is "fire," "flame," or "combustion." But the aesthetic stance heightens awareness of the words as signs with particular visual and auditory characteristics *and* as symbols. What is lived through is felt constantly to be linked with the stimulus of the words.

This is one of the reasons why the frequently cited parallel between ritual and art raises some questions. Such a parallel is useful in the history of drama and in speculations on the genesis of art as a human activity. The reading process is so sophisticated, however, that we must insist on those aspects that make the parallel with ritual least suggestive. The element of absorption in the moment is present in ritual activity, but the medium that excites this state is in itself expendable, one may say. Hence the relative unimportance of repetitiveness or even unintelligibility of the words of many religious incantations. Services in an archaic or dead language may thus perform a ritual function. Poets like Swinburne who lean heavily on the incantatory potentialities of words tend often to defeat their own literary purposes, as the incantatory effect hinders the necessary attention to the referential function of their words.

Ideas recurrently emphasized in various philosophies of art may help to isolate the element that I am seeking especially to highlight. Contemplation as a main characteristic of art experience is one such formulation, for example—it might seem a congenial one, since it is concerned with the attitude of the observer or audience. Schopenhauer's "will-less" state of contemplation explicitly contrasts aesthetic contemplation with a practical, volitional orientation. This is, however, basically a negative distinction. Vivas's term, "intransitive" reading has similar negative implications. The concept of "psychical distance" also assumes contemplation removed from practical ends. But the character of contemplative, "autonomous" aesthetic activity requires more than such negative explication. Perhaps for this reason Dewey found Kant's concept of aesthetic contemplation too passive, even though Kant's other key concept, *Zweckmässigkeit ohne Zweck*, purposiveness without practical purpose, has more dynamic overtones.

In such formulations, the question of *what* is being contemplated, or the nature of the activity, remains clouded. More positive differentia are the notions of intense concentration and heightened consciousness as traits of artistic contemplation. Yet here again, how exclude, say, the botanist's intense concentration on his specimen? Even the insistence that instrumental, scientific contemplation requires a shearing away of everything but the practical or operational implications of what is perceived is still negative so far as defining the difference between scientific and aesthetic contemplation is concerned.[5] Hence my insistence that aesthetic concentration differs from nonaesthetic contemplation by virtue of the shift of the direction of attention toward the qualitative lived-through experience.

"The object" of aesthetic contemplation takes on a different character. A certain confusion—particularly for the aesthetics of reading—results from the fact that the general aesthetic paradigm usually offered is the contemplation of some "art object" such as a painting or statue. Yet intense concentration on an "object," such as Brancusi's famous sculpture entitled *Bird in Space*, can, as we know, entail two different kinds of activity: the customs officer, efferently oriented, may see only a mass of taxable metal, while the art critic, attending to his own responses to its lines, its texture, its color, the associations aroused in him, will organize them into an aesthetic experience.[6]

It would be less confusing to use the reading act itself as the general paradigm of the aesthetic experience; it would then become clear that the "object" of aesthetic contemplation is what the perceiver makes of his responses to the artistic stimulus, no matter whether this be a physical object, such as a statue, or a set of verbal symbols. The reader contemplates his own shaping of his responses to the text, a far from passive kind of contemplation.

Another constantly recurrent theme is the distinction between the work of art and the "real world," sometimes referred to as the fictionality of the work, sometimes as its imaginative character. Such a distinction between the real and the fictional does not, however, suffice to differentiate the work of art. For example, whether the reader assumes that there was ever a person, Sherlock Holmes, who existed in the real world is of minor importance in answering the question as to whether Conan Doyle's text gives rise to a literary work of art. We are reasonably sure that Julius Caesar did exist in the real world. Yet this does not affect the attitude that the reader takes toward what is evoked for him and in him by the text of Shakespeare's play. Perhaps a more accurate formulation would be: during the evocation of the literary work of art from the text the question as to Caesar's existence in the "real world" becomes irrelevant or secondary. The reader may later apply insights derived during this experience to the practical historical figure; but this would involve a nonaesthetic attitude.

The aesthetic stance brings with it a certain distancing from "reality," *because* it is known that the experience is generated by the words and not by such images, situations, characters, actions observed directly without verbal mediation. The attention is consciously focused on what the words are stirring up. This may be felt to correspond to what is known as actual reality—realism derives from such a judgment, but such realism is not confused with actuality.

Coleridge invoked his powerful formulation—"the willing suspension of disbelief"—to explain how he and Wordsworth had apportioned their contributions to *The Lyrical Ballads*. Coleridge was to treat the supernatural—hence his need to effect the suspension of the reader's disbelief.[7] But Wordsworth, in his effort to "give the charm of novelty to things of everyday, and to excite a feeling analogous to the supernatural" was also concerned with leading the reader to suspend his ordinary attitudes, in this instance his attitudes toward practical reality. The frequent tendency to extend Coleridge's formulation to all poetry and indeed all literary art reflects awareness of the need to differentiate the reader's attitude even when supposedly realistic or "natural" experiences are offered by the text.

Interpreting the image on the retina of the eye, as Adelbert Ames has taught us, is not a simple thing; we may discover that the three-dimensional chair before us is an arrangement of strings. The presence of a text fortunately signals to us that, in a sense, we are indeed dealing with an artful arrangement of stimuli, that our experience may be vividly savored, but that its connection with actuality is a special one, a question to be held in suspension, to be answered subsequently by other means.

The evocation of a work of art is itself a form of experience in the real world, one that can be related to the other forms of experience. Sometimes what has been lived through is felt to be a version of the real, as in naturalistic fiction. Sometimes it is felt as an escape from it, an experiencing of alternative possibilities. What makes it art rather than, say, history, is that a particular kind of relationship with a text has been lived through.

The term, "imagination," so closely linked to art in the post-Lockean period, also creates problems. The capacity of the human being to evoke images of things or events not present, and even never experienced, or which may never have existed, is undoubtedly an important element in art. It is especially important in the experiences generated by speech and by verbal texts. Yet this imaginative capacity is not limited to art but is basic to any kind of verbal communication. It is sometimes seen as the essence of language, which enables us to deal with things and events that are not present or that may not have occurred. Is not imagination required in any reading—history, science, legal or philosophic persuasion—since it requires the reader to conjure up the referents for the verbal symbols and to entertain new ideas? But in scientific reading, attention is efferently focused on theoretical implications or on the relations between phenomena rather than on the immediacy of the experience engendered by what is imagined. In other words, the term "imagination" covers both the aesthetic and the efferent attitudes, which must be further differentiated by the particular focus of the reader's attention.

The fictional or imaginary are often considered parasitic on the real world, since the fictional contains many elements drawn from the world of sense experience. Here, again, perhaps too sharp a distinction is being made; philosophers, psychologists, and anthropologists have led us to question how much of what we take to be "reality" has been structured by the human organism and the assumptions of our culture. Our vision of the "real" world often depends on what we bring to it not only from past "reality" but also from the world of fiction or the imagination. Literature especially invites confusion about its relation with reality.

Words, the medium of the literary work, are used in our everyday life; moreover, as we have seen, words, unlike musical sounds, point to something outside themselves, often to something that has a separate existence in real life. Hence, it is tempting to think of the poem as also having a separate existence "out there" in whatever materials of life are treated or used in the poem. Wallace Stevens rejects this view of the poem:

> Poetry is the subject of the poem,
> From this the poem issues and
>
> To this returns. Between the two,
> Between issue and return, there is
>
> An absence in reality,
> Things as they are. Or so we say.
>
> But are these separate? Is it
> An absence for the poem, which acquires
>
> Its true appearances there, sun's green,
> Cloud's red, earth feeling, sky that thinks?
>
> From these it takes. Perhaps it gives,
> In the universal intercourse.[8]

Stevens's poem balances two kinds of perception, two modes of experience. He does not fall into the usual fallacies either of equating reality and the world of the poem or of assuming that because they are different and autonomous, they are not related.

In these images of the interplay of reality and poetry, more is involved than the relationship between two entities, the poem and something called reality. Though Stevens's poem simply takes them for granted, either an author or a reader is also implied. In the creation of the text of a poem, the author's perception of reality is the link. In the reading relationship, the reader brings his sense of something called reality, to which words point; this may become transmuted into something "rich and strange" under the magnetism of the patterned words of the text. Thus, the reader also is a link in the "universal intercourse" between the world of "reality" and the world of poetry.

Those who seek the essence of the poetic or the aesthetic in the text itself often end up emphasizing such matters as deviations from normal syntax, ordinary diction, and grammaticality. Departures from normal discourse are indeed frequent in the literary canon, yet no single one of these is essential to poetry or other literary works of art. The same is true of other frequent attributes of poems, such as repetitions of sound in rhyme or alliteration. Just as we reject the notion of a specifically "poetic" diction, so we find it impossible to make any other such aspect of the text the essential and differentiating sign of poetry.

Stylistic deviations or other stylistic devices are sometimes said to be "poetic" because they "call attention to themselves." The reader's attention is "called," however, not to just the words themselves, but to their potentialities for qualitative response. The presence of such striking stylistic or formal devices is one of the ways of alerting the reader to adopt the aesthetic stance.

Emphasis on the reader's role does not in any way minimize the importance of the text. When the reader adopts the aesthetic stance, clearly some texts will yield a greater reward for his attention than others. To adopt an aesthetic stance toward the items in a newspaper or toward the directions for constructing a radio, is possible, but would usually be very unrewarding. And a Rod McKuen text offers less potentiality than a Yeats text. Often the literary experience is indeed more complex, more nuanced, more intense, because of the presence of certain stylistic devices or formal traits. Yet the introduction of syntactic deviations from the norm, or rhyme or alliteration, into texts would not be sufficient in itself to raise their aesthetic value.

Similarly, some have sought the essence of poetry in certain subjects or themes. Although the "content" of the text usually plays a primary role in the literary experience, content cannot be dissociated from the form in which it is embodied. It would be fallacious to seek some essentially poetic content or themes such as Poe deemed the death of a beautiful young woman to be. No matter how much certain themes may recur in good and great literature, their presence cannot guarantee poetry. It seems impossible to think of any subject that can be dealt with poetically that could not also be dealt with efferently or scientifically. By the same token, the readers who approach the texts of *The Divine Comedy* or *The Magic Mountain* seeking linguistic or sociological information will not elicit works of art. Their efferent attitude will prevent it.

Thus far, extreme forms of relationships with texts have been contrasted. Actually, no hard-and-fast line separates efferent—scientific or expository—reading on the one hand from aesthetic reading on the other. It is more accurate to think of a continuum, a series of gradations between the nonaesthetic and the aesthetic extremes. The reader's stance toward the text—what he focuses his attention on, what his "mental set" shuts out or permits to enter into the center of awareness—may vary in a multiplicity of ways between the two poles.

One of the perennial problems in the theory of literature is raised by such works as the Book of Isaiah, Emerson's essays, or Gibbon's *Decline and Fall of the Roman Empire*. The usual definitions of literature-as-art have not provided a satisfactory basis for categorizing them. Distinctions between the aesthetic and nonaesthetic based on such matters as the author's purpose or methods, the linguistic devices present in the text, the fictionality or nobility or emotional intensity of the contents, have not been able to encompass such works. Wellek and Warren, for example, having opted for fictionality as the essential component, simply give up and exclude works such as those mentioned above from consideration in their *Theory of Literature*.[9] Recognition of a continuum of possible stances that the reader might adopt during his relationship with the text provides, however, for a systematic understanding of such writings.

Since each encounter between a reader and the text is a unique event, it is not possible to simply look at the text of Gibbon or Emerson or, to cite a more recent work, Loren Eiseley's *The Immense Journey*, and assign it a particular place in the spectrum. But we know that texts like the ones cited above tend often to produce literary experiences that fall somewhere in the middle of the continuum. The differences reside in the range of elements permitted into the center of attention—in the manner, say, of the enlarging or narrowing of the shutter-opening in a camera. While the reader focuses mainly on the ultimate external import of the text, he is often also aware of the qualitative responses aroused in him. This experiential awareness is fused with the acquisition of the information or practical implications derived from the text and bestows on the resulting work its "literary" value. The reader's dominant concern usually continues to be the information to be retained after the reading, yet at the same time he is aware of, is paying some attention to, the actual experiential aspects of the reading, and deriving satisfaction from them. Later, he may subject the information to the usual critical, scientific tests and reject or modify it, but he will continue to value the "literary" experience the work provided.

Many texts are susceptible of being experienced at different points of the continuum by different readers, or even by the same reader under different circumstances. The same text may even be recreated variously as an efferent utterance or a poetic experience. For instance, some works, viewed originally as religious or hortatory—hence read mainly efferently—may, under different conditions or by people with different urgencies, be experienced as works of art. The Book of Isaiah and the Song of Songs have been transformed in this way by many contemporary readers. Lincoln's Gettysburg Address seems to be undergoing such a shift in response. The change, of course, occurs in the attitude of the reader, in what dimension of his response to the text becomes central to him. The religious or political implications may persist, but of primary importance will be the awareness of the qualities of thought and feeling generated by the words during the reading of the text; the aesthetic reading of Lincoln's Address would find its place in our continuum somewhere near the reading of, say, Mark Antony's speech in *Julius Caesar*. Thus, too, some historians—from Herodotus to Parkman—though superseded by later research, continue to be read perhaps more for their immediate experiential values than for the information they present.

All of this raises doubts about the usual tendency to think of the nonaesthetic or efferent or informative as the basic form of reading, with the reader automatically looking outward to the referents to which the words point. Language is thus seen as a basically impersonal medium, with the affective and sensuous or "feeling" elements added on to the so-called literal meaning. The aesthetic mode is then considered secondary. According to this view, the progression in complexity of reading operations would be from the nonaesthetic to the aesthetic end of the continuum. This ignores the fact that in the reading of a scientific text, there may have to be an active shutting out of personal attitudes or associations. The use in some disciplines of special symbolic systems, of codes or terminology separate from ordinary linguistic usage, may be an aid to such an exclusion of personal responses. But the reader has to be seen as carrying on such exclusions or inclusions.

Perhaps we should think rather of most reading as hovering near the middle of our continuum. This would do justice to the fact that a reader has to learn to handle his multiple responses to texts in a variety of complex ways, moving the center of attention toward the efferent or aesthetic ends of the spectrum.

John Dewey, denying a break between ordinary life and art, stressed that *an* experience, an aesthetic experience, was simply the stuff of ordinary day-to-day experience defined, heightened, complete. His much-needed insistence on the continuity with ordinary life did not, however, rule out emphasis on the heightened awareness characteristic of the aesthetic experience. Dewey says somewhere that there is nothing to prevent the man sipping his tea from also enjoying the shape of the cup. But, one must add, his pleasure cannot be taken for granted; he must turn his attention to his response to the contours of the cup in his hand. Without reinstating a break between art and life, we need to recognize that if there is the aesthetic element in day-to-day life, it depends on a certain shift of interest, attention, or awareness from the purely practical or referential to the immediately experienced qualitative aspects. This play of attention back and forth between the efferent and the aesthetic is undoubtedly much more characteristic of our daily lives than is usually acknowledged. Similarly, in much of our reading, there is a to-and-fro movement of the attention from one aspect to another of the responses activated by the text. Thus, where we might place a particular reading on our continuum would be a matter of the relative emphasis or incidence of one or the other stance.

The Reader, the Text, the Poem

In actual literary experiences—experiences which do justify the label "aesthetic"—various factors enter to diminish the moment of perfect equilibrium so often posited as the distinguishing trait of the art experience. One frequently recognized is that the reader may not respond to, or assimilate, all the cues offered by the text: the experience may not be complete, or fully integrated. Second, as the reader draws upon his past life for the substance from which, under the guidance of the textual signs, to build up the work, special and sometimes tangential preoccupations, preconceptions, and misconceptions emerge. Such intrusions may interrupt the experience, and even when recognized as irrelevant to the text, may still provide overtones, diversions, interruptions, that diminish the wholeness and integrity of the experience.

Still, an absolutely unbroken texture need not be achieved before we can speak of an aesthetic experience. My solution is to ask about the kinds of activity engaged in by the reader—and to see this as a matter of varying degrees of concentration on what he is shaping out of his responses and sees as the equivalent of the text. Moments may intervene in a generally aesthetic reading when the reader is more concerned with the information being acquired, than with the experienced meaning. Thus parts of the text, though integral to the work, may in themselves not reward qualitative attention, being introduced to provide the reader with background information, or a conceptual framework, as a necessary foundation for the parts in which the work is to be more immediately experienced. The introductory chapters in nineteenth-century novels, a Scott novel, say, require more of the efferent stance, a concern for registering the information being provided, so that it may later be assumed in the actual events of the novel.

Yet even here—and certainly in the interspersed essaylike chapters of Fielding's *Tom Jones* or in even the opening, information-giving chapter of Camus's *The Plague*—in addition to the major information or ideas being acquired the reader is also developing and attending to attitudes, a sense of the tone and character of the narrative persona, that have to be experienced rather than simply cognized, and that add to the quality of the experience being evoked. The various indications of tone and substance suggest the need primarily in these parts of the text for interest in what is being referred to and its practical import. But the reader has already been alerted to the need to adopt a dominantly aesthetic stance; hence, the ideas and information are assimilated as preparation for the reader's adopting the appropriate aesthetic attitudes toward the characters and events to follow. We are dealing here with a matter of degree. In contrast, in a scientific treatise, for which the efferent stance is paramount, any qualitative experiences evoked by the text may even have to be actively discounted as irrelevant and confusing.

Because readers are usually not aware of adopting one or another stance, this element of choice usually does not come into consciousness unless there is some inappropriateness to text or context. In a paper presented at the Modern Language Association, a speaker told about an eight-year-old boy's response as he was being read to: "But rabbits don't run around pulling watches out of their pockets!" The rejoinder was, "Shut up! in this story they do." The speaker's purpose was to underline the need for a suspension of judgment while reading a literary work. Sound as the advice to suspend judgment is (though one might object to the tone!) that does not get at the heart of the boy's problem. He was entirely correct in his statement that rabbits do not carry watches. His real problem was that he was listening with an efferent attitude. In that kind of listening or reading, he would deserve praise for his refusal to accept everything unquestioningly—for his "critical reading," aimed at clarifying the information that should remain at the end of the reading. A suspension of judgment—Coleridge's "willing suspension of disbelief"—was indeed needed, but required first of all was a change of focus, so that the boy would have been content to live in the moment, devoting his attention to experiencing the story fully without concern for its connections with practical reality.

It is strange that the young boy had not developed, or perhaps he had lost, a habit of mind, whether we call it fantasy or imagination, that seems very much a part of many young children's initial use of language. The following may throw some light on how such literal-mindedness may develop: In a series of reading workbooks for the primary grades, the first inclusion of a poem occurred in the third grade book. The poem, describing a cow standing in a stream, was introduced by "What facts does this poem teach you?" This, unfortunately, guaranteed that the children would *not* read the text as a poem, since the question instructed them from the start to adopt an efferent, fact-accumulating, attitude. It explicitly contradicted what should have been stressed: that the external clues announcing a poem—the wide margins, the patterned lines, the rhymed words—

were signals alerting them to adopt an aesthetic stance. Their attention should have been focused on what the words could make them see and hear and feel and think.

Some, perhaps for reasons of temperament or early environment, seem to adopt the aesthetic stance instinctively or intuitively. But, perhaps because this distinction has tended to be taken for granted and has not been made explicit, many never learn to read aesthetically. Those people often consider poetry a pretty silly kind of convention. Why not give information about cows directly? They have not learned that poetry is primarily a source of a special kind of experience. They have not been led to direct their attention to the qualitative responses going on during the reading itself. The question arises: to what extent do environmental pressures—home, school, societal—lead the child to focus attention on the efferent handling of language and to push the richly fused cognitive-affective matrix into the fringes of consciousness?

"The meaning of meaning" and the place of language in human life has increasingly concerned philosophers, psychologists, and social scientists during this century. The past few decades have produced a welter of theories and schools of thought approaching the problem from almost diametrically opposed positions, whether the intuitionism of a Husserl, the behaviorism of a Skinner, the geneticism of a Piaget, or the "ordinary language" approach of a Wittgenstein.

P. W. Bridgman made a significant semantic formulation when he spoke of meaning as "operationally" defined—defined, that is, by the kinds of operations or actions the words stand for. This provides a useful criterion for the communication of scientifically precise meanings: we can agree on what a "yard" is by pointing to the measure to be used, or we might even try to define democracy operationally. But some, like the earlier logical positivists, carry this concern for operational definition to an extreme, calling anything that cannot be so verified, "nonsense." Behaviorist psychologists have propagated a similar intolerance, refusing to deal with the fact that ultimately an individual consciousness is in some way involved even in "objective" semantic activities.[10]

Paradoxically, the linguists and the critics have until recently remained aloof from the problem of meaning and the individual consciousness. Linguists have not been unaware of it, of course, but the structural linguists limited themselves to the more easily studied manifestations of language in external linguistic behavior in spoken or printed texts. They have evaded the question by claiming that they dealt only with the theoretical construct, the system of signs shared by the users of the language, termed by de Saussure *langue* as distinct from the actual human manifestations of language, *parole*.[11] And, we have seen, the New Critics, fearful of falling into the "affective fallacy" and subjectivism, also limited themselves to analysis of the attributes of a fictive entity, the autonomous "poem itself," "the verbal icon."

Even these fields demonstrate the general trend away from logical positivist narrowness. In criticism, there is a widespread reaction against the sterility of formalist dogmas, and the hegemony of the New Critics is a thing of the past. In linguistics, the behaviorist notion that the structure of language can be studied without reference to meaning has been found to apply with profit only to certain limited types of linguistic behavior. The transformationalists have found it necessary to stress increasingly the "intuitive" basis of the native speaker's "competence," to introduce the concept of creativity in the individual speaker's articulation of unique sentences, and even to hypothesize the existence of innate linguistic ideas and linguistic universals.[12] Without necessarily agreeing with all of the pendulum-swing reversals, one can welcome the increasing willingness to recognize that the human element cannot be abstracted out.

The emergence of psycholinguistics as a discipline is in itself a favorable sign, and its work is beginning to reinforce the transactional approach. A recent article, part of a publication designed to emphasize various neglected aspects of "language as a human problem," states: "In the past twenty years of psycholinguistic investigation into what the listener does when he understands a sentence, we have come to understand that there is no simple correlation between the properties of the acoustic stimulus and the listener's interpretation of the sentence. The listener makes an active contribution to what he hears and understands, and it is this contribution which makes the problem of comprehension both difficult and interesting."[13] The reader's activities, as I have postulated them in these chapters, can be regarded as at least parallel to those of the listener in ordinary talk.

Always there is the human being mediating between the linguistic symbol and its referent. No one denies this relationship, though often only symbol and referent are actually acknowledged. The verbal symbol activates something within the reader that is somehow linked for him with what we call the referent of the word. Without falling into the extreme intuitionism or subjectivism of some recent thinkers, and without reifying "consciousness," students of language should inquire more deeply into how the abstracting and conceptualizing activities involved in the use of language are related to the stream of feeling in which they are embedded.

The complex nature of the linguistic process is beginning to be investigated from this angle. Methods of determining the "affective meaning space" of words are being experimented with (e.g., Osgood's semantic differential).[14] Studies of children's acquisition of language have led to the suggestion that there is an early stage in which the word form is "a peculiar fusion of processes which later will branch off into referential, emotive, and associative part processes. Thus, the initial sphere of reference will be indistinguishable from the associative network of the word."[15] Emotive meaning will be fused with such mixed referential-associative processes, moreover, until affective response patterns are singled out as distinctively internal, expressive components. In short, the child has to learn to sort out the various responses. Studies by Vygotsky and Piaget also suggest an internal process of differentiation of various components of meaning, carried out by the child in the original context of a diffuse network of perceptions and feelings.[16] Though often the attention of the psychological investigator is directed toward the development of mathematical or logical thinking, the important point for our purposes is that the individual "subject" is seen as the center of activity, the mediator among the various structures that present themselves to consciousness.

Thus we find the idea that linguistic operations are carried on within an experiential matrix is again becoming acceptable. William James, in his great pioneering work on psychology, refers to the stream of thought "as part of the consciousness of self." This stream metaphor still seems the best way to suggest the continuing flow of sensations, feelings, attitudes, ideas, and funded or latent memories. James introduced another concept, the phenomenon of "selective attention," which seems especially useful as a phrasing for the process that I have stressed as distinctive of the literary experience, involving, first, adoption of a focus of attention, or a stance, and, second, selection of responses relevant to the text.

James emphasizes this selective activity of the human creature, both in his dealings with the outside world and in his inner life. One of the major characteristics that James postulates for the stream of thought is a continuing process of bestowing interest on particular thoughts or elements of consciousness, which then seem to be independent of the general stream of consciousness. "It is interested in some parts of these objects to the exclusion of others, and welcomes or rejects—*chooses* from among them, in a word—all the while."[17] This is the sense in which I speak of the efferent reader screening out all but the needed end result or residue. Similarly, the aesthetic reader bestows his attention on a fuller arc of his response to the verbal symbols, selecting out what can be woven into the relevant structure of idea, feeling, and attitude. He feels this to be independent of the general diffuse stream of consciousness—to be, in short, the poem for which the text stands.

These concepts provide support for the formulation of the nature of literary experience that I am advancing. Recognition of the individual consciousness mediating between symbol and referent is essential to an understanding of any reading and especially of aesthetic reading. The concept of the transaction with the environment provides the model for the process in which reader and text are involved. Each becomes in a sense environment for the other. A two-way, or better, a circular, process can be postulated, in which the reader responds to the verbal stimuli offered by the text, but at the same time he must draw selectively on the resources of his own fund of experience and sensibility to provide and organize the substance of his response. Out of this the new experience, the literary work, is formed.

The concept of selective attention is central to my definition of the aesthetic experience. It is helpful also in eliminating the notion of a necessarily conscious choice. The selective process operates in weighting responses to the multiple possibilities offered by the text and thus sets the degrees of awareness accorded to the referential import and to the experiential process being lived through. Hence, my phrasing of an efferent or an aesthetic *stance*, since that term suggests a readiness to respond in a particular (efferent or aesthetic) way.

The concept of the experiential matrix or stream of thought and feeling within which this complex selective activity occurs provides

43

the basis for freeing "meaning" from its purely conceptual overtones and permitting rather the view of meaning as experienced. The reader of the text not only brings the poem into being by responding to the verbal symbols with the resources of his own personality and experience but also focuses his attention on the very work that he is shaping. Within this awareness of the live circuit between himself and what the text points to, he lives through the experienced meaning that is for him the poem. The dimensions of this experience will be treated more fully in the next chapter.

The view of the literary experience presented here rejects many assumptions that have tended to dominate critical theory in recent decades. One is that to deal with the reader's response is to inevitably end in pure subjectivism and a "purely affective" concept of poetry. Under the label of "the affective fallacy," as a most influential statement phrased it, concern for the reader's response became for years almost taboo in critical and educational circles: "The Affective Fallacy is a confusion between the poem and its *results* (what it *is* and what it *does*). . . . It begins by trying to derive the standards of criticism from the psychological effects of the poem and ends in impressionism and relativism. The outcome . . . is that the poem itself, as an object of specifically critical judgment, tends to disappear."[18] The basic false premise here, that the poem is a separate "object," will be dealt with further in chapter 6. At this point, I am especially concerned to dispel the notion that insistence on the reader's contribution produces "sheer affectivism," a preoccupation with emotion as opposed to thought, with the affective as opposed to the cognitive. One exponent of this view, for example, claimed that my position would lead to concentration on "me, my viscera, and *Hamlet*." Auden, in his elegy on Yeats, provides a fitting riposte to this contention.

> Now he is scattered among a hundred
>   cities
> And wholly given over to unfamiliar
>   affections;
> To find his happiness in another kind
>   of wood
> And be punished under a foreign code
>   of conscience.
> The words of a dead man
> Are modified in the guts of the living.[19]

To recognize that, as Auden phrases it in the same poem, the poet "became his admirers" does not necessarily condone irresponsible emotionalism in the reading of the poet's words. Nor does recognition of the poem as a special mode of experience in itself constitute setting up "standards of criticism." In starting with the transaction between reader and text, we are simply reporting the basic conditions for approaching all of the other problems of critical theory, such as by what criteria one reading can indeed be deemed more valid than another.

The still very influential "objective" critics' readiness to attack the straw man of art-as-pure-emotion may also lead to the misapprehension that my distinction between efferent and aesthetic reading is equivalent to a distinction between, on the one hand, referential or cognitive, versus on the other, affective or emotive, uses of language. I reject this because even what seem to be the most purely referential uses of language proceed within an ever-present matrix of feeling, which the nonaesthetic, efferent stance pushes into the fringe of awareness. Even more important: the reader evoking a work of art is not focused only on the affective impact of verbal symbols, but must attend to their cognitive import, often as the core of the other dimensions of consciousness. Precisely because this is so, the distinction between nonaesthetic and aesthetic lies not in the presence or absence of emotive or cognitive elements but in the primary direction or focus of the reader's attention.

Hence the transactional view does not share the neoromantic tendency to make degree or intensity of emotion the criterion of the presence of a work of art, of an aesthetic reading. The writings of a Hitler might arouse powerful emotions of hate in a reader, but this would still be an efferent reading, which might, for example, lead him to rush out and engage in mob action. My remarks earlier about borderline cases such as the Book of Isaiah or the Gettysburg Address also had to do with the reader's stance toward what he evoked from the text, rather than with the presence or absence of referential and emotive elements. The whole concept of the reading continuum negates this distinction. As we have seen, a reading of Rachel Carson's *Silent Spring* could be primarily cognitive in the sense that the reader was seeking verifiable ecological knowledge, but this does not necessarily imply absence of awareness of affective elements generated by the words and their referents during the process of reading.

When poems such as Shakespeare's lyrics or Mallarmé's *Un Coup de Dés* are said to require an extreme aesthetic stance, this should not be interpreted as implying that these are purely emotive. Even in such works there is a cognitive element, in the sense that at the very least the individual words have clear referents. The aesthetic stance is mandatory simply because practically the only way for the reader to organize the cognitive elements is through primary attention to the experienced meaning. However, a sonnet, for example, may have a strong ideational structure, which may be an important means of synthesizing the affective and cognitive elements. Nor do I mean to suggest that the best literary works of art are instances of what George Moore and others have called "pure poetry." On the contrary, it seems to me that many good and great poems, and certainly the good and great stories, novels, and plays, possess a strong cognitive or intellectual or ideational element. The mark of the reader's aesthetic activity is precisely that he does not respond to either of these elements separately but, rather, fuses the cognitive and the emotive, or perhaps more accurately, apprehends them as facets of the same lived-through experience, thus giving it its special meaning and quality.

Apprehension of what a poem is "about," what a novel "says," the human meaning, the "sense" of the words, what they refer to "in the world" is an essential element, which cannot be dissociated from the affective impact on the reader, given an aesthetic orientation. The concept of the aesthetic stance is in harmony with T. S. Eliot's much-debated idea of the "unified sensibility." As I understand it, Eliot was at various times reacting against both the Romantic glorification of emotion and the Victorian preoccupation with "message." The reader who adopts the aesthetic stance can pay attention to all of the elements activated within him by the text, and can develop the fusion of thought and feeling, of cognitive and affective, that constitutes the integrated sensibility. Out of these he will structure the experience that for him corresponds to the text of *King Lear* or *Emma* or *The Waste Land*.

In this chapter, I have been especially concerned with differentiating aesthetic from nonaesthetic or efferent reading. Concepts have been developed that are crucial to an understanding of the nature of the literary work of art: "selective attention," which makes possible the adoption of an aesthetic or efferent stance, and the modulation of interest in specific details. And, most important of all, "aesthetic

46

reading," characterized by the reader's turning his attention toward the full lived-through fusion with the text. The way has been cleared for a rounded consideration of the complexities of the reader's activities during the literary transaction.

4

EVOKING

A POEM

*A*T least two streams of response are involved in any reading-event. Thus far, we have concentrated on the reader's evocation of the poem or novel or play from the text. This is usually thought of as encompassing the entire reading process. Once the work has been re-created, it seems, the reader-critic can respond to it, evaluate it, analyze it. To limit the reading process to the production of the work, however, with the critical responses a purely subsequent activity, oversimplifies the actual reading transaction. Even as we are generating the work of art, we are reacting to it. A concurrent stream of feelings, attitudes, and ideas is aroused by the very work being summoned up under guidance of the text. This chapter will attempt to sketch some of the main dimensions of the reader's activities, although it will inevitably simplify the awesome complexity of the process.

This dual stream of responses may not always be apprehended as separate. The reaction to the emerging work may be felt merely as a general state of mind, an ambiance of acceptance, approval, incredulity. Such responses may be momentary, peripheral, almost woven into the texture of what is felt to be the work itself. Or the reaction may at times take more conscious form. The range of potential responses and the gamut of degrees of intensity and articulateness are infinitely vast, since they depend not only on the character of the text but even more on the special character of the individual reader.

Once this complexity of the reading process is acknowledged, it becomes possible, for the sake of clarity, to deal with each of these aspects separately, though never in isolation from the other. In this chapter, I shall first attempt to develop a fuller account of some of the activities involved in evoking the literary work of art. Then it will be possible to relate these processes to the accompanying current of responses.

The reader's role is often disposed of through one or another general analogy with the much more fully explored activities of the author. In the effort to vindicate the importance of the reader, we should not, however, award him the reflected glory of duplicating the author's initial creativity. For instance, it is sometimes claimed that the reader seeks to recapture the author's original emotions and state of mind. This equates the author's final text with its germinal impulse, and disregards the groping, developing, trial-and-error revision characteristic of much creative activity, in the course of which the initial motivation may become transformed. Keats's love of Fanny Brawne or Auden's feelings at the death of Yeats may have generated their poems, but the texts that resulted had an evolution and a character of their own. The nature of the language in which an author is writing, and the literary and cultural conventions he is either following or modifying, play an important role. Beyond this, the very emotions and thoughts ultimately expressed through the text may have undergone a development or even transformation.

The view that the reader in re-creating the work reenacts the author's creative role superficially seems more reasonable. But this, too, ignores actuality. The end result of the poet's creative throes is a text, a pattern of verbal signs. This is the reader's starting point. His

49

relationship to the text is different from the author's, depending on a more modest, but happily more widespread, kind of ability. Each reader, we have seen, assuming that the signs before him represent an organized verbal structure, feels his way toward a vital principle of coherence for his own inner responses to these particular words in this particular order. He evolves an impalpable experiential structure which he apprehends as the poem or novel or play. He will be conscious always that the words of the author are guiding him; he will have a sense of achieved communication, sometimes, indeed, of communion with the author. But it will be by virtue of the reader's own unique form of literary creativity. Thus, the differences between the activities of author and reader require as much attention as the similarities. Still, the analogy with the author's creative process does provide a baseline from which to proceed in defining the reader's task.

Coleridge's discussion of the creative process in his famous chapter 13 of the *Biographia Literaria* continues to be especially pertinent. For Coleridge, the poetic imagination flowers from the primary creative process involved in all human perception. In this, he foreshadowed the recent developments in psychology and philosophy that emphasize the contribution of the perceiving organism, a concept that is central, we have seen, in the transactional approach. We are usually not aware of the organizing or constructive process—the fitting-together and interpretation of visual clues—which results in the act of perception. It is noticed, perhaps, when there is a mistaking of the signals—when, say, someone thinks he recognizes a friend approaching and then discovers a stranger. Or we look at a black-and-white checkerboard and "see" the pattern change as our attention shifts. In the secondary or poetic imagination, Coleridge found operating not simply a putting-together or patterning of remembered elements but an organic and vital kind of synthesis: "It dissolves, diffuses, dissipates, in order to re-create: or where this process is rendered impossible, yet still at all events it struggles to idealize and to unify. It is essentially *vital*, even as all objects (*as* objects) are essentially fixed and dead."[1] Contemporary psychologists may find the term imagination itself embarrassing, with its overtones reminiscent of the older views of psychological faculties. Yet Coleridge's fundamental insights remain cogent.

The concept of organic form which "shapes as it develops itself from

50

within and the fulness of its development is one and the same with the perfection of its outward form," is central to Coleridge's view of the poetic imagination. Shakespeare, he said, evolved "the germ from within by the imaginative power according to an idea." Literary creation is, after all, basically the making of choices. No matter whether the poem seems to have sprung full-blown for recording in the poet's manuscript, or whether dozens of versions and revisions exist, a process of selection from the resources of the language has occurred. Something, no matter how dimly sensed, must have guided the choices, some evolving feeling, emotion, attitude, or idea, that dictated selection of the vitally relevant word and rejection of the one that blurs or weakens. At various points, Coleridge stresses the power of reducing multitude into unity of effect and modifying a series of thoughts by some one predominant thought or feeling. Authors' accounts of the genesis of a literary work and evidence concerning the "making of a poem" found in textual revisions add up largely to the authors' striving constantly—often by trial and error—to achieve, and then to satisfy, some such organizing or synthesizing urge.[2]

The organic unity of a work is for Coleridge the outward and visible sign of the synthesizing, creative power of the poet's imagination. This metaphor of organic unity, dating back at least to Plato and Aristotle, though mainly for us the legacy of the Romantics, has been one of the shibboleths of contemporary criticism. All the more strange, therefore, is the general failure to do justice to the parallel synthesizing, organizing activity of the reader in his evocation of a poem.

The analogy between the process of visual perception and the primary imagination holds for reading also, even though the reading process is much more complex than any act of simple perception. In reading, we also perceive cues or clues—in this instance offered by the verbal symbols, which in turn have been derived from the printer's signs—and we must also "put the clues together." There is an element of creativity in even the simplest reading act. Further, Coleridge saw the difference between the poetic imagination and ordinary perception as residing in the organic and vital nature of the poet's imaginative synthesis. So too the reading which results in the literary work of art requires something more than an ordinary putting-together of clues. As we have seen, the aesthetic stance

51

provides the differentiating factor as the reader builds up and con-templates a unique synthesis of his responses which is for him the poem.

This active, synthesizing aspect of the reading process has been largely neglected. "Could a rule be given from without, poetry would cease to be poetry, and sink into a mechanical art," said Coleridge. By the same token the reader who seeks to participate in a poem or novel or play must face ultimately a unique task of selection, synthesis, and interpretation. As "information theory" studies remind us, there is an element of experiment, trial and error, in construing even the most banal verbal communication. In the reading of a literary work of art, this activity is raised to the level of creative adventure. In this sense, the "shaping spirit," the "synthetic and magical power," of the imagination, which Coleridge attributed to the poet, can also be claimed for the reader.

Actually, as Coleridge suggested, not only poetry, but ordinary linguistic activity also has much of this character of spontaneous creation. The psycholinguists concern themselves with its humble manifestation in the utterance of a simple sentence. How is it, they ask, that when we begin a sentence we have no conscious notion of how it will end, yet we do end it in a coherent way?[3] The speaker, the linguists remind us, possesses "linguistic competence." We may afterward analyze the structure and semantic makeup of our sen-tence, but this is a separate and subsequent activity, not to be confused with the production of the sentence itself. Similarly, the writer may plan, analyze, revise his work, but this is not to be confused with its actual creation, with the activities carried on under the guidance of the "shaping spirit of the imagination." In Shake-speare, Coleridge says, "all is growth, evolution, [genesis];—each line, each word, almost, begets the following, and the will of the writer is an interfusion, a continuous agency, and not a series of separate acts."[4]

The reader is no less immersed in a creative process that goes on largely below the threshold of awareness. He is conscious of the resulting images, ideas, states of mind, even physical states, that are generated by his reading, but he is not aware of the individual responses or of much of the process of selection and synthesis that goes on as his eyes scan the page. Like the speaker, he is able of course to stop the process, to shift his attention from the actual literary experience, and to engage in an analysis of the words, the syntax and possible alternative responses. Still, we should not confuse these analytic activities with the experienced literary work.

Someone perusing a book often seems hypnotized by the text, completely oblivious of everything except the printed page before him. Anything else that might enter into awareness—a physical sensation, a noise, will be shut out, as he attends only to what the symbols before him bring into consciousness. But just as the noise of a passing car is irrelevant, so are some of the images, feelings, and ideas welling up under the sequential stimulus of the words. This imposes the delicate task of sorting the relevant from the irrelevant in a continuing process of selection, revision, and expansion.

The verbal symbols of the text are part of a linguistic system by virtue of their potentiality for evoking in listeners or readers referents commonly accepted by those sharing the language. These the reader has presumably assimilated in past experiences with language in life situations and in reading. But out of these past encounters with the particular verbal symbols has crystallized for him not only their publicly accepted content and overtones but also a special personal feeling-tone and significance. There will be a common reference for "home," say. But the individual will have learned this in specific life-situations and in various specific verbal contexts, spoken and written. Hence the general usage will be embodied for each in a personal matrix, varying from reader to reader. This quality of language—essentially social yet always individually internalized—makes the literary experience something both shared and uniquely personal.

The poet fashions a text in which any one word is dependent on its interrelationship with the other words. Our transactional point of view leads us to see that it is not the words, essential though they are, that—to use Richards's term—"interinanimate" one another. The reader, assuming the aesthetic stance, selects out and synthesizes—interinanimates—his responses to the author's pattern of words. This requires the reader to carry on a continuing, constructive, "shaping" activity.

The lexicographer attempts to record in his dictionary the different possible referents and associations that have generally become associated with a particular verbal symbol. The reader must seek guidance toward which of these meanings is appropriate within the context provided by the other words of the text. Moreover, out of this particular collocation of words, a special unprecedented variant set of overtones and meanings may emerge. (Coleridge saw the presence of a high degree of such contextual determinism as the trait of the truly successful work of art.) The more closely knit the text, the greater the reader's need for refinement of synthesizing response. We have seen that, in the aesthetic reading especially, while holding on to the sound and the primary reference of the words, he must pay attention to the shimmering interplay of meanings, associations, feeling-tones.

As one decodes the opening lines or sentences and pages of a text, one begins to develop a tentative sense of a framework within which to place what will follow. Underlying this is the assumption that this body of words, set forth in certain patterns and sequences on the page, bears the potentiality for a reasonably unified or integrated, or at the very least coherent, experience. One evolves certain expectations about the diction, the subject, the ideas, the themes, the kind of text, that will be forthcoming. Each sentence, each phrase, each word, will signal certain possibilities and exclude others, thus limiting the arc of expectations. What the reader has elicited from the text up to any point generates a receptivity to certain kinds of ideas, overtones, or attitudes. Perhaps one can think of this as an alerting of certain areas of memory, a stirring-up of certain reservoirs of experience, knowledge, and feeling. As the reading proceeds, attention will be fixed on the reverberations or implications that result from fulfillment or frustration of those expectations.

In broadest terms, then, the basic paradigm of the reading process consists in the response to cues; the adoption of an efferent or aesthetic stance; the development of a tentative framework or guiding principle of organization; the arousal of expectations that influence the selection and synthesis of further responses; the fulfillment or reinforcement of expectations, or their frustration, sometimes leading to revision of the framework, and sometimes, if necessary, to rereading; the arousal of further expectations; until, if all goes well, with the completed decoding of the text, the final synthesis or organization is achieved.

The desire "to see what happens next" in a narrative is the most obvious version of the basic forward movement of the reading process. In another phrasing, texts are said to be more or less effective in eliciting and holding the interest of the reader. Of course, not only the unfolding of a story but many other kinds of stimuli generate such interest, which embodies both intellectual and emotive elements. Indeed, interest seems to be the name given to the reader's need to live through to some resolution of the tensions, questions, curiosity or conflicts aroused by the text. This need to resolve, to round out, gives impetus to the organizing activity of the reader. What we call a sense of form also manifests itself in such progression, the arousal of expectations, the movement toward some culmination or completion. Rhythm, meter, rhyme, for example, depend on some kind of anticipation of repetition of sensed elements, or perception of variation on a recurrent pattern.

Aristotle's articulation of the need for a beginning, middle, and end of an action is relevant here. His theory of tragedy as exciting and providing a catharsis for emotions of pity and terror—no matter whether catharsis is understood as a purification or a purgation—may also be viewed as a special type of the arousal-resolution pattern. Underlying all this organizing activity, as I have said, is the assumption that the text offers the basis for a coherent experience. It may seem to "organize itself" if the reader proceeds smoothly with the process I have sketched above. Sometimes the reader may read quickly to grasp the framework—as in sensing the tone, the mood, the voice of a poem, or in establishing the general drift of a narrative—before rereading it more slowly, to attend to all the details and finer shadings. Or there may be unfulfilled expectations, unanswered questions, details that cannot be assimilated, so that much is held in suspension until it all "falls into shape," or there is a "click" of insight, to cite phrases that report this aspect of the reading event. If such a putting-together, such a com-position, does not eventually happen, the cause may be felt to be either a weakness in the text, or a failure on the reader's part. In some recent French and American writings—as in Laurence Sterne's *Tristram Shandy*—the frustration of the reader's desire for resolution becomes itself the "organizing principle."

"Cues" or "clues" have been used as the most general terms for designating the textual signs to which the reader responds. If we try to sort out the various types of cues, we usually start with language. The reader, we have said, must possess competence in the phonemic and syntactic systems of the language, as well as the system of visual symbols. What the words stand for—the semantic "code," to use a fashionable, though rather loosely used, term—obviously also is involved. The literary "code" of vocabulary and subject embedded in the text and the patterns of literary convention signal the aesthetic stance or alert the reader to construct a particular genre, a poem, say, or a play. Moreover, the verbal symbols activate a structure of ideas and attitudes that grow out of and around the concepts of social life. Most readers tend to operate within the literary codes rather automatically and to begin by reflecting on these human considerations.

We may borrow from the anthropologists or the sociologists their classifications of the many different codes or mores or systems of ideas and values that apply to the world evoked by the reader.[5] Some of the most usual are assumptions about the universe, about "human nature," about the structure of society, about the roles of men and women, children and adults, about moral and social and religious imperatives. The text presents us with a whole network of such codes, embodied explicitly or implicitly in its personae and its situations. The reader draws on his own internalized culture in order to elicit from the text this world which may differ from his own in many respects. Moreover, the text may yield glimpses of the personality and codes of the author. The literary transaction may thus embody, and probably to some degree always embodies, an interplay between at least two sets of codes, two sets of values. Even when author and reader share the same culture—that is, when they live in the same social group at the same time, and the text directly reflects that culture, their uniqueness as individual human beings would insure this interplay.

The problem created by the fact that a text has been produced by an author living in a different time or place—that is, in a different culture—thus is largely only an extreme instance of the tensions implicit in any literary transaction. (In chapter 6 we shall explore some of the alternative approaches to the question of the author's intention, and in chapter 7, the critical implications of the relationship between author's and reader's codes.)

The very general term "framework" has served to cover the great variety and complexity of kinds of organizing principles that the reader may require. At the beginning of a reading, a number of different choices are being made at the same time. As we have observed, verbal clues (e.g., diction or syntax) and content clues arouse expectations concerning the stance to be adopted. If the aesthetic stance seems indicated, clues are noted concerning the genre to be expected. In chapter 2, for example, we found that some of the readers did not at first sense the Frost quatrain as a poem and had to reread it with revised stance and with their attention (or expectations) focused differently. Others responded to the visual clues, the wide margins and lines of print. We saw them applying first one and then another tentative sense of a subject, a situation, a setting, a persona or voice that might make it possible (provide the framework within which) to develop a consistent and coherent "meaning" for the four lines. The beginning of a narrative will be signaled by clues as to situation, setting, characters, and incidents that stir the expectation of further events. Other clues—first of all, visual clues, the disposition of the words on the page—will announce whether a prose fiction or a play is opening.

Past literary experiences serve as subliminal guides as to the genre to be anticipated, the details to be attended to, the kinds of organizing patterns to be evolved. Each genre, each kind of work (e.g., a sonnet or an ode, a detective novel, a picaresque novel, a psychological novel) makes its own kinds of conventional demands on the reader— that is, once he has set up one or another such expectation, his stance, the details he responds to, the way he handles his responses, will differ. Traditional subjects, themes, treatments, may provide the guides to organization and the background against which to recognize something new or original in the text.

Early in this process, too, the reader weaves his responses into an utterance sensed as a particular voice of a particular kind of persona. Embedded in the text also are felt to be clues as to the attitudes of that persona toward what is being uttered and toward the reader-listener. Should he, for example, be the kind of trusting listener who hears what is being set forth as a neutral, impersonal, or at least a direct, utterance, or should he listen for ironic overtones?—to cite only two of the myriad possible alternatives of tone or point of view.

Memory functions in an important way in this selecting, synthesizing, organizing process. I refer here not simply to the overall role of the linguistic- and life-memories the reader brings to the text, but to the way in which during the reading the reader keeps alive what he has already elicited from the text. At any point, he brings a state of mind, a penumbra of "memories" of what has preceded, ready to be activated by what follows, and providing the context from which further meaning will be derived. Awareness—more or less explicit—of repetitions, echoes, resonances, repercussions, linkages, cumulative effects, contrasts, or surprises is the mnemonic matrix for the structuring of emotion, idea, situation, character, plot—in short, for the evocation of a work of art.

E. M. Forster, in his laudable effort to categorize types of fiction by the demands made on the reader, listed "Curiosity" as the trait the reader needed to bring to "story," the simple chronological presentation of events answering the question, "And then? And then?" "Memory" and "Intelligence" were the capacities demanded by a fiction with a "plot," that is, a sequence causally determined. Undoubtedly, these types of narrative may be characterized by a greater dependence respectively on the appeal to curiosity or to memory and intelligence. But this demarcation should not blur the fact that even the simplest narrative, the simplest stringing together of "actions," to use Aristotle's term, requires of the reader a degree of organizing ability, and a degree of memory of what has preceded. And curiosity, in the sense of a desire to see what comes next, is present in the reading of the most causally complex and value-laden novel. The transactional point of view permits us to recognize the diversity in the quality and complexity of stimuli offered by different texts, but at the same time it prevents our ignoring the complexity of even the most naïve reading of a text presenting a simple fictional narrative or other genre.

For the experienced reader, much of this has become automatic, carried on through a continuing flow of responses, syntheses, readjustment, and assimilation. Under such pressure, the irrelevant or confusing referents for the verbal symbols evidently often are ignored or are not permitted to rise into consciousness. Referents that fit together from the same area of experience or that share the same kinds of feeling-tones, often "come to mind" without conscious selection. The baseball reference of "home," to take an extreme example, will not have to be consciously rejected when, say, reading in Ecclesiastes "man goeth to his long home, and the mourners go about the streets."

Sometimes, as Empson has so elaborately pointed out, different referents and associations may simultaneously suggest themselves and by "ambiguity" give depth and complexity to the experience lived through in the involvement with the text. When, in the course of reading, such multiple referents and associations do arise, there still remains the need for acceptance or rejection. Hence the controversy over Empson's much-cited passage concerning his associations with the fourth line of Shakespeare's Sonnet 73.

> That time of year thou may'st in me behold
> When yellow leaves, or none, or few, do hang
> Upon those boughs which shake against the cold,
> Bare ruin'd choirs, where late the sweet birds sang.

Empson writes:

The comparison holds for many reasons; because ruined monastery choirs are places in which to sing, because they involve sitting in a row, because they are made of wood, are carved into knots and so forth, because they used to be surrounded by a sheltering building crystallised out of the likeness of a forest, and coloured with stained glass and painting like flowers and leaves, because they are now abandoned by all but the grey walls coloured like the skies of winter, because the cold and Narcissistic charm suggested by choir-boys suits well with Shakespeare's feeling for the object of the Sonnets, and for various sociological and historical reasons (the protestant destruction of monasteries; fear of puritanism), which it would be hard now to trace out in their proportions; these reasons, and many more relating the simile to its place in the Sonnet, must all combine to give the line its beauty, and there is a sort of ambiguity in not knowing which of them to hold most clearly in mind. Clearly this is involved in all such richness and heightening of effect, and the machinations of ambiguity are among the very roots of poetry.[6]

In a prefatory note for his third edition (1956), Empson found it necessary to reply to objections to his reference above to the protestant destruction of the monasteries. He claims that he "mainly meant to illustrate the familiar process of putting in a little historical background," and that the line is "still good if you don't think at all about the Destruction of the Monasteries." But this begs the question of whether this association, no matter how historically or sociologically logical, is relevant to, or strengthens, the contribution of this particular line in this particular sonnet. The alternatives, for either a contemporary of Shakespeare or a twentieth-century reader, would be: 1) to accept the historical association into the center of awareness and seek to relate it to the primary level of meaning; 2) to leave it as a peripheral association, an overtone felt to be emotionally in tune with the ideas and attitudes central to the sonnet; or 3) to repress and reject the association as irrelevant or even disturbing or inharmonious. Such decisions are constantly and often automatically being made.

In probably many instances, the tentative guiding or organizing principle activates mainly relevant ideas and associations. But when elements appear that do not fuse with or relate to what precedes, either emotionally or in terms of "sense," there may be a retreat, a rereading, an effort to sense new guidelines within the context. Something such as Empson's political association with "bare ruin'd choirs" may bring the problem of selection to consciousness, and after a process of reflection on various alternatives a linkage or choice may crystallize. Usually, however, the choice depends on selective attention to components of consciousness rather than on logical analysis. Reflection may later explain analytically why, say, the political association has been rejected. It may be pointed out that the first line has focused attention on the age of the persona and has aroused expectations that the following lines will fill in or particularize the idea; that the second and third lines have called forth images of decline and decay caused by natural forces—the passage of time, the wintry season, the effect of the elements—and that these arouse feelings and thoughts applicable to old age; that the notion of the expropriation of the monasteries moves into a different kind of destructiveness (political) that has no ready connection with natural aging due to passage of time and has dissonant overtones that do not blend with the feelings and attitudes aroused by the other associations. But as Empson would agree, this logical explanation, like much of Empson's own analysis, differs from the actual selective, synthesizing process. Empson's reference, in the excerpt above, to the difficulty of knowing which idea to "hold most clearly in mind" suggests something of what I mean by the process of allowing compatible associations into the focus of attention.

Obviously, a great many different factors, dependent on the text *and* on what the reader brings to it, will affect both conscious and unconscious choices. Modulations of attention will occur. Different texts certainly have different potentialities for generating multiple levels of association. Moreover, readers evidently vary greatly in the extent to which they hold fast to a central structure of ideas and attitudes while sensing a penumbra of overtones and associations. General habits of reading in different literary epochs vary too in this respect. Note the actual cultivation of ambiguities, tensions, paradoxes, puns in recent years, of which Empson's work is only one prime example.

Nor does all of this activity, we have seen, go on in a simple linear progression. As the text unrolls, there is not only the cumulative building-up of effect through the linking of remembered earlier elements to the new ones. There is sometimes a backward flow, a revision of earlier understandings, emphases, or attitudes; there may even be the emergence of a completely altered framework or principle of organization. Sometimes this very act of revision of the framework becomes an important aspect of "the meaning" of the work. Swift's "A Modest Proposal" comes to mind, and indeed all satire requires an awareness of a double set of organizing principles.

A much-anthologized contemporary short story, Shirley Jackson's "The Lottery," can provide a fairly simple example of the reader's (nevertheless still very complex) activity. The opening paragraph offers typical clues of tone and subject that alert the reader to expect a story. One assimilates the general setting of a quiet village, and the general situation, that this is a pleasant day when the villagers will briefly interrupt their usual activities in order to participate in a traditional lottery.

> The morning of June 27th was clear and sunny, with the fresh warmth of a full-summer day; the flowers were blossoming profusely and the grass was richly green. The people of the village began to gather in the square, between the post office and the bank, around ten o'clock; in some towns there were so many people that the lottery took two days and had to be started on June 26th, but in this village, where there were only about three hundred people, the whole lottery took less than two hours, so it could begin at ten o'clock in the morning and still be through in time to allow the villagers to get home for noon dinner.[7]

Within this framework, the reader proceeds to incorporate more and more details that reinforce and enlarge the pleasantly prosaic picture. The villagers gather on the green, some of them chatting desultorily about the customary event. Mrs. Hutchinson even jokes about her last-minute arrival: " 'Wouldn't have me leave m'dishes in the sink, now, would you, Joe?' " At a certain point, somewhat different for different readers, details become less and less amenable to absorption into the earlier rather relaxed and matter-of-fact picture. Winning the lottery seems less and less the pleasant affair one might have expected. Then comes the shock of realizing what it all had been leading to—the stoning to death of the "winner," Mrs. Hutchinson. One detail after another that the reader had earlier given neutral or pleasant overtones or had slurred over now is recalled and seen to prepare for the lottery as a ritual sacrifice. Old Man Warner's jingle, for instance, "Lottery in June, corn be heavy soon," undoubtedly would stir the memory of any reader at all knowledge-able about anthropology, but without reinforcement. Now in retro-spect it is seen to be a clue linking this lottery to primitive ritual in which success of the crops is assured by sacrifice of a scapegoat, a ritual that might once have had meaning but is now being followed out of the inertia of custom. It is as though one had organized a pattern by paying attention only to the white squares in a checkerboard and now must reorganize by making the dark squares dominant.

The reader has lived through the villagers' routine, almost un-thinking acceptance of a rite of traditional brutality. For many adult readers, I have found, the traumatic realization of this constitutes "the meaning" of the story, felt in an intensely personal way. The question is often raised: How much of our own culture involves routine acceptance of similar callousness and brutality?

The way in which Jackson has "taken advantage" of the reader's habits of organization and the relative simplicity of this story makes it particularly useful for our purpose. Jackson's ending forces her reader to think back over the process that he has been carrying on and to see how his expectations had led him to link some details together and to ignore or underemphasize others. As in a slow-motion replay of a film, he can see something of the kind of process that he engages in even in those readings that do not require such "a double take" or reorganization but develop in a straightforward way: the tentative creation of a framework, a setting, a situation, a tone, and the reader's tendency to pay attention to those details that fit, until inassimilable details require reorganization of the synthesizing framework. This kind of tentative synthesis and revision goes on in less drastic ways in all reading, and especially in aesthetic reading, with its attention to fine shades of thought, sensation, and feeling. Much of this activity seems to occur on the periphery of conscious-ness, while the reader's attention is focused on the work he is shap-ing.

Of course, sometimes the reader does not relinquish his tentative framework but, instead, ignores the untractable details. Or perhaps he does not sense a viable organizing principle at all. The process I have sketched is equally illustrated by such misreadings; as in biol-ogy, pathological developments often throw light on healthy function-ing. Richards, in *Practical Criticism*, categorizes some of the many reasons for failure to do justice to a text. These categories in large measure describe some aspect of the reader's attitudes or modes of response (e.g., "irrelevant associations and stock responses," "sentimentality and inhibition," "technical presuppositions and critical preconceptions"). Ironically, the New Critics derived from Richards his high standards of interpretation but in their effort to exorcise such misreadings somehow focused on the text and ignored the reader. Perhaps they were misled by the emphasis on readers' failures into forgetting that if readers do succeed, they accomplish this through the kind of positive handling of their own responses that I have been outlining.

Recent studies of children's errors in reading have had a more constructive result. Misreadings, it has been discovered, are often due to the development of misleading expectations or frameworks rather than to the mistaking of an individual word. Sometimes the grasp of the correct framework may even lead to the substitution of another word that fits it as well as the actual word of the text. These studies in "miscues," though mainly concerned with efferent reading, have brought welcome reinforcement to my view of the reading process.[8]

The importance of the reader's contribution—the mnemonic baggage, so to speak, that he brings to the text—and its influence on all dimensions of the reading process can be illustrated by readings of Emily Dickinson's poem:

> I heard a Fly buzz—when I died—
> The Stillness in the Room
> Was like the Stillness in the Air—
> Between the Heaves of Storm—
>
> The eyes around—had wrung them dry—
> and Breaths were gathering firm
> For that last Onset—when the King
> Be witnessed—in the Room—
>
> I willed my Keepsakes—Signed away
> What portion of me be
> Assignable—and then it was
> There interposed a Fly—
>
> With Blue—uncertain stumbling Buzz—
> Between the light—and me—
> And then the Windows failed—and then
> I could not see to see—[9]

Over the years, I have observed many students, graduate and undergraduate, encounter this text, and have been struck by the importance of the associations that the intruding insect has for readers. I shall not here attempt to report on the whole range of interpretations nor on the evidence concerning the tremendously complex process of creating from the verbal clues a sense of the situation—a dying person, surrounded by mourning friends or relatives—but shall dwell rather on the general attitudes and ideas that blend with these specifics. Nor do I propose to expound a paraphrase or a normative reading. The aim is rather to outline the broad movement and structure of some readers' contrasting experiences during their evocation of the poem.

The opening line, with its juxtaposition of death and the fly, is striking no matter what the associations. The rest of the work is felt as a flashback, retracing the moments before the coming of death. For some, the fly in that opening statement is simply an insignificant, weak creature. The stillness image of the first stanza, sensed as a moment of intense quiet between moments of great agitation, generates expectancy of some thunderous sequel. This flows into the tension of the hushed awaiting of "the King," felt as the advent of the awesome, and for some, godlike, majesty of death. The very casting away of all worldly interests, the cessation of all conventional bedside expressions of grief as inadequate to the occasion, strengthen the tense expectation of an overwhelming, momentous event.

"And then it was"—at this high point of expectation—"there interposed a Fly," with its anticlimactic aura of something inconsequential, weak, mundane. The failing light and vision of the remaining lines bring nothing to change—indeed for some they reinforce—this sense of anticlimax. The very repetition of "and then" in this version of the text strengthens the feeling of a turning point, from initial awestruck anticipation to the humble resolution. The last line, "I could not see to see," parallel to the homely "I could not see to read," seems to distinguish between the act, the effort to see, and the actual seeing, and thus enhances the felt value of the mere physical senses that are being extinguished.

Many of my students, however, brought to the word "Fly" a very strong association with filth, germs, and decay. For them, the first line immediately links the thought of death with strong feelings of revulsion, which color the ensuing lines and create an ambivalence throughout. Underlying the potentially positive sense of the coming of "the King" is the association with giving up the body to loathsome decay, of which the fly, the feeder upon putrefaction, is the harbinger. "And then it was" signals a fulfillment of this morbid presentiment.

For those with an originally neutral reaction to the fly, the image of a creature "with Blue—uncertain stumbling Buzz" usually suggests its weakness and adds a somewhat sympathetic, even pitying overtone. But as many readings demonstrate, the line does not alter the negative feelings of those who responded initially with loathing. Reserving the question of relative validity of readings for later discussion,* we can recognize that what the reader brings to the text enters into both streams of response—the evocation and the reaction. Given the negative response to the first line, the very structure of the work is affected, and the last stanza becomes not an anticlimax, but a crescendo, fulfilling the ambivalent anticipations elicited by the first line. Although, of course, the individual readings vary in a multiplicity of ways, in these instances two basically different poems are lived through. Even the structure of the poem changes with what the reader brings to it.[10]

Many other elements of Dickinson's text have similar potentialities for decidedly diverse personal responses which become woven into the texture of the experienced poem. To mention only a few: the thought of death, the image of the willing away of wordly goods, the expressions of conventional sorrow, the religious or legal overtones of "witnessed," the positive or negative attitudes toward "King," the tendency to merge the thoughts of death and of God or Heaven, or to focus on one or the other. Nor is this the place to discuss the differences between readings due to differing literary sophistication, for example, knowledge of other poems by Dickinson and others, understanding of her use of capitals, openness to departures from usual syntax. I have touched on this text mainly because it lends itself to rather schematic treatment of the intensely complex process of reading a poem.

We have come far indeed from the notion of "the work" as an object, existing "out there" for the enterprising reader and critic to illuminate. I have sketched something of the process of reading a poem or novel or play as a structured experience corresponding to the

---

*What Dickinson's own reading might have been is of course a valid question, as is the whole problem of validity of interpretation. These are separate questions, however, which I treat in chaps. 6 and 7.

signs of the text. Yet one can understand why this experience can be thought of as an "object" of attention and reflection. William James, in speaking of the stream of thought, mentioned our tendency to perceive whatever is at the focus of attention as having an objective existence.[11] This is, of course, true of our retinal images of the book in our hand or of the tree outside the window; we "see" them as "out there." In focusing our attention on the poem or play or novel, we are saved from confusion with that kind of external, "objective" reality by our awareness that although the images and characters of, say, a story are at the focus of our attention, their existential contours are delimited for us by our transaction with the text. This evocation, then, becomes the "object" of the concurrent stream of responses that, though usually ignored, often contributes greatly to the texture and the impact of the literary transaction.

Another relatively simple illustration of how the reader's response to some aspect of the emerging work will become integrated into the work as perceived: The opening scene of *King Lear,* in which the egotistical old king calls on his daughters to declare their love for him, has drawn similar responses from generations of my students, who almost universally manifested some degree of disapproval of the traditional image of the authoritarian father. They sympathized with Cordelia's refusal to emulate her sisters' fawning protestations of love and admired Cordelia's statement about the amount of love due a father in a life that should admit also love of a husband. They saw Cordelia as faultless, the innocent victim of her domineering father's lack of wisdom. A. C. Bradley, writing early in this century, reported both this reaction and another one.[12] Some readers, he said, felt Cordelia's reticence to constitute a failure to rise to the demands of the situation. She should have been able, they claimed, to reassure her father that he was fondly loved, even while refusing to appear to compete for a reward. Other heroines, such as Desdemona, were temperamentally capable of accomplishing this, Bradley suggests. He points to elements in the text that show Cordelia to be extraordinarily reserved, proud, withdrawn, laconic, almost inarticulate, unable to express her love. Such a reserved response makes the tragedy a dual one, in the sense that the sequence of events is unleashed not only by Lear's errors but also by Cordelia's inflexibility toward an aged and erring father. One might say that readers with different attitudes toward parental authority and filial piety reacted differently to the words and actions of Lear and Cordelia. But these attitudes of approval or disapproval actually seem to become woven into the "meaning" of the scene. Moreover, the way in which the first scene is regarded throws a different light on everything that follows and especially, of course, on the scenes involving Cordelia and her fate. It becomes difficult in this instance to separate out the process of evocation from the stream of concurrent response.

The blurring of the boundary between the two aspects of the reading process is illustrated also by the different ways in which characters are evoked. Some theorists stress the tendency of the reader to empathize or to identify with the characters and their experiences. Others see the reader of a literary work as a spectator, not directly involved in the events, as he might be in real life. Actually, these are not mutually exclusive notions. Texts differ widely in the stimuli they offer toward the participatory or spectator attitude. But even given the same text, readers differ in their degree of empathy. Moreover, within the same work, the reader may adopt a variety of attitudes toward the same character or toward different characters, varying from identification to hostile spectatorship. In some instances, the reader feels himself at one with the attitudes or experiences called up. The "I" of a lyric may seem to be himself, the images and feelings aroused may occupy the whole span of attention, as though he himself were uttering the words. At other times, he may feel himself to be looking on at the scenes in, say, a Dickens novel, amused at the pomposity of a Micawber or approving or disapproving the behavior of Pip. Again, the reader may adopt sometimes one and sometimes the other attitude, identifying with one character, seeing glimpses of a relative in another, impersonally sitting in judgment on a third.

Both the capacity to empathize and the ability, as William James noted, to shift the focus of attention toward different elements in the stream of consciousness, certainly enter into this feeling of nearness or distance from the characters. Perhaps our sense of identification with a character is due to a relatively complete merging of evocation and response. Such a character arouses no qualifications, questions, doubts, but on the contrary fits our preconceptions, our needs, our own conscious or unconscious potentialities.

Even when we feel ourselves simply spectators, we are also participants. I regret having in the past written of literature as providing "vicarious" experience. The term, derived from the Latin for "substitute," seems to me to be appropriate when we speak, for example, of someone vicariously undergoing punishment for another's crime. But in a literary work there is no one else for whom we are substituting. We are not vicarious or substitute Juliets or Leopold Blooms; we are living in the world of the work which we have created under guidance of the text and are entering into new potentialities of our own natures. Hence the necessity for suggesting the complex dimensions of the reading process, with all the possible nuances of concurrent response to what we are evoking. I do not expect to affect usage in this instance, but I believe it important to counteract the implication that the literary work is only substitute or even "virtual" experience and to insist that it is a unique mode of experience, an expansion of the boundaries of our own temperaments and worlds, lived through in our own persons.

The concurrent stream of responses manifests itself in various other ways. The reader may stop at times simply to register more fully the experience that has been elicited—to savor the qualities of the images or state of mind produced, to clarify the relationships that have been sensed, or to see implications. What is being structured may startle because it violates the reader's expectations; a character, for example, may behave in ways not prepared for in the text. Or the text may imply assumptions about human behavior different from those the reader has brought to the transaction. Accompanying responses may thus lead to periods of reflection on the emerging work, clearly divorced from the evocative process.

In the transaction with the text—of, for example, *Othello*—the reader envisions the characters, participates in their uttered thoughts and emotions, and weaves the sequence of events into a plot. Living through this, one will be aware of feelings of tension or foreboding. One will not merely develop an image of a character, say, Iago; one will feel him as a negative element within the play, providing conflict, tension, and suspense. We usually phrase this as feeling Iago to be an evil character. A reader might respond to Iago on two planes, seeing him as a dark color in the total picture, but on a separate level being aware of a feeling about him, amazement at his evil machinations, or, it might be, perverse admiration for his ruthlessness, even though this response would be recognized as irrelevant to the dramatic function of the character.

Or the actual technique of the text—linguistic or dramatic—may capture the attention, and there may be awareness of, or even reflection on, the sources of the effects being sensed: the technical traits of the text, the fresh image, the subtle rhythm, the variations on conventions. I am not referring here to the more or less systematic analysis of technique that, say, the New Critic or the structuralist exemplifies as he "works over" the text after the reading, but rather to a heightened awareness of word or phrase or action, an admiring recognition of the author's strategy (or, *per contra*, irritation at it) that are a concurrent part of the total reading experience.

The various strands of response are often simultaneous, often interwoven, and often interacting. The dynamics of the literary experience include, then, first the dialogue of the reader with the text as he creates the world of the work. We have followed through some of his activities—responding to cues, adopting a predominantly efferent or aesthetic stance, developing anticipatory frameworks, sensing, synthesizing, organizing and reorganizing. Second, there is the concurrent stream of reactions to the work being brought forth: approval, disapproval, pleasure, shock; acceptance or rejection of the world that is being imaged; the supplying of rationales for what is being lived through. There may also be awareness, pleasant or unpleasant, of the technical traits of the text.

"Pleasure" has traditionally been associated with the idea of art, yet attempts to define aesthetic pleasure by specifying its peculiar sources in the text have been inconclusive. It is not the purpose of the present discussion to deal with such questions, but I should like to suggest that perhaps much aesthetic pleasure consists in satisfaction derived from the varied kinds of activity that I have been sketching. The reader's main purpose is to participate as fully as possible in the potentialities of the text. But much of the interest and vitality and texture of the total literary experience arises from the intensely personal activity of thought and feeling with which the literary transaction is impregnated and surrounded. And the matrix of this is, of course, the personality and world of the individual reader.

Throughout, I have used the term "evocation" to refer to the lived-through process of building up the work under the guidance of the text. My purpose is to differentiate between the reader's evocation of the work and his interpretation of that evocation.

The tendency is to speak of interpretation as the construing of the meaning of a text. This conceals the nature of the reader's activity in relation to the text: he responds to the verbal signs and construes or organizes *his responses* into an experienced meaning which is for him "the work." This, we have seen, is a process in time. The reader ultimately crystallizes his sense of the work; he may seek to recall it or to relive different parts of it. (Have we not all recaptured episodes, characters, even speeches with voices reverberating in the inner ear?) All of this can be designated as the evocation, and *this is what the reader interprets*. Interpretation involves primarily an effort to describe in some way the nature of the lived-through evocation of the work.

It is possible that a reader may be satisfied simply with the evocation and response dimensions of the reading process, turning his attention completely away at the end of these dynamic activities without further reflection. Perhaps this is what happens when we read an almost-immediately-forgotten detective story or some other text purely for "escape." But in many or most instances, there is reflection on the experience and an effort at interpretation.

Chapter 7 will treat the process of interpretation in greater detail and will develop the implications of this view of the reading process for ordinary readers and for critics. Before that, it seems necessary to clarify the role of the text and to look at some of the theoretical objections to the transactional view of the literary work.

5

THE TEXT:

OPENNESS

AND CONSTRAINT

*W*HEN critics are moved to cele-
brate the joys of literature, they often remind us of the wonderful
opening lines or sentences in great poems or novels or plays. All of us
undoubtedly have been gripped by the opening words of some great
or good work and have read on almost helplessly, it seemed, under
the control of the text. There are those who, far from thinking of the
reader's activity as free, speak of the domination of the text, the
submergence of the reader in what sounds in their phrasing almost
like a brainwashing dictated by the text. The very intensity of one's
aroused interest in the particular unique combination of words before
one, so unexpected, and yet so perfect, is indeed often so compelling
that it seems to call for full credit for the text. Although affirming its
essentiality in the literary transaction, the preceding chapters have

shown us, however, how illusory is the seeming passivity of the reader. In this chapter, I should like to focus more squarely on the text, on both its constraints and its openness.

The notion of the text as sole dictator of the work has analogies with the now fairly discredited notion that words are inherently either referential or emotive. It may be useful to look at the problem first in terms of words before going on to consider them in the context of the total text. Most words, Edward Sapir pointed out years ago, "like practically all elements of consciousness, have an associated feeling-tone."

Not only may the feeling-tone change from one age to another (this, of course is true of the conceptual content as well), but it varies remarkably from individual to individual according to personal associations of each, varies, indeed, from time to time in a single individual's consciousness as his experiences mold him and his moods change. To be sure there are socially accepted feeling-tones, or ranges of feeling-tone, for many words over and above the force of individual associations, but they are exceedingly variable and elusive things at best. They rarely have the rigidity of the central, primary fact.[1]

And he reminds us of the importance of this personal aura of words for art.

Usually, the contrast between referential and emotive language is based on the "socially accepted ranges of feeling tone" and the fact that some words have acquired much more of this aura in general usage than others. "Mother" has much more of this emotive potential than does "hypotenuse." Recall, however, that it is not the words but the individual reader who has acquired the associations with them, and who pays attention to these associations or shuts them out of awareness. Sometimes he may share the socially accepted feeling-tone, at other times he may modify or even diverge sharply from it. The cues offered by the text on the one hand excite his response and on the other hand lead him to eliminate what is irrelevant from what is to be incorporated into his sense of the "meaning" of the text. To speak of the denotations or connotations of words, or to speak of emotive or referential language, therefore, is only a shortcut for differentiating between the selective ways in which readers handle their responses to verbal symbols.

In scientific communications, we know, the purpose is to use symbols that can be, as Bridgman formulates it, "operationally defined" in terms of procedures to be carried out or data to be observed. In order to insure such freedom from personal elements, some disciplines, such as mathematics, chemistry, and symbolic logic, have created special language systems. The symbols themselves are presumably neutral. For example, it probably would not matter to the reader if the following statement was expressed through one or another set of symbols: $2 + 3 = 5$ *or* $a + b = c$. And the choice of letters, $a + b = c$ *or* $d + e = f$, would not affect response to the algebraic statement. (Though the recollection of Arthur Rimbaud's sonnet about the color associations produced for him by the different vowels may suggest that even here there may be elements in the fringe of consciousness that must be actively ignored. And we have noted the well-worn example of the mathematician's pleasure in his elegant demonstration.)

In a scientific reading, then, the reader must adopt the attitude of mind, the stance, that will lead him automatically to reject or inhibit any personal associations activated by the symbols. He will then attend only to the referents that can be publicly or operationally tested or defined. This must be especially true of those disciplines that use words that occur in both scientific and nonscientific vocabularies. Thus, the ordinary word *salt* carries varied potentialities of response—as in "He is the salt of the earth," in contrast to the neutral symbols "NaCl" or "sodium chloride."

Although some disciplines provide systems of neutral symbols that make it easy for the reader to ignore anything but the purely referential or cognitive, we cannot think of even such symbols as inherently, purely, efferent. Even symbols of this kind may be responded to aesthetically. Take, for example, Einstein's formula, $E = mc^2$.

$E = mc^2$

What was our trust, we trust not;
  What was our faith, we doubt;
Whether we must or must not,
  We may debate about.

The soul, perhaps, is a gust of gas
  And wrong is a form of right—
But we know that Energy equals Mass
  By the Square of the Speed of Light.

What we have known, we know not;
  What we have proved, abjure;
Life is a tangled bowknot,
  But one thing still is sure.
Come, little lad; come, little lass—

Your docile creed recite:
"We know that Energy equals Mass
By the Square of the Speed of Light."[2]

The witty effect results, of course, largely from the reader's response to the abstractness of the formula: the very lack of connections with the emotive life of human beings, with all their personal and cosmic yearnings and queries, becomes the source of an affective response to that formula. Even a statement in the abstract language of a science can lose its neutrality. The notion of inherently poetic or emotive or inherently referential language breaks down.

Assumption of the appropriate mode of response to the symbols probably often takes place automatically and below the level of consciousness. Yet the medical student, for example, who will need later to identify the diagnostic symptoms explained in the following passage from a medical text, must often learn to scrupulously ignore any feelings or attitudes that the word "heart" might arouse in him and focus his attention entirely on the operational referents of the words: "Although during the acute stages [of a rheumatic infection] it cannot be said that a heart which is normal in size is not diseased, it may be safely accepted that, if the size of the heart increases or is greater than normal in size, it is diseased."[3]

Note Dylan Thomas's "My busy heart who shudders as she talks/ Sheds the syllabic blood and drains her words." Here the reader probably still holds on to the reference to the heart as an organ, but permits an awareness of feeling-tone that may even have a strong kinesthetic element. When he encounters the word in the first stanza of Whitman's "O Captain! My Captain!" feeling-tone probably predominates.

> But O heart! heart! heart!
> O the bleeding drops of red,
>   Where on the deck my Captain lies,
>   Fallen cold and dead.

Metaphor—live or even "dead"—requires the reader to carry out a diversity of complex operations: "Recognition of the dignity of the individual is the heart of democracy"; or "His office is in the heart of the financial district."

The use of the word *heart* in a long series of contexts might be cited, to demonstrate the many different shades of response possible for the reader, who in each instance carries on a highly selective process. As

Sapir pointed out, the precise feeling-tone or associations that each reader will have for the word *heart* in each of these examples will be unique. Some associations will be due to the general history of the use of the word—in some instances perhaps deriving from the old notion that the heart was the seat of the emotions. But in addition, each reader will have had a personal history of experiences with the word, both in everyday life and in literature.

We are here not concerned with the source of the associations but rather with the wide range of referential and affective responses that might be activated, and the fact that the reader must manage these responses, must select from them. When words are not viewed as in themselves inherently scientific, informative, referential, or inherently imaginative, suggestive, emotive, they can be seen as potential stimuli for the reader's engaging in various kinds of selective activities. Different "meanings" can be phrased as different kinds of operations carried out by the reader in response to linguistic symbols.

Whether or not the reader's stance permits one or another element of the referent and its feeling-tones to become activated is the crux of the matter. All reading is carried on in a matrix of experienced meaning: efferent reading gives attention primarily to the referent alone; aesthetic reading places the experienced meaning in the full light of awareness and involves the selective process of creating a work of art.

Of course, the preceding illustrations of the different ways in which a reader might respond to the same word present the word in different contexts. The word, it is usually said, derives its meaning from its context or linguistic environment, the other words or sentences within which the specific verbal symbol is embedded. A more dynamic phrasing, we have seen, is that the context guides the reader in the process of selecting out—from the range of inner possibilities—the kinds of responses, referential and affective, that are appropriate. The flexibility of individual words, the wide range of possible responses, might seem in this way to be relatively delimited or stabilized within each individual text. This is indeed the basis of the extreme importance of the particular pattern of linguistic symbols which constitute the literary text. But, we know, not even the total text represents an absolute set of guides; multiple and equally valid possibilities are often inherent in the same text in its transactions with different readers under different conditions.

The general concept of the text as a guide and gauge offers no problem. Difficulties arise, however, when one seeks to specify the degree of constraint. Formulations present themselves, such as that the text delimits an arc or area within which meanings may be organized, or that it offers a pattern that, like the cutout portion of a stencil, may be applied to a wide range of surfaces or filled in with a variety of colors and still retain its basic form. Yet all of these suggest a more rigid outline or constraint than seems appropriate to the actual process and to the wide range of readings possible for single texts. The notion that at least the literal or referential meanings of the words remain constant offers little support, not only because of the fluidity of language but mainly because to consider the literal apart from the total import of a word is to destroy it as an aesthetic entity.

So interwoven are the aesthetic responses to a text, that when the response to one word is changed, it may affect the organization or structure of the whole work. Instead of a rigid stencil, a more valid image for the text seems to be something like an open-meshed woven curtain, a mesh of flexible strands that hold a certain relationship to one another, but whose total shape and pattern changes as any one part is pulled or loosened. One can imagine the reader peering through the curtain, affecting its shape and the pattern of the mesh by the tension or looseness with which he is holding it, and filling in the openings from his own palette of colors. Perhaps most actual readings lie somewhere between the rigidity and flexbility of these two images. We shall have an opportunity to consider these questions more specifically in the following chapters.

Concentration on the reader has led us arbitrarily to start with the text as given. Usually, the relationship between author and reader is considered from the point of view of the writer. His problem is to find words that he hopes will communicate his intended meaning to a reader. Even the author who declares that he writes without concern for any potential reader writes "for himself alone"—as a reader. The author must more or less consciously create the image of the reader he is addressing. How much this guides him in the process of artistic creation—in addition to the inner state or ideas that have initiated the process—is a complex question, perhaps not sufficiently studied in discussions of the creative process. But for the reader, as the preceding chapters have shown, the process of communication with the author becomes in fact a relationship through the text.

Since the reader ultimately has only the text to guide him, his task is indeed complex. Nor does a more excellent text make his task less complex. In order to decode the message he must also re-create from the text a speaker or a persona, and sometimes behind that an author. And in the aesthetic reading, in order to sense the voice, the intention, of the hypothetical speaker, the reader must often also supply a setting, a situation, a general context.

The reader, it is sometimes objected, does not *choose*, say, the aesthetic stance, but assumes it because the text imposes it. William James's concept of selective attention may help us to see that choice does not necessarily involve a conscious pondering of alternatives. The reader is simply responding to cues set forth in the text, and because he has developed the habit of such response to such cues seemingly automatically adopts a particular stance. Yet the element of choice between alternative stances still is present. Actually, it will be useful to spell out some of the kinds of cues that are often taken for granted but that still alert the reader to take one or another attitude toward the text.

The non-verbal setting may play a role in the process. In information theory, the listener is said to have "decoded" the "message" when he has reconstructed the sounds and has recognized them as a pattern of words. This view is understandable when it is recalled that information theory originally was mainly concerned with such matters as the transmission of utterances over the telephone. But, of course, workers in this field are quite ready to admit that in any actual communication, the process must be carried through to an interpretation of the meaning of the sounds heard. And even on the level of recognizing the sounds, evidence exists to demonstrate that the listener's present expectations and past experience are important. For example, experiments have revealed that once a listener is aware of the general subject matter of an utterance, he is more likely to recognize the words in spite of distorting interference or "noise."[4] Herein lies the reason for the already mentioned deficiency in the simple information-theory diagram for our purposes, a deficiency shared by most scientific efforts to schematize the relationship between speaker and listener. Usually lacking is the sense of the transactional, two-way situation within which any actual transmission of meaning takes place.

Like the information theorists, the linguists also have found it useful to eliminate from the purview of their theories the complexities of actual linguistic behaviors under particular conditions.

Seeking general predictive rules or common psychological mechanisms, the linguist exercises the scientist's right to delimit his problems to manageable factors. He cannot avoid assuming the "intuitive" activities or "competence" of the native users of spoken or written language, but he restricts himself to studying hypothetical utterances apart from actual speakers or listeners. His aim is to develop a structural model that will cover the generation of all types of syntactic structures possible in that language. When he moves into the semantic dimension and starts to develop a philosophy of language, the scientific linguist again seeks to eliminate the factors that require recognition of the "socio-physical setting" of utterances.[5]

Such abstraction may yield more refined analytic categories for the various components of meaning that words carry, and may produce improved ways of organizing dictionaries. So far, the analytic apparatus developed only makes more evident the complexity of the selective process required in all actual uses of language. The possible ultimate value of such abstracting analyses should not meanwhile lead to neglect of the fact that language actually functions—that utterances become speech acts—through the selective activities of specific users in specific "socio-physical settings."

Given the assumption that the text offers a potentially meaningful set of linguistic symbols, the reader is faced with the adoption of either a predominantly efferent or a predominantly aesthetic stance. The "socio-physical" setting, the nonverbal situation, may dictate the choice. Or the reader may have to depend on the text alone, on nothing but the pattern of verbal symbols to provide the basis for arriving at a tentative context that will guide him in selecting meanings for the words and also lead him to take a particular attitude toward what he is eliciting.

The nonverbal setting can be understood to include all of the possible factors outside the verbal symbols themselves that might influence the interpretation of their meaning. We take for granted that the actual circumstances surrounding a spoken utterance often provide the basis for understanding. If "Don't step on the train" were uttered on a railroad platform, it is unlikely that anyone would look around for a woman wearing a garment with a piece of cloth trailing behind. Much of our reading also is influenced by the setting, by nonlinguistic factors of which the reader is aware. Since this point is so often assumed and then neglected, it seems necessary to underscore the elements other than the text itself that may enter into the reading transaction and may affect the approach or stance of the reader.

A few illustrations will show how the setting may contribute to the adoption of one or another, predominantly efferent or aesthetic, attitude toward the text. For instance, if there is a fire, and one is struggling to understand the directions printed on the label of an unfamiliar type of fire extinguisher, one's attention—and whole muscular set—will be focused on the operations to be performed as soon as the reading ends. One will not be paying attention to the particular sound or rhythm of the words or to fine shades of idea and feeling associated with the words themselves—"flames," say, as against "fire." The situation will have determined one's stance.

A similar automatic adjustment of stance, prior to the encounter with the actual text, occurs when someone seeks out a novel, a play, a collection of poems. Something in the mood of the reader or the "socio-physical setting" has initiated the search for a text that will be particularly rewarding for the aesthetic stance. Various signals have been developed to alert readers to the types of texts and hence to the appropriate stance: the categories under which books are shelved in libraries, the differences between titles of nonfiction and fiction, the reports of book reviewers, the frequent use of headings such as "Fiction" or "Poetry" in the tables of contents of magazines—even, sometimes, the insertion of the phrase "a story" after a title. This may be an adaptation to the fact that readers themselves often are not conscious of the difference in stance required by different texts, but need such prior signals to adjust their approach to such materials.

Indeed, one is sometimes led to wonder how many adults may never have learned to make such a shift from the efferent toward the aesthetic end of the spectrum. I mentioned earlier the boy who responded efferently to *Alice in Wonderland.* In our schools, the emphasis in the teaching of reading is almost entirely on the efferent stance. Comprehension in reading tests is assumed mainly to be of this type. It is not possible here to detail the methods of the teaching of literature in school and college that tend often to develop an efferent attitude, even toward the literary work of art. Still, despite these obstacles, either because of the accident of temperament, favorable family or social background, or good teaching, some have developed the ability to take the most advantageous stance in rela-

79

tion to various texts. Our concern at this point is with the ways in which readers are given cues extraneous to the text that help them to adopt one or another stance in relation to it.

The importance of such extraneous factors is most easily seen in relation to texts that we consider definitely to be in the aesthetic category. For example, many students these days encounter Carroll's "Jabberwocky" for the first time in a course in linguistics, when the verses are offered as an illustration of how language provides "markers" and "slots" that identify the various kinds of units in the structure of the sentence without dependence on the meaning of the words.

> 'Twas brillig, and the slithy toves
> Did gyre and gimble in the wabe;
> All mimsy were the borogoves,
> And the mome raths outgrabe.

In the linguistics class, the instructor implicitly specifies that an efferent stance is to be adopted toward these lines, since he invites the students to focus on the devices, such as word order, word endings, and articles, by which different parts of speech are indicated.[6] Such analytic reading involves a very different kind of activity from the responses generated by an aesthetic stance, in which the grammatical structure would be intuited, as the reader paid attention primarily to the sounds, the associations, the ideas and feeling-tone activated by these verses. He would be absorbed in the actual sensing, interpreting, and organizing of what is aroused in him by the text.

A decision to "go to the theatre" is another definite prior choice of stance, implying a readiness to adopt an aesthetic attitude. Yet even in the theatre, occasional episodes occur in which the spectator reacts efferently to what he perceives. The old woman sitting next to me in the pit of the Old Vic in London years ago, who seemed to have wandered in mainly to rest her weary feet, became so involved that I thought I was going to have to physically restrain her from leaping on to the stage to warn Othello of the web of evil being woven around him. At a New York performance of Osborne's *Look Back in Anger* in 1957, a spectator did jump onto the stage to intervene in defense of the wife. The audiences of radio and television "soap opera" are evidently especially prone to such confusion of stance: it has been reported, for instance, that when the heroine becomes pregnant, gifts for the baby arrive at the studio. In recent years, dramatists have even played with the audience by having events occur in the theatre pit, so that the audience responds practically until it becomes apparent that the quarreling spectators, say, are actually part of the play. Here, the audience become conscious of their need for a shift of stance. The adoption of an appropriate or inappropriate stance is equally involved in any reading. Like so many linguistic processes, this activity is often automatic and unconscious.

If we think of the total literary transaction, we must recognize that the reader brings to or adds to the nonverbal or socio-physical setting his whole past experience of life and literature. His memories, his present preoccupations, his sense of values, his aspirations, enter into a relationship with the text. I shall later return to this broader aspect of his contribution. At this stage of our discussion, I am still mainly concerned with the processes by which the reader actively commits himself to the aesthetic undertaking.

Verbal cues are, of course, ultimately the most pervasive. In arguing for the importance of the reader's contribution, I have stressed the extent to which the reader's stance may be determined by factors in the broader environment or within himself even before he sees the text. Since, however, I spoke of inappropriate attitudes—efferent, for example, rather than aesthetic—I have assumed all along that some texts call for, or are designed for, or serve better, one or another type of reading. Thus, when we turn from the broader environment of the reading act to the text itself, we need to recognize that a very important aspect of a text is the cues it provides as to what stance the reader should adopt.

Various conventions associated with writing or printing provide such cues. The arrangement of words on the page may do this. This is especially true for poetry, with the text broken up into lines which are marked off by spacing and broad margins. This visual signaling to the reader to adopt an aesthetic stance is the main device used by certain "pop" poets. They take sentences from a newspaper or some other such source and break them up into lines arranged on a page in a way that announces this to be free verse. This invites the reader to pay attention to the experience evoked even by these seemingly banal words. The following was found as an advertisement in a London newspaper and transformed into a text calling for the aesthetic stance by the rearrangement of the words on the page:

81

The Headmistress
Of a successful independent
Girls' preparatory
School
Now retiring
After a long career
Of creative teaching
And cooperative achievement
Seeks to leave
Her grateful governors
With a capable
And imaginative
Successor.[7]

Such "found poetry" illustrates in most obvious ways the dependence of the literary work of art on the focus of the reader's selective attention. Similarly, the famous "pop" image of the magnified soup can invites the viewer, without ignoring the practical nature of the pictured object, to concentrate on the qualitative experiencing of it. (These so-called avant-garde artists seem to be rediscovering the basic alphabet of aesthetics; though their works are often very minor indeed, they may be performing a function by educating a public largely wedded to purely efferent attitudes to begin the slow development of aesthetic attention to an awareness of their own responses.)

Readers learn to react to such visual cues without conscious thought. The seventeenth-century poets whose verses fall into the shape of a cross or of a tree, and the presentday "concrete poets," bring this visual aspect into the reader's consciousness and try to lead him to merge it with what is being derived from the verbal symbols.

Conventions governing the printing of plays undoubtedly also serve as signals to trigger the reader's imaginative activities. The divisions into acts, the printing of dialogue with the names of each speaker, the descriptions of stage settings, the parenthetic stage directions, alert the reader to adopt the aesthetic stance. A reader's failure to do this would be like the failure of some spectators to take an aesthetic attitude toward events on the stage, referred to earlier. They had failed to respond, among other things, to the convention of the proscenium arch. The assumption that the audience is looking on at a four-walled room, with one wall miraculously transparent, carries with it the assumption that the spectator will adopt an aesthetic attitude toward whatever goes on in that room. Recent dramatists have eliminated the proscenium arch and have substituted "theatre in the round" and other conventions that are said to "break down" the barrier between audience and play. Their purpose is not to induce an efferent attitude, however, but rather to heighten aesthetic participation in the world of the play. Similarly, the conventions of the dramatic text alert the reader to adopt an actively aesthetic stance.

Some of the readers of Frost's quatrain realized that they were being called upon to make a poem of it only when they became aware of the rhymes. Other such traditional cues that trigger an aesthetic attitude are a decided or regular rhythm, special kinds of diction, devices such as alliteration, and, in both traditional and more recent writing, decided departures from normal syntactic patterns.*

Even certain types of material may signal the need for an aesthetic response. Though the old "once upon a time" beginning that heralded a story to be enjoyed is now archaic, there are other conventional ways of opening a story or a novel; introducing us into the mind of a character, describing a setting, giving necessary information about the time, and creating a noninstrumental atmosphere and tone. This kind of material or "content" gives notice of the appropriate receptive attitude to adopt.

Those who place all the weight on the text may mistake these remarks for an implicit acceptance of their views, an admission that the text itself—what the work "says"—automatically imposes an aesthetic response. Transactional theory, they must be reminded, recognizes the text as a necessary, but not sufficient, condition for any literary work of art. Even within the confines of the text, the reader's role should not be underestimated. What the reader brings to the text will affect what he makes of the verbal cues. Assumption of an aesthetic stance does not depend entirely on the cues offered by the text, but depends also on the reader's being prepared to act on them. The reader does not simply reflect the text. It is necessary to belabor this point because this aspect of the reading process is so persistently ignored.

A New England farmer told me about the man he had hired to clear

---

*The frequency of such cues has led some to make deviations from "normal" usage the special mark of poetry. Often such departures from the expected alert the attention to qualitative overtones and thus reinforce the aesthetic stance. Though frequent, such deviations are not, however, essential to poetry or other literary works of art. Poems, stories, plays can be cited that do not depend on such verbal deviations. See chaps. 3 and 6.

his land. "He dawdled about all day. And he never lifted up a single stone." Few would recognize in the preceding sentence the line in Wordsworth's "Michael": "And he never lifted up a single stone." Matthew Arnold quoted this line as typical of Wordsworth's style, simple, yet "of the highest and most truly expressive kind."[8] How can the same words function in such different ways?

Arnold was using the quotation from Wordsworth in much the same way that he had offered brief quotations from the great masters as "touchstones" or standards of high poetic quality to apply to other poetry. These touchstones, it has often been pointed out, do not always in themselves possess the great poetic power he felt in them; they owe it to their contexts, to the lines of the text that led up to them. In "Michael," the stone sheepfold that the old shepherd plans to build while his beloved only son is away in the great city, and that was a commitment to their future reunion, remains unfinished after news comes of the son's downfall and disappearance. The line that Arnold justifiably singles out has acquired its expressiveness from its context, from the lines that have preceded—the account of the pastoral life, the great dignity and moral strength of the old man, his love of his son, and his hopes for the son's inheritance of the land that he and his forefathers had labored for.

This should be rephrased transactionally: The touchstone line, the words, "And he never lifted up a single stone," do not in themselves have a special power; they acquire the capacity to evoke an intense response because of what the reader has lived through under guidance of the text before he encounters these particular words. The actual context of the words is the sequence of experiences that the reader has had under the influence of the particular sequence of linguistic symbols in the preceding lines. The efferent stance was appropriate for hearing the words as the New England farmer uttered them; all that was involved was a certain bit of information. The aesthetic stance of the reader toward the text of "Michael" involves the keenest attention to experienced meanings, to the sound and pace of the verse, the overtones of sensation, feeling, and association. Then the very words of the quoted line take on a rhythm, a resonance, and a weight appropriately absent from the farmer's querulous remark. The reader brings to the line a whole fund of understanding and feeling that makes it possible for those simple words to elicit the poignant response that won Arnold's admiration. The experiential context is provided by the reader as he brings an aesthetic orientation to the pattern of symbols which is the text.

Context is usually thought of as sequential—earlier words and sentences excluding certain possible meanings from subsequent words, and leaving certain other possibilities open. In aesthetic reading, as the earlier discussion of the Frost quatrain demonstrates, context operates in more complex fashion, verbal context eliciting experiential responses that may reflect back as well as forward, to create a contextual ambiance.

William Empson's brilliant *Seven Types of Ambiguity* offers elaborate testimony to the openness of texts. One instance is his much-cited discussion of the Arden edition note on "rookie" in Macbeth's speech, "Light thickens, and the Crow/Makes wing to th' rookie wood." Empson quotes the editor's list of his predecessor's interpretations of the word:

> This somewhat obscure epithet, however spelt (and it should be spelt *rouky*), does NOT mean "murky" or "dusky" (Roderick, quoted by Edward's *Canons of Criticism*, 1765); NOR "damp," "misty," "steamy with exhalations" (Steevens, also Craig); NOR "misty," "gloomy" (Clar. Edd.); NOR "where its fellows are already assembled" (Mitford), and has NOTHING to do with the dialectic word "roke" meaning "mist," "steam," etc. . . . the meaning here . . . I THINK, is simply the "rouking" or perching wood, *i.e.*, where the rook (or crow) perches for the night.

Empson ends by suggesting that, instead of assuming that only one of these is acceptable, all may be, and that a reader can entertain a great many of the alternatives at once.[9] In analyses of this and other texts, Empson shows how different referents and associations may present themselves simultaneously and give depth and complexity to the reader's evocation of the passage.

However, Empson's sometimes overwhelming pursuit of ambiguities is not always a report on immediate poetic experiences. His speculations about potential multiple meanings often derive from investigating such sources as the just-mentioned footnotes of Shakespeare's editors or alternative definitions in the New Oxford Dictionary. On the efferent-aesthetic continuum, his analytic method reflects a stance rather remote from the aesthetic. Of course, Empson recognized this and reminded his readers that "the process of getting to understand a poet is precisely that of constructing his poems in one's own mind" (p. 79). Still, Empson hoped that his analytic criticism might affect readers' sensibilities and in that way influence their later actual readings of texts. Much recent critical writing attests to the influence of his book, but unfortunately in many instances only his analytic method has been imitated, despite his warning against confusing the analysis and the evocation of a poem. Empson's discussion mainly demonstrates the extent to which texts may provide room for alternative responses, sometimes simultaneously by the same reader, sometimes by different readers, shaping qualitatively different experiences from the same words. Hence my belief that the method of his book offers not so much models of the aesthetic reading process as evidence concerning the openness of texts.

The importance of the text is not denied by recognition of its openness. The text is the author's means of directing the attention of the reader. The author has looked at life from a particular angle of vision; he has selected out what he hopes will fulfill his aim, as Conrad phrased it, to make you see, to make you hear, to make you feel. The reader, concentrating his attention on the world he has evoked, feels himself freed for the time from his own preoccupations and limitations. Aware that the blueprint of this experience is the author's text, the reader feels himself in communication with another mind, another world.

In the aesthetic transaction, the text possesses an especial importance. In the efferent situation, a paraphrase or summary or restatement—in short, another text—may be as useful as the original text. Someone else can read the newspaper or a scientific text for you and paraphrase it quite acceptably. But no one can read a poem for you. Accepting an account of someone else's reading or experience of a poem is analogous to seeking nourishment through having someone else eat your dinner for you and recite the menu. The summary of a biology text, the rephrasing of the technical language of a law, may serve but only the relationship between the reader and the actual text, his attending to and synthesizing his own responses to the particular words in their particular order, can produce the poem for him.

The paraphrase, it is generally agreed, does not equal the poem. "B" below can in no sense be considered equivalent to, or a substitute for, "A":

A.   That time of year thou mayst in me behold
     When yellow leaves, or none, or few, do hang
     Upon those boughs which shake against the cold,

Bare, ruined choirs, where late the sweet birds sang.
In me thou see'st the twilight of such day
As after sunset fadeth in the west,
Which by and by black night doth take away,
Death's second self, that seals up all in rest.
In me thou see'st the glowing of such fire
That on the ashes of his youth doth lie
As the death-bed whereon it must expire,
Consumed with that which it was nourished by.
    This thou perceiv'st, which makes thy love more strong
    To love that well which thou must leave ere long.[10]

B.   In me you behold that time of year when a few yellow leaves or none at all hang on the branches, shaking in the cold, like bare, ruined choirs, where lately birds were singing. In me you see such twilight as there is after the sun has faded in the west, which by and by is extinguished by night—image of death, that seals up all in rest. In me you see the glow of embers, the ashes of my youth, dying out as on a death-bed, consumed by that which fed it and gave it life. Seeing this increases your love and makes you value more that which you must take leave of before long.[11]

The paraphrase may restate some thoughts or aspects of the evoked poem. It is erroneous to say that it sums up the "meaning," even if qualified by the term "literal." A list of the sequence of feelings or moods elicited by the text would not be mistaken for a statement of its "meaning." No more is a list of the ideas suggested by the text a statement of the poem's meaning. This must encompass the sum total of lived-through ideas, feelings, and attitudes relevant to Shakespeare's words in their particular order. The paraphrase is simply another, a different, text. No matter how similar the general ideas expressed in the text and in its paraphrase, the reading of each would involve a relationship to two different texts and would give rise to two different experiences for the reader.

To change a text in any particular is to direct us to elicit a different poem. For instance, we undergo something different in relation to the first and second versions of the opening line of Keats's *Endymion*. "A thing of beauty is a constant joy" was changed to "A thing of beauty is a joy forever." The simple paraphrasable difference between *constant* and *forever* does not fully account for the great difference in effect. Even the transposition of the words, "A thing of beauty is forever a joy" produces a different experienced meaning. The difference in lexicographical meaning between *constant* and *forever* does contribute something to the difference in impact, although this is not sufficient to explain the total difference. The reader pays attention to all the kinds of responses involved, sensuous and affective, as well as cognitive. (Here, again, we find that at the very moment of emphasizing the extreme importance of the text, we must also deal with the reader's contribution. The symbols on the page are, at best, only partial indicators of the linguistic referents.)

The view of reading that I have been espousing is now receiving confirmation from psycholinguistic research on reading. Some experts are, as we have noted, actually asserting that "comprehension" of the text starts "from the outside in." That is—to use their jargon—from "the semantic input," from what the reader brings to the page. Moreover, they conclude, it is "not simply a question of meanings for words but the much larger question of the reader having sufficient experience and conceptual background to feed into the reading process so that he can make sense out of what he is reading."[12] Even in efferent reading, then, the reader's role is beginning to be recognized: the words on the page leave much open for him to fill in and structure.

In the evocation of the literary work of art, this openness of the text takes on especial importance, while at the same time the reader must pay especially close attention to the exact words of the text. As with all texts, the reader must bring more than a literal understanding of the individual words. He must bring a whole body of cultural assumptions, practical knowledge, awareness of literary conventions, readinesses to think and feel. These provide the basis for weaving a meaningful structure around the clues offered by the verbal symbols. But in the aesthetic reading, the reader must focus his attention on the precise responses generated by that particular pattern of words. The reader, on the one hand, respects the limitations set by the verbal cues, and on the other, draws on his own resources to fill in the gaps, to realize the blueprint provided by the text. Recognizing the essential role of the text as the stimulus to the creativity of the reader has as its corollary recognition both of the openness of the text, on the one hand, and on the other, its constraining function as a guide or check. The text of a poem may indeed offer us a "closed form" within which to organize a work—yet at the same time, it is open to the contributions of the reader in his relationships to his own world and the world of the author.

Form, it is claimed, is the mark of the work of art, and form is to be found in the text, in its arrangement of sounds, its syntax, its figures of speech, its configurations of ideas, in short, in the way the words have been patterned. When the transaction between reader and text is thus ignored, the formal aspects of the text come to be viewed as essentially static. Rhetorical* and critical terms become mainly classificatory and anatomizing, a naming of static components. Such terms should, on the contrary, be conceived dynamically, as the names of cues for the reader to carry out certain operations.

The distinction between efferent and aesthetic reading is crucial to this dynamic approach. Such a distinction is tacitly present, for example, in the various categories that have often been suggested for such basic concepts as "form" or "structure" or "unity." For example, "external form" and "internal form" are sometimes used to distinguish between the results of systematic analysis of syntax, rhyme, metrics, or diction, on the one hand, and, on the other, the substance, the themes, the events, embodied in the work. "Formal structure" and "nonformal structure" are used to make a similar distinction. "Unity" also involves such notions as "inner coherence" in contrast to syntactic or metrical or other external aspects.[13]

Now, these various so-called external forms or structures are all arrived at by *efferent* reading and analysis of the charted symbols. The text is viewed as a set of signs whose arrangement is to be described in some objectively verifiable way. The analyst approaches the text with some systematic code or framework of selection, such as phonemic or morphemic categories, a grammatical system, a metrical code, stanzaic patterns, a set of semantic categories (e.g., concrete or abstract nouns), types of images (e.g., the five senses, nature, animal, human, etc.), or kinds of topics or ideas. The analyst is not reading the text in order to create a work of art; he is reading it efferently in order to make a systematic classification of elements. This means that he must pay equal attention to each of the elements of the text for the purpose of determining objectively which is relevant to his particular preordained system of selection. Hence the increasing useful-

---

*It is perhaps regrettable that Aristotle did not prevail in his restriction of "rhetoric" to persuasive speech or writing. (Aristotle, *Rhetoric*, bk. II, chap. 2). This would reduce confusion between efferent and aesthetic reading. In persuasive speech or writing, the author seeks to act on the listener or reader through specific (rhetorical) uses of language. The aim is to lead the listener or reader to reach certain conclusions or engage in certain actions. Emotions are to be aroused, but in order to affect judgments and decisions. The listener or reader is being called upon to adopt a predominantly efferent stance, with the argument the focus of attention.

ness of computers programmed in advance to mechanically select out such items of the text. The aesthetic reader, on the contrary, responds to the verbal symbols, we have seen, with varying resonances and emphases, under the guidance of emerging expectations and tentative organizations.

The term "significant form" has satisfied many as a definition of the essential requirement of works of art. This tends to be translated into external description of the "art object"—the vase into account of line and texture and color, or the poem into analysis of verbal recurrences and variations. The stimuli presented by the text can be efferently abstracted out into different configurations. But the test of significance lies in whether these stimuli or cues permit or help viewers or readers who have adopted the aesthetic stance to organize their responses into a coherent, shaped, "formed" experience. To say that a text possesses "significant form" seems actually tautological, a judgment on the quality of the potential transaction.[14]

Coleridge spoke of the poem "proposing to itself such delight from the *whole*, as is compatible with a distinct gratification from each component *part*."[15] In one way or other, of course, the idea of the relationship of the parts constituting the whole enters discussions of the form, the unity, or the structure of the work. Coleridge's emphasis on gratification from each component part adds an important qualification, because it means that the reader senses a qualitative unity. What in most discussions has been tacitly assumed is here stressed: only a reader in aesthetic transaction with the text can synthesize the parts into a "whole" or structure which is a work of art. The reader draws on his own reservoir of past life experience; he has notions of what to expect of a novel or poem or satire. But he has to use whatever he brings to the text and build out of his responses to the patterned verbal cues a unifying principle. The structure of the work of art corresponds ultimately to what he perceives as the relationships that he has woven among the various elements or parts of his lived-through experience. Instead of thinking of the structure of the work of art as something statically inherent in the text, we need to recognize the dynamic situation in which the reader, in the give-and-take with the text, senses or organizes a relationship among the various parts of his lived-through experience.

Such a phrasing does more than reiterate the contention that in a work of art, form and matter cannot be separated, that one is an aspect or function of the other, that to change the form is to change the "meaning." The dynamic phrasing makes explicit what remains only tacit, implicit, and often quickly ignored in many theoretical statements of the interdependence of form and matter. First of all, the dynamic transactional phrasing brings into the forefront the idea of the reader's aesthetic stance as essential to the solution of the question of form and matter, or inner and outer form. Second, it makes clear that the "structure," the "form," the "unity" of the work are terms applied to the results of the reader's structuring, forming, unifying activities under the stimulus and guidance of the text.

The patterned symbols of the text are absolutely essential, of course, but as a constituent of the transactional synthesis. It is relevant to ask whether the work-as-evoked corresponds to the text; the reader may not "do justice to" it. He should be able to point to the elements of the text that have given rise to the interrelated or interwoven "whole" or structure. Yet no efferent analysis can predict the work. And we are left with the question, how fully the efferently objective analyses of the structure of the text can explain the nature of the work-as-evoked. We shall return to this question in chapter 7. At this point, our concern is to set forth the need for a dynamic, reader- as well as text-oriented understanding of rhetorical or critical terms such as form or structure.

A concept such as "plot" offers another illustration of this view. It involves a series of actions or events, which can be efferently itemized or listed. But the term implies also that these permit a certain kind of activity on the part of the reader—namely that he will be able to relate them to one another experientially, usually as a sequence in time, although other time-relationships are possible. He will need first to envision a situation with potentialities for further events or further developments. As the text unfurls, he is able to move into the new actions, the new situations, and to feel them as related to what he has already participated in. This process is repeated from event to event as the reader builds up a sense of sequence and perhaps consequence—of chronological or causal or other relationships.

Plot is often discussed in terms of exposition, rising action, crisis, falling action, and denouement. These, and a term such as climax, imply, and indeed require, the understandings and awarenesses and responses of a reader. The rising action is felt by the reader as a rise or increase in tension, or at the very least in interest or curiosity, about what he is calling forth from the text. "Climax" refers to the highest point of interest and is related to a reader's lived-through response. (We may later efferently discern that a certain event was the turning point, but this does not seem to be a term as necessarily dependent on the reader's active evocation as is the term "climax.")*

In other words, essential to "the plot" is the action of the reader in relating one episode or one element or one aspect of the events to the others decoded from the text. A child may look at the separate squares of a comic strip, and see them as separate and distinct. Plot begins to emerge when he sees that the characters and situation of the second square can be related to the first, usually as later in time and as developing from the situation indicated in the first and so on, so that the comic strip becomes a narrative. This is a simpler version of a process carried on in the reading of a play or a novel. To speak of the plot of *Othello* or of *Tom Jones* as particularly tight is to say that the words of the text have enabled the reader to live through a series of events, to relate them clearly, chronologically, and causally, and to organize his own emotional responses to this experience. The reader not only responds to the textual cues by generating the characters, situations, actions, they signify; he also retains in his memory and attitudes the basis for interpreting the sequence of events as they unfold, and he provides the experiential ligatures between them that constitute plot.

Many of the terms most frequently applied to narrative form depend on the cues provided (or not provided) for the reader—that is, on the kinds of activities the reader is called on to engage in for the production of the narrative.[16] Much twentieth-century art, in contrast to earlier periods, relies quite overtly on the reader's or perceiver's contribution. In the novel, the decline of the omniscient narrator—the recourse to the participant-narrator or to the point of view of one character, as in James's *The Ambassadors*, or to the multiple point of view, as in Faulkner's *Absalom, Absalom!*—has made for greater demands on the reader to weave the clues together. Terms naming innovations such as "spatial form in the novel"† or "the

---

*The structuralist effort to develop a "grammar of plot" seeks a system of signs, or code, underlying narrative, analogous to the linguist's search for "deep structure." My concern here is with actual readings of texts, which occur at a particular time, in a particular cultural context. See chap. 7.

†Joseph Frank, in his deservedly famous essay on ,"Spatial Form in Modern Literature," recalling Lessing's treatment of aesthetic perception, explains the shifts in literary form by repeated references to its demands on the reader. E.g., "The reader is forced to read *Ulysses* in exactly the same manner as he reads modern poetry, that is,

anti-novel," also point ultimately to the operations that the reader performs. "Spatial form" denotes a reading in which efforts at a linear, sequential synthesis are suspended as the various parts of the "picture" open up. The tentative framework that emerges may depend less on time- and causal-sequences and more on other kinds of relationships among the characters or incidents. The reader orders the component lived-through episodes or scenes into a meaningful configuration in a way analogous to the viewer's relating the component parts of a painting. The "anti-novel" purports to offer only objective details without interpretation.[17] Yet these newer types of texts simply demand more explicitly the kind of "filling-in" and organizing activity that we have seen the reader performing even in texts with explanatory omniscient narrators like, for instance, Thackeray's *Vanity Fair.* The traditional novels that give the reader the usual clues as to narrative sequence still require a fitting-together of elements, a memory of earlier episodes and details, an awareness of allusions, a looking-backward to sense the structure of the whole reading experience.

"Metaphor" is another term that, viewed transactionally, refuses to remain riveted to the text. The diverse efforts to explain metaphor have usually sought to specify a relationship between the textual elements. (Richards's terms for them, the *tenor* and the *vehicle,* are most often, though not always consistently, used.) Many of the definitions name some logical relationship between them, for example, similarity, contrast, dissimilarity, resemblance, substitution, interaction, paradox, inappropriate combination.[18] Yet, as Richards long ago pointed out, "there are few metaphors whose effect, if carefully examined, can be traced to the logical relations involved."[19]

Even when, for example, a metaphor is expressed in the grammatical form of a comparison, that is, as a simile, it is still a metaphor only by virtue of a very special mode of handling on the reader's part: "O,

---

by continually fitting fragments together and keeping allusions in mind until, by reflexive reference, he can link them to their complements" (*The Widening Gyre* [New Brunswick: Rutgers University Press, 1963], p. 18). As usual, however, the emphasis is on the text *forcing* the reader to perform, with little recognition of the positive, active, contribution of each reader in any reading.

Wayne C. Booth's classic, *The Rhetoric of Fiction* (University of Chicago Press, 1961), is even more deeply permeated by awareness of the reader. It would be possible to rephrase many of Booth's points in transactional terms. However—perhaps because he adopts the stance of the rhetorician—his ultimate concern is with the author's point of view and techniques, the production of a text that will have the desired "effect" on the reader.

my luve is like a red, red rose, / That's newly sprung in June." If the reader stops to consider in what logical ways a woman might be "like" a rose, the metaphor has vanished; an efferent attitude is being brought to bear as he sorts out their possible similarities from their dissimilarities. A metaphor is not a Q.E.D. arrived at after efferent analysis.* Indeed, the metaphor "happens" because something in the preceding text or in the combination of elements makes the efferent attitude unsatisfactory.

Does not the metaphor reside in the reader's generating a state of mind arising from the juxtaposition of the loved one and the rose? I may later analyze what permitted me to hold them together, I may later find similarities, though in this instance they would be mainly of the order of potentiality to arouse similar feelings—again a matter of the reader looking inward. Whatever the relationship between the two elements of the figure, the essential point is that the reader's attention be turned toward a qualitative synthesis, cognitive and affective, that can be experienced conjointly.

Again, it is necessary to spell out what is tacitly understood: metaphor requires, first of all, the aesthetic stance. And this, we know, means that the reader is primarily paying attention, not to logical connections, but to what the juxtaposition of these terms is calling forth within him. He is selecting out, from the reverberations of both members of the metaphor, attitudes, feelings, images, associations, that can be synthesized within the context of the total lived-through experience. The amount of selectivity and adjustment—the focusing on some aspects and the relegation of others—that goes on in such a response to a metaphor is staggering to consider.

Shakespeare's satire in Sonnet 130 on the overworked metaphors of the Elizabethan sonneteers depends largely on its insistence on a logical efferent comparison: "My mistress' eyes are nothing like the sun." A refusal to carry out the metaphoric activity of selective adjustment and fusion of attitudes or associations can reduce the analogy or juxtaposed elements to literal (logical) absurdity.

The linguist's illustrations of combinations of words that do not meet our intuitive norms for grammaticality are nevertheless often

---

*Even metaphors that are used to characterize scientific theories—the wave theory of light, say—seem to be the result, not of the efferent working-out of analogies, but of "flashes of insight." This is suggested by Konrad Lorenz's statement, "No important scientific fact has ever been 'proved' that had not previously been simply and immediately seen by intuitive Gestalt perception." Repeatedly, accounts of scientific discoveries offer instances of experimental testing of metaphoric insights.

entirely appropriate for metaphoric reading. Take, for instance, a statement such as "My spinster aunt is an infant." From the strictly "grammatical" point of view, this is a nonsense statement.[20] The word spinster, indicating a person of marriageable age, rules out the statement that she is an infant. In a metaphorical reading, the implications of chronological age are ignored, and attention is focused on notions of helplessness, innocence, inability to manage her own affairs. Chomsky's often-cited illustrations, "growling flowers," and "green ideas sleep furiously," also have been rescued by the aesthetic stance. One can place them in a context in which one can fuse the juxtaposed associations and ideas into a meaningful, by no means ridiculous, experience. From an efferent stance, Chomsky's phrases must be rejected. From an aesthetic stance, they permit the kind of meaningful activity that we call metaphoric, since the reader can be primarily concerned with awareness of his own intellectual and emotional associations or responses to this particular conjunction or juxtaposition of ideas or images.

In a particular context, one of the elements may assimilate the result, as does "my love" in Burns's lines or the trees with Shakespeare's "bare ruin'd choirs." The possible combinations of similarity and dissimilarity seem endless. And the clusters of metaphor in such a text as Shakespeare's Sonnet 73 (see above) require still further syntheses into a state of mind that characterizes the whole literary transaction. It is not my purpose here to choose among the various efforts at defining the precise relationship between the elements of the metaphor. The assumption that there can be a single descriptive term to cover the various kinds or degrees of disparity may very likely be erroneous. It is sufficient for purposes of the present discussion to have underlined the fact that when we point to a metaphor in a text, we are saying that these words constitute a cue for a special kind of activity: metaphor ultimately derives from or depends on the capacity of readers to hold disparate ideas or images and their overtones or associations in the focus of attention and to create from this a qualitatively unique state of mind. Thus it is impossible to find criteria for metaphor entirely within the text itself. A basic requirement is that there should exist the conditions for a particular kind of process in which the reader, attending to and selecting from his responses to the individual elements, fuses these thoughts and feelings or transcends them in a qualitative "meaning" not susceptible of direct statement. Whether we shall judge the metaphor successful or not depends, of course, on how this metaphoric synthesis fits into the total context of the literary work of art, and whether it adds to or illuminates the experience and knowledge we brought to the text.

A transactional view would also once and for all destroy the naïve tendency to think of works of literary art as made up of a literal sense, to which the "poetic" or "literary" overtones can be added. Richards may have unintentionally contributed to this confusion by listing as the first of readers' weaknesses their failure to make out the "plain sense." He later in his book—but too late—cautions that sometimes we cannot arrive at the plain sense until we have achieved the appropriate feeling-tone.[21] The situation concerning the concept of "tone," another widely used critical term, is summed up in the following: "We are brought back then to tone as a determining element of meaning. It is tone which tells us what the author feels about his subject, his audience, and himself. But tone is located in no specific element of the poem; it arises from diction, images, figures of speech, structure, even rhymes and meter—in short, from the whole. If we miss any part of this whole, we may miss the tone of the poem. And if we miss its tone, we miss its meaning."[22]

To say that tone is located "in no specific element" of the text is to admit the inadequacy of the efferent analysis of those elements. The conventional emphasis on literal meaning is shown to be counterproductive, since it implies an efferent stance, whereas in the dynamic process of the aesthetic reading, tone and plain meaning may crystallize simultaneously. What is assumed throughout—and should be made explicit—is the reader's weaving his responses to all of these cues into an attitude, a voice, that can be named "the tone" of the work, and that enters into "the meaning."

The inadequacy of the notion of the "plain sense" of the work and of "meaning" as applied to metaphor—that is, meaning stated in direct or efferent discourse—leads us into the even more theoretically belabored term, "symbol" or "symbolic." Suffice it to say that I am not concerned with the linguistic usage which refers to a verbal sign as a symbol of its referent. Nor am I concerned with other symbolic codes, in which a word and its referent have come to "stand for" something with which it is associated—such as the Cross. Nor is the kind of code utilized by Freudians or Jungians for analysis of dreams or myths relevant here. Such systematizations offer comparatively few problems. Moreover, terms such as "metonomy" or "synecdoche" simply classify the kind of association that has crystallized in a symbolic usage—for example, "sail" for "ship." The real problem inheres in the kind of process involved, say, in our reading of Blake's "The Sick Rose":

> O Rose, thou art sick!
> The invisible worm,
> That flies in the night
> In the howling storm,
>
> Has found out thy bed
> Of crimson joy;
> And his dark secret love
> Does thy life destroy.[23]

Of course, we find in this text many cues that lead us to reject an efferent reading. The very title, with its use of an adjective usually applied to human beings, may be enough to trigger the aesthetic stance. But as we read we cannot confine our responses within the scope of the ideas and images directly evoked from the words. The emotional overtones are, we may say, too powerful. And we find ourselves fitting our responses into contexts not at all directly indicated by the text. For some readers, for example, the overtones have sexual relevance. The poem "symbolizes," they say, a lustful passion that corrupts or a thwarted passion that engenders deceit and jealousy or, it may be, "the ambiguity of love." Others have incorporated the experience into a more general context, such as "natural joy corrupted by stolen and perverted joy," or "an account of Beauty, destroyed by Evil," suggesting "the fatal attraction felt by evil for the innocent, passive, helpless, and beautiful."[24]

The narratives of Kafka often give rise to similar symbolic extensions. Thus, for some, living through *The Castle* brings with it an expansion of the context into political significance; for others it has religious symbolism.

One may indicate the words and images in Blake's text that generate sinister overtones or sexual overtones and an intensity of feeling that require a broader context than that provided by the basic image of the rose and the worm. Many such commentaries on this text exist. The very differences in the explications point to the part of the process usually ignored: the reader, in order to handle his responses to these special words of this text, in their sequence—in order to find an adequate organizing principle for these responses—finds it necessary to engage in a symbolic or symbolizing process. *He pro-*

vides a context; this is drawn from his own past experience, and depends on his own attitudes and values.* Similarly, readers of *The Castle* fit the concrete, practical, often homely details of the surveyor's frustrations into broad "symbolic" religious or political contexts.

Note that this context should not be confused with the statements about sex or beauty or politics or religion reported above. In the actual reading, certain overtones and ideas have been singled out and reinforced as the organizing principle. The stated theme is an effort to describe the lived-through experience, and is derivative from the selective process described in chapter 3.

The Blake and Kafka illustrations are rather extreme instances of what the reader does in evoking any "symbolic" work. The cues are more or less explicitly present in the text, but the reader must impose the broader context, the additional "level of meaning" that will effectively synthesize all of the responses triggered by the text.

Again, one marvels at how the story of a vain, authoritarian, quick-tempered old man like Lear can, by the end of the play, take on such dimensions that his fate seems not one man's tragedy but expressive of the human condition. Of course, reasons are to be sought in the text, the precise sequence of words found in the text—no mere summary of the play would have such an effect. One can point out how various elements—from the sound and movement of the verse, the images of storm and physical suffering, to the double strands of conflict between fathers and children, and Lear's growing compassion for other human beings—permit us to live through a cumulatively powerful experience. I need not repeat the many subtle and humane readings of this great text. Yet the many critics who have analyzed this work have tended to take for granted their own contributions, their own emotional and intellectual endowment, that permitted them to transcend the limits of Lear's acts and mythical kingdom and provided a context that encompassed a sense of the fate

---

*If we want to know what this text may have symbolized for Blake, we again shall have to go outside the text, to see in what other contexts he used these and similar images. The argument then draws on other somewhat analogous texts, such as "A Chapel All of Gold" and poems in the Rossetti Manuscript that help understand Blakean connotations of "Night," "crimson Joy," "invisible worm," or "dark secret love." But even such evidence cannot guarantee a single definitive interpretation of Blake's reading. The following chapter treats the general question of "the author's meaning."

of mankind. Shakespeare's text still must be seen as both controlling and yet open.

If we must admit the openness of even the most closely knit pattern of verbal signs, can we not at least console ourselves with the stability of the text itself? Anyone trained as a scholar tends to make responsibility to the precise words in their precise order a basic criterion of adequacy in reading. The best interests of communication and of the cumulative sharing of culture justify the concern for accurate replication of texts as they were first conceived by their authors. Recognition of the importance of the text leads to recognition of the contribution of textual critics, who concern themselves with establishing definitive versions, especially of those texts whose publishing history has created problems or whose authors produced variant versions. Part of the work of deciphering manuscripts depends, of course, simply on visual acuity in detecting the typical formations in the handwriting of the author. But (unless the deciphering is being done by someone who does not know the language of the manuscript) decisions as to the verbal signs depend ultimately on a reading process such as was suggested in chapter 4. The words that come to the decipherer's mind as possibilities are those that tend to fit the framework of thought and feeling that he as a reader has developed from the preceding text, no matter what extrinsic help he may derive from other texts of the same author or of his contemporaries. And obviously the same process enters into textual criticism of printed works.

Shakespearean textual scholarship, which to many of us takes pride of place in its effort to establish the author's original words, surely reinforces the transactional view. For in many instances, as any volume of the Variorum Edition attests, it is the editor-as-reader-evoking-the-work who makes the decision. Thus Falstaff comes to "babble" of green fields, and the choice is made between "sullied" and "solid" in Hamlet's soliloquy.

Recall Fredson Bowers's demonstration that a particularly subtle interpretation of a passage in *White-Jacket* was based on a misprint.[25] Was this a reduction to absurdity of the critic's interpretation? Could it not be argued that the words on the page, whether or not the author's, had constituted the text for that reader, whose report of his experience with *that* particular text had its own validity? Of course, if the critic claimed that his interpretation reflected Melville's intention, he would be open to ridicule; the distinction between the defective and the definitive texts would have to be scrupulously admitted. But here we are ready to face the problem of validity and the quest for "the poem itself."

6

THE QUEST FOR
"THE POEM ITSELF"

HE dominant critical climate of the midcentury, it is usually pointed out, was largely shaped by reaction, on the one hand against the academic preoccupation with literary history, and on the other hand against romantic impressionism. A third influence often cited is the prestige of objective scientific modes of thought. All of these militated against recognition of the important role of the reader. A reaction, in turn, against the hegemony of the New Critics has now gained momentum. Yet resistance to emphasis on the reader's role still persists. In this chapter, I shall deal with two major current views of the nature of the literary work that rule out the transactional emphasis.

Excessive concern with the history of literature or with literature as an expression of biographical and social factors, the New Critics claimed, led to neglect of literature as an art. Building on one facet of I. A. Richards's work, they did much to rescue the poem as a work of art from earlier confusions with the poem either as a biographical document or as a document in intellectual and social history. A mark of twentieth-century criticism thus became depreciation of such approaches to literature and development of the technique of "close reading" of the work as an autonomous entity. The extraordinary success of some of the critical works and textbooks presenting this general approach established it as practically an unquestioned orthodoxy, if not for whole generations of readers emerging from our schools and colleges, certainly for those trained as specialists in literature.

The reaction against romantic impressionism fostered the ideal of an impersonal or objective criticism. Impressionist critics were charged with forgetting "the poem itself" as they pursued the adventures of their souls among masterpieces. Walter Pater, seeking to make of his own criticism a work of art, became (with only partial justice, I believe) the exemplar of the reader too preoccupied with his own emotions to remain faithful to the literary work. As so often happens, the reaction produced an equally extreme counterposition—emphasis on something called "the work itself," treated as if it were an object whose parts could be analyzed without reference to the maker or the reader.

This trend in criticism undoubtedly paralleled, and was reinforced by, the ideal of the "impersonality" of the poet to which T. S. Eliot brought so much prestige. Spurning romantic self-expression, he declared poetry to be "not a turning loose of emotion, but an escape from emotion; it is not the expression of personality, but an escape from personality."[1] Thus, the literary work is seen as existing apart from the immediate circumstances in the poet's personal life that gave rise to it.

Eliot's famous phrase "the objective correlative"—despite the rather confused concepts associated with it, or perhaps because of its ambiguities*—also undoubtedly strengthened the view of the literary work as something existing in isolation. Eliot's definition of his

*In "Hamlet and His Problems," Eliot uses the term in two ways. Part of the time he is discussing whether the situation and facts presented in the play justify Hamlet's emotions as expressed in the play. But Eliot primarily raises the question whether the total play is an adequate "objective correlative" for the author's emotions. Eliot argues that the difficulty of interpreting the play demonstrates its inadequacy in relation to Shakespeare's confused generating emotions.

key term does imply the presence of a reader, since the adequacy of the objective correlative depends on what it can evoke: "The only way of expressing emotion in the form of art is by finding an 'objective correlative'; in other words, a set of objects, a situation, a chain of events which shall be the formula of that particular emotion; such that when the external facts, which must terminate in sensory experience, are given, the emotion is immediately evoked."[2] In this phrasing, however, the implied reader seems passively to wait for the signal or formula for a particular and already completely determined emotion. This is an oversimplification not only of the reader's response to a highly complex work like *Hamlet* but even to a simpler one—say, a lyric about life "under the greenwood tree." Even this, we have seen, requires the reader's active contribution. The danger of this formulation is the general assumption that the more uniform and automatic the response to an image or a scene, the better it is as an "objective correlative" and the better the work. This would reduce literature, at worst, to a series of automatic signals, like traffic lights, and, at best, to a collection of static symbols or emblems.

Eliot's basic contention is, rather, that, whatever the author's personal emotion, he must rely on the text to embody it. Reacting against the romantic emphasis on the poet's self-expression, Eliot is actually concerned with communication, and—a point in harmony with the transactional theory—he equates this with finding "a set of objects, a situation, a chain of events," that will enable *the reader* to produce the desired emotions. These were not the emphases generally drawn from the much-cited concept of the objective correlative, however. Freed from romantic identification with the biography and day-to-day personality of the author, the work, it seemed, existed objectively, impersonally, autonomously.

By analogy and example, evidently, rather than as the result of a clearly developed theory, the notion of the impersonality of the literary work of art was paralleled by the ideal of an impersonal, objective criticism. This tended to focus on explication, elaborate formal analysis, and discussion of the technique of the poem, viewed as an autonomous object. The author having been eliminated, the reader, too, was expected to approximate the impersonal transparency of the scientist.

Theory of Literature, by René Wellek and Austin Warren, published in 1949, contributed probably the clearest and most influential theoretical framework for concentration on "the poem itself," as against its study as a document in literary or social history. This work did much to provide a scholarly basis for consideration of major problems of critical theory. Yet, dominated by the notion of something nonpersonal, something apart from particular readers, which "is" the poem, their book has undoubtedly reinforced a narrow view of literary objectivity and a reluctance to recognize the contribution of the reader. Aware of the philosophical difficulties implicit in this problem, Wellek and Warren survey the various positions concerning the nature of the poem, and in their famous chapter 12 develop a sophisticated theory to support their view of "the mode of existence of the poem." Their arguments present in a more developed form what in the writings of their contemporaries is often merely arbitrary dictum or unquestioned assumption.

In the following statement, Wellek and Warren at first glance might seem to be attacking the position developed in the preceding chapters. But they set up as their target an extreme, even caricatured, version of the approach to the poem as embodied in unique evocations: "The view that the mental experience of a reader is the poem itself leads to the absurd conclusion that a poem is non-existent unless experienced and that it is recreated in every experience. There would thus not be one *Divine Comedy* but as many Divine Comedies as there are and were and will be readers. We end in complete scepticism and anarchy and arrive at the vicious maxim of *de gustibus non est disputandum.*"[3] One of the fallacies illustrated by this excerpt is the assumption that the title of a work or the term "the poem itself" must necessarily refer to an entity. Critical practice and literary pedagogy are frequently confused by this assumption. "The real poem," "the true poem," "the novel as it really is," "the genuine novel," "the poem itself," such phrases constantly invoked in *Theory of Literature* and other critical discussions, beg the question concerning whether there is indeed any single thing to which such a term might point. Thus, instead of the first sentence in the above excerpt, the problem should be phrased: "Given the fact that a poem is re-created each time it is read, can we validly speak of anything as being 'the poem itself'?"

The statement by Wellek and Warren illustrates another current confusion—the assumption that recognition of the reader's activity in evoking the poem inevitably implies that any reading is as valid as any other. Any such view would of course lead to critical chaos. *But nothing in my insistence on the reader's activity necessitates such a conclusion.*

It is hard to liberate ourselves from the notion that the poem is something either entirely mental or entirely external to readers. "The poem" cannot be equated solely with *either* the text *or* the experience of a reader. Something encapsuled in a reader's mind without relevance to a text may be a wonderful fantasy, but the term "poem" or "literary work," in transactional terminology, would not be applicable to such a "mental experience" any more than to an entity apart from a reader. As soon as "poem" is understood to refer to the relationship between a reader and a text, the threatened critical anarchy does not follow; this and the following chapter will show that the basis exists for orderly and systematic criticism.

What each reader makes of the text is, indeed, *for him* the poem, in the sense that this is his only direct perception of it. No one else can read it for him. He may learn indirectly about others' experiences with the text; he may come to see that his own was confused or impoverished, and he may then be stimulated to attempt to call forth from the text a better poem. But this he must do himself, and only what he himself experiences in relation to the text is—again let us underline—*for him,* the work.

This point is frequently glossed over, evidently out of fear that it will lead to an assertion of brash literary egalitarianism. The solution is, rather, to face the uniquely personal character of literary experience, and then to discover how in this situation critical discrimination and sound criteria of interpretation can be achieved.

Wellek and Warren are much too sophisticated to deny completely the fact of the reader's activity. But their assumption that there must be something which is "the poem itself," external to any particular readers, repeatedly creates a theoretical dilemma. "It is true, of course, that a poem can be known only through individual experiences," they concede, "but it is not identical with such an individual experience. Every individual experience of a poem contains something idiosyncratic and purely individual. . . . Every experience of a poem thus both leaves out something or adds something individual. The experience will never be commensurate with the poem" (p. 146).

In their quest for "the poem itself" Wellek and Warren quickly dismiss the absurd notion that "the genuine poem" is the common denominator of all experiences of it. Also rejected as a fallacy is

105

equating *the* poem with the experience of "the right" or best reader, whether this be the author or someone else. The superiority of the reading of the individual designated as the right reader would still have to be justified. Wellek and Warren insist, however, on the "normative character of the genuine poem" (p. 150), although the existence of "the genuine" or "the true" poem is precisely what is in question. They attempt to evade such difficulties by relying on the idea of a set of norms: "In every individual experience only a small part can be considered as adequate to the true poem. Thus the real poem must be conceived as a structure of norms, realized only partially in the actual experience of its many readers. Every single experience (reading, reciting, and so forth) is only an attempt—more or less successful and complete—to grasp this set of norms or standards" (p. 150). The nature of these norms, and "where and how these norms exist" is not made clear.

Drawing on Roman Ingarden, the Polish philosopher, Wellek and Warren suggest that the system of norms would be made up of several strata, each implying its own subordinate group. Such strata are the sound patterns; the units of meaning or syntactic structure; the objects represented, for example, "the world" of a novelist; the particular viewpoint (e.g., an event presented as seen or as heard, a character seen in his inner or his outer traits); and "metaphysical qualities" (e.g., the sublime, the tragic, the terrible, the holy). Obviously, the idea of "norms" or "standards" becomes increasingly difficult to apply in the last three suggested strata, and especially in the last two.

"The unsound thesis of absolutism and the equally unsound antithesis of relativism must be superseded and harmonized in a new synthesis," the authors declare (p. 156) and suggest that their idea of a stratified scaffolding opens the way to this. Unfortunately, their claim is not substantiated when we consider the actual reading of specific works of art—that is, the actual responses to texts, or, in Wellek and Warren's term, to the "systems of norms." The authors seem repeatedly to assume a single ideal "system" organizing the various strata of norms implicit in the text. If so, a hypothetical or actual reader must be postulated from whose point of view the multiple possibilities of the text could be synthesized into an ideal and "complete" system. But even a hypothetical ideal reader implies a particular hypothetical language system, a particular hypothetical culture and ethos, a particular set of hypothetical personal values.

The Quest for "the Poem Itself"

In the preface to the Third German Edition of *Das Literarische Kunstwerk* (p. lxxix of *The Literary Work of Art*)[4] Ingarden complained that Wellek had not fully acknowledged indebtedness and also had misinterpreted the concept of strata as constituting norms. Because of the widespread influence of Wellek and Warren's book in this country, I am concerned with their general position rather than their fidelity to their sources. Moreover, they and Ingarden agree on the major point—on the assumed existence of "the poem itself" apart from its individual readings. Ingarden, while applying the phenomenological approach of Husserl, rejects his transcendental idealism and claims that the literary work of art is neither "real" nor "ideal" (i.e., timeless and permanent). Like Wellek, Ingarden creates a false dilemma for himself, however, since as late as 1969, he still postulates the literary work of art as some kind of entity, having recourse to such terms as "essence" or "schematic entity" to characterize the work apart from its "concretizations." His analyses of the processes involved in the creation and the reading of the text often present views with which I agree (e.g., on the indeterminateness of the text), but the argument is constantly vitiated by an insistence on the postulated work as separate from its concretizations.

When Ingarden attempts in *The Literary Work of Art* to clarify the relationship between "the literary work" and the concretizations, the arbitrariness of his view becomes patent: "the literary work inheres, so to speak, as a skeleton in every adequately constituted concretization, which only clothes this skeleton with various features and particulars as with a living body. The work is, as it were, visible through the clothing, but distinguishable from it—this clothing, which, among other things, contains aesthetically valuable qualities and depicts the aesthetic value found in them. It is only when this skeleton is both contained and visible in the concretization that the identity of the work is demonstrably assured in all its changes during its life in the course of history" (pp. 8–9). This metaphor, no matter how generously interpreted, suggests either implicit but unspecifiable norms of "adequacy" or a common denominator, and makes no provision for the fact that the "meaning stratum" is shaped, first of all, by whether or not the reader has adopted the aesthetic stance.

As soon as any reader selects out from the possibilities of one stratum—say, the syntactic—he has automatically reduced the possibilities from which he can select for the semantic stratum, and this in turn narrows the ways in which he will synthesize these to call forth his sense of a "world." Moreover, the "strata" are only logical fictions or, better, categories for analysis *after* the text has been read. The whole analogy of strata or layers, because it is too static, falsifies the actual process of evocation. As we have seen, the reader seeks to apprehend the work as an organized whole. The limiting influences work not simply from the linguistic-semantic level upward but from the other direction, too: The "world" which the reader brings to the text will affect what he makes of all the so-called strata. Two readers of *Hamlet* in 1623 would differ in some ways. Given all the changes during four centuries, in all strata, from the "sound-structure" to world view, we can be certain that the *Hamlet* of each Elizabethan differed from that of a twentieth-century reader. The notion of even a hypothetical reader who will make the most "complete" synthesis of the various "levels" brings us back therefore simply to the problem of justifying a single "right" reader.

How, then, face the fact that there are as many *Divine Comedies* as there are readers? Wellek and Warren's effort to establish "an iden-tify between the *Iliad* as the contemporary Greeks heard or read it and the *Iliad* we now read" again leads to the unfortunate postulation of an ideal *Iliad* toward which all individual readings evidently as-pire. Thus we are told that the work has "a life of its own," a "development which can be described." The work is said to have "a substantial identity of 'structure' which has remained the same throughout the ages," but which is somehow also "dynamic"; it "changes throughout the process of history while passing through the minds of its readers, critics, and fellow artists" (p. 155).

This reference to the minds of readers is immediately qualified by the description of the work as "a system of norms" which is "growing and changing and will remain in some sense, always incompletely and imperfectly realized." True, there is a disclaimer of the need "to hypostatize or 'reify' this system of norms to make it a sort of archetypal ideal presiding over a timeless realm of essences" (p. 153). Unfortunately, this denial cannot counteract the cumulative effect of repeated references to the "real," the "genuine" poem, and recurrent negative remarks about the reader as distorting or falling short of the "full" meaning of "the poem itself."

Wellek and Warren's effort to maintain the autonomy of "the work itself" apart from author and readers, does not succeed theoretically. Yet for at least a generation such arguments satisfied those who sought a rationalization for a formalistic criticism. In the recent reaction against the narrowness of the New Criticism, the historical and biographical approaches are being newly defended. Ironically, however, Wellek and Warren and the New Critics are being attacked for being too flexible in their view of the identity of the work, for conceding too much to the reader! For example, E. D. Hirsch, in his impressive *Validity in Interpretation*, not only insists on the identity of the work but condemns the New Critics for their "banishment of the author."[5] Since Hirsch is even more stringent than Wellek and Warren in his rejection of the reader, I shall briefly sketch some of his arguments and especially cite some of his applications. My main purpose is to make clear what the transactional view offers that is lost in concentration either on the hypostatized poem or on the author.

Hirsch also accepts the fact of the openness of the text, the fact that the same sequence of words can sponsor different meanings. But he rejects as leading only to critical confusion the idea that there can be more than one "correct" interpretation of the text. When the author wrote the text, he "meant" something by it; that must be the sole acceptable meaning. "For if the meaning of a text is not the author's, then no interpretation can possibly correspond to *the* meaning of the text, since the text can have no determinate or determinable meaning" (p. 5). His purpose is to develop principles that will counteract skepticism concerning the "conception of absolutely valid interpretation" (p. viii).

Hirsch deplores the effects of the famous essay by W. K. Wimsatt and Monroe Beardsley, "The Intentional Fallacy," with its reminder of the distinction between an author's intention and his actual accomplishment in the text.[6] Agreeing that we "cannot get inside" the author's head and can never be certain of his intended meaning, Hirsch nevertheless argues that "common sense" tells us that author's meaning is the only universally acceptable norm. If genuine certainty in interpretation is impossible, the "aim of the discipline must be to reach a consensus, on the basis of what is known, that correct understanding of the author's meaning has *probably* been reached" (p. 17). This, of course, reflects a highly admirable scientific approach to knowledge in which valid conclusions are drawn on the basis of the available evidence and revised as new evidence emerges. If Hirsch settles on the question, what did the author mean to convey? as the *only* acceptable question, it is evidently because it lends itself to such a method. This search for correctness of the kind that, for example, we desire in interpreting a scientific formula or a logical statement, is precisely what ultimately vitiates much that is insightful in Hirsch's discussion.

Of course, Hirsch cannot, we have seen, completely ignore the fact of the readers' experiential evocation of the work. His method is to relegate it to a theoretical limbo, as self-confirmatory imaginative guesswork,* which then must be scientifically tested against all the relevant knowledge available. The real work of arriving at the author's meaning is seen in the process of validation, which can be carried on "in the light of day" (p. 206). This sets up an arbitrary break between the process of shaping what I call an experienced meaning, and the process of critical validation.

In the course of scientific discovery, the scientist often proceeds by intuition and imagination to arrive at an idea or hypothesis which he then must test by evidence and logical principles.[7] The scientist retains and reports only the logical and evidential proof; the prior intuitive creative process is taken for granted. Hirsch seems to want to do the same thing for the literary work of art—and in stressing so much the logical processes of validation he has forgotten the essential difference between science and art. In dismissing the creative evocation of the poem as mere imaginative guesswork, Hirsch has thrown out the experienced work of art and retained only the scholarly apparatus.

Citing Edmund Husserl's analysis of the meaning process in his *Logische Untersuchungen*, Hirsch differentiates between nonverbal and verbal aspects of the speaker's (or writer's) "intention." Husserl's use of this term is interpreted by Hirsch as "roughly equivalent to 'awareness.' "

But [says Hirsch] the noteworthy feature of verbal meaning is its suprapersonal character. It is not an intentional object for simply one person, but for many—potentially for all persons. Verbal meaning is, by definition, *that aspect of a speaker's "intention" which, under linguistic conventions, may be shared by others.* (p. 218)

However, by content he [Husserl] does not mean simply intellectual content, but all those aspects of the intention—cognitive, emotive, phonetic (and

*Northrop Frye, in *Anatomy of Criticism* (Princeton University Press, 1957), similarly dismisses the actual evocation of literary works to the limbo of "history of taste" (pp. 9–10). In his effort to develop a pseudoscientific taxonomy of literature, he sets up for his treatment of literature the model of the physicist analyzing nature. (Frye shows himself very much out of touch with contemporary philosophy of science, which would have shown him that the physicist's "nature" is no more completely "out there" than is our transactionally understood literary work.)

in writing, even visual)—which may be conveyed to others by the linguistic means employed. (p. 219)

In using these terms, Hirsch indulges in extraordinarily circular thinking.* He commendably stresses language as a means of communication but leaves wide open, and consistently ignores, the basic question: How does verbal meaning in aesthetic communication or sharing differ from verbal meaning in ordinary or nonaesthetic communication?

In Hirsch's terminology, the problem of the interpretation of a literary work of art could be stated as the relationship between the author's intention (what the author perceives as the content conveyed by the words) and the reader's intention (what the reader perceives as the content conveyed by the words). We find that operationally, despite the disclaimer of the intentional fallacy, Hirsch's position makes the interpretation of a text largely an exercise in research into extrinsic evidence concerning what might have been in the author's mind, call it intention in whatever sense one wishes.

Hirsch draws on Gottlob Frege's distinction between *Sinn* and *Bedeutung* to buttress the view that there is a *constant* public and sharable aspect of each literary work. Frege's terminology makes it possible, for example, to say that "the morning star" and "the evening star" have a different *Sinn*, but point to the same *Bedeutung*, that is, the same planet, Venus. Hirsch argues that a statement similarly can have a constant "meaning," but shifting "significances." When there is a changing interpretation of a work from age to age such as Wellek and Warren cite for the *Iliad*, Hirsch uses Frege's distinction to argue that "the change could be explained by saying that the meaning of the text has remained the same, while the significance of that meaning has shifted" (p. 213). And that unchanging meaning is, for Hirsch, "what the author meant." Hence, external

*I am concerned with Husserl here only to the extent that Hirsch involves him in the argument concerning the author's meaning. It is not necessary for purposes of this discussion to go further into why Hirsch's views on Husserl seem to me to be questionable. My impression is that Husserl's phenomenological concepts in general are closer to my own position. That, as I indicated earlier, draws on William James—to whom, incidentally, Husserl expressed indebtedness (Herbert Spiegelberg, *The Phenomenological Movement* [The Hague: Martinus Nijhoff, 1971], I, 111 ff.; II, 580). Still, the phenomenologists seem to me less congenial than James and Dewey in providing a live context within which to place the aesthetic event. See chap. 3, passim, and n. 17.

clues to the author's intention become essential in determining the relative "correctness" of differing interpretations of a text, which otherwise is, to Hirsch, intolerably indeterminate, open to any interpretation.

Hirsch's basic error, again, is his failure to make the distinction that I elaborated in chapter 3 between nonaesthetic and aesthetic reading—which, in essence, distinguishes between nonaesthetic and aesthetic "meaning." Hirsch strangely ignores Frege's own warning about this difference and hence makes an erroneous use of Frege's terminology. Frege specifically limits his distinction between *Bedeutung* and *Sinn* to scientific statements, that is, to statements whose truth or falsehood can be ascertained. Frege's *Bedeutung* thus resembles Bridgman's "operational meaning"—the stable referents of a statement that can be tested or observed. *Frege explicitly rules out aesthetic texts:*

> In hearing an epic poem, for instance, apart from the euphony of the language we are interested only in the sense [*Sinn*] of the sentences and the images and feelings thereby aroused. The question of truth would cause us to abandon aesthetic delight for an attitude of scientific investigation. Hence it is a matter of indifference to us whether the name "Odysseus," for instance, has a referent [*Bedeutung*] so long as we accept the poem as a work of art.[8]

For Frege, the aesthetic verbal sign has only *Sinn* (in a footnote, he even suggests that there ought to be a special term for this). In the literary work of art, then, what the words point to, their referents, can be distinguished but cannot be considered apart from what they stir up in the reader's consciousness. The important thing is not a scientifically determinable, constant reference (or à la Hirsch, meaning) but rather the conception (Frege's *Vorstellung*) produced by "the sense of the sentence and the images and feelings thereby aroused." Surely, Frege's formulation fits my transactional view perfectly: that the sense *and* what it arouses in the reader's awareness are the "object" of his attention as he shapes responses to the text into a work of art. Hirsch's desire to dissect out an unchanging public meaning of the text apart from its aesthetic embodiment by readers not only is false to his authority, Frege, but simply violates the transactional nature of literary experience.

Nothing that I have said should be interpreted as a rejection of the validity of the desire to ascertain the author's intentions. What is more natural than to sense the author behind the words to which we have vividly responded? Indeed, with most texts, the naïve reader automatically assumes that his interpretation approximates to the author's "meaning," to "what the author had in mind." The more sophisticated reader knows, however, that there may be a great gap between his interpretation and the author's intention. That this is often the case, Hirsch's and other works on hermeneutics attest—to unravel the author's probable intended meaning is often a complex task. However, much as we share Hirsch's interest in the author's intention, we must assert that the error lies in the assumption by Hirsch and others that the author's reconstructed intention must be the only—and universally accepted—criterion of the sole "meaning" of the text when it is read aesthetically.

Those who seek a unitary criterion of interpretation fear that the alternative is complete subjectivism, the reader "alone." This is a false dilemma: we do not need to accept as the sole criterion either the banishment of the author or the absolutism of the author's intention. The following discussions of differences in the interpretations of specific poems illustrate the dangers inherent in both of these views and clarify the transactional solution to the problem of validity in interpretation.

F. W. Bateson has been, like Hirsch, a defender of the primacy of the author's meaning. One such instance is a series of interchanges between him and others in *Essays in Criticism*, of which he was editor.[9] Blake's lines from *Milton* (often entitled "Jerusalem") were at issue.

> And did those feet in ancient time
> Walk upon England's mountains green?
> And was the holy Lamb of God
> On England's pleasant pastures seen?
>
> And did the Countenance Divine
> Shine forth upon our clouded hills?
> And was Jerusalem builded here
> Among these dark Satanic Mills?
>
> Bring me my Bow of burning gold:
> Bring me my Arrows of desire:
> Bring me my Spear: O clouds unfold!
> Bring me my Chariot of fire.
>
> I will not cease from Mental Fight,
> Nor shall my Sword sleep in my hand
> Till we have built Jerusalem
> In England's green and pleasant Land.

The Reader, the Text, the Poem

Bateson, in his *English Poetry: A Critical Introduction* (p. 7), had stated that these lines have a meaning very remote from anything imagined by the "millions" who "chant these lines every year." They need to learn, he claimed, that the phrase "ancient time" refers to a legend relating Pythagoras to the British druids, that "Jerusalem" means, not an ideally happy England, but "something more abstract," for example, sexual liberty, and that by "dark Satanic Mills" Blake refers to the altars of the churches.

John Wain published a criticism of this in *Essays in Criticism*,

> I am far from wishing to dispute that this is the real meaning of Blake's verses—if we reserve the term "real" for the meaning which the author himself attaches to the work. But are we to do so? The lines themselves would never, in a thousand years, yield this meaning; it has to be supplied from outside. But few would oppose Coleridge's "Every work must contain within itself the reason why it is thus and not otherwise."

Bateson pressed his views further, however, citing Northrop Frye's various findings, among them that "the mill also represents the dissolving of 'living form' and 'the dark Satanic Mills' in Blake mean any unimaginative mechanism." This, or something not unlike it, wrote Bateson, is what the phrase meant to Blake.

> To Mr. Wain, on the other hand, Blake's mills are, I suppose, a nineteenth-century textile factory: "dark" with soot from its steam-engines, "Satanic" because of capitalism's indifference to human suffering. . . . There can be no question of Blake or his original readers giving "dark Satanic mills" . . . the sense that Mr. Wain prefers. There *were* no grim steam-driven textile factories when Blake wrote Milton (1800–4), nor apparently did capitalism, as a coherent economic theory, ever penetrate his consciousness.

Bateson accused Wain of encouraging the modern reader to engage in the inadmissible activity of rewriting Blake's poem. Bateson's basic assumption is that the essential meaning of the particular work under discussion "remains continuously the *same.*"

What is the solution? First of all, we can agree that two different poems have indeed been created from the same text. If we wish to know what Blake probably sought to express and perhaps communicate—and this is indeed of great interest—we should follow the path of the scholar-critic, as he engages in various historical, linguistic, literary, and biographical investigations. We should analyze Blake's various works in the effort to arrive at his private system of symbols and his implicit intentions as he wrote the text.

114

Interest in Blake's personality and in his relation to the social currents and nascent Romanticism of his day has indeed stimulated an extraordinary amount of such research, some of it very illuminating.[10]

But what about John Wain's interpretation? Presumably he has organized into a meaningful experience the sensations, understandings, and attitudes generated within him by the words of Blake's text. Note that neither Wain nor I claim that anything any reader makes of the text is acceptable. Two prime criteria of validity as I understand it are that the reader's interpretation not be contradicted by any element of the text, and that nothing be projected for which there is no verbal basis. We have, for the sake of the argument, assumed the accuracy of Bateson's historical and biographical information; let us assume also that Wain's reading meets these two criteria of soundness. Indeed, would not some agree with him that, bringing the twentieth-century world to the text, he has made a better poem than the more esoteric interpretation? For example, does not the factory image suggested by "dark Satanic Mills" set up more reverberations in opposition to "green and pleasant land" than does the notion of the church altars or any other suggested abstract symbolic reference? How can Bateson legislate that Wain's report of his transaction with that text is totally unacceptable?

Yet Wain, too, must be careful not to claim that what he makes of the text is the sole valid reading, or necessarily the intended meaning, or one of the intended meanings, of the author. That, as we have agreed, is a matter of linguistic, historical, and biographical research.

Surely, nothing is more natural than interest in what the author "meant" to express. This does not, however, justify, first, the denial of validity to any meaning other than what is reconstructed as the author's, and, second, the refusal to deal with the realities of the transactions between the author's text and readers of his own and later generations. We have in this instance been dealing with a text produced in an earlier century. But the problem of the relationship to the author exists in this sense for texts produced in our own age also.

Concentration on extrinsic evidence concerning the author's meaning unfortunately tends to lead to neglect of the poem or novel or play as primarily a work of art. (The New Critics were correct in this contention, although their solution, the fiction of a supposedly autonomous work, had its own unfortunate limitations.) In adjudicating

115

between two contradictory interpretations of a text by Wordsworth, Hirsch exemplifies the way in which such disregard of the aesthetic event comes about (pp. 227 ff.).

> A slumber did my spirit seal;
>   I had no human fears:
> She seemed a thing that could not feel
>   The touch of earthly years.
>
> No motion has she now, no force;
>   She neither hears nor sees;
> Rolled round in earth's diurnal course,
>   With rocks, and stones, and trees.

Hirsch presents excerpts from commentaries on the last two lines of this poem. The first is by Cleanth Brooks.

[The poet] attempts to suggest something of the lover's agonized shock at the loved one's present lack of motion—of his response to her utter and horrible inertness. . . . Part of the effect, of course, resides in the fact that a dead lifelessness is suggested more sharply by an object's being whirled about by something else than by an image of the object in repose. But there are other matters which are at work here: the sense of the girl's falling back into the clutter of things, companioned by things chained like a tree to one particular spot, or by things completely inanimate like rocks and stones. . . . [She] is caught up helplessly into the empty whirl of the earth which measures and makes time. She is touched by and held by earthly time in its most powerful and horrible image.

The second excerpt is from F. W. Bateson.

The final impression the poem leaves is not of two contrasting moods, but of a single mood mounting to a climax in the pantheistic magnificence of the last two lines. . . . The vague living-Lucy of this poem is opposed to the grander dead-Lucy who has become involved in the sublime processes of nature. We put the poem down satisfied, because its last two lines succeed in effecting a reconciliation between the two philosophies or social attitudes. Lucy is actually more alive now that she is dead, because she is now a part of the life of Nature, and not just a human "thing."[11]

Somewhat too generously, in the light of his later comments on Bateson, Hirsch grants that "both the cited interpretations are permitted by the text." He proceeds to demonstrate that it is not possible validly to reconcile or fuse the two as somehow inherent in the ambiguity of the text. He then repeats his argument that the text can mean only what its author intended. Hence he argues from extra-textual knowledge about the author: that is, that Wordsworth's "characteristic attitudes are somewhat pantheistic. Instead of regarding rocks and stones and trees as inert objects, he probably regarded them in 1799 as deeply alive." Hirsch is forced to concede, however, that "Bateson fails to emphasize the negative implications in the poem. He overlooks the poet's reticence, his distinct unwillingness to express any unqualified evaluation of his experience." Yet Hirsch concludes: *"Nevertheless, in spite of this, and in spite of the apparent implausibility of Bateson's reading,* it remains, I think, somewhat more probable than that of Brooks." (Italics added.)

Hirsch recognizes (rather belatedly) that "a poet's typical attitudes do not always apply to a particular poem." Why, then, can he not recognize that even a pantheist might undergo the initial shock of realizing the absence in death of the usual physical attributes of the live being? And why should Wordsworth not have recaptured that traumatic moment in a poem? Later, of course, he might find consolation in a pantheistic view of death, to be expressed in other poems. Nevertheless, Hirsch insists that Bateson's reading (despite its acknowledged failure to do justice to the negative aspect of the text) is more "probable" because he grounds it in external "data" concerning the poet's typical outlook. How far removed this is from any actual experienced meaning derived from the verbal stimuli! The impact of the exact words of the total text has been overshadowed, thrust aside, in the preoccupation with extrinsic information about the author. Arriving at an interpretation thus becomes an exercise in the logic of evidence. The essentiality of both reader and text is ignored.

Even if a letter were discovered tomorrow, in which Wordsworth stated his intention to express a consolatory pantheistic view of death in this poem, we should still have to ask: does the total text permit the evocation of such a poem? Would we not have to point out that the words of this text focus our attention on a mistaken lack of "human fears" of death and on death as an inert state, sans energy, motion, sight, or hearing? There is nothing *in the text* to arouse the feeling that rocks and stones and trees are "deeply alive, part of the immortal life of nature." On the contrary, their being "rolled round in earth's diurnal course" reinforces the link with the effect of inertness produced by the first lines of the stanza, so that even the trees are assimilated to the inert immobility of stones and rocks. If Wordsworth "meant" an optimistic, pantheistic poem, he did not provide a text that enables a reader not already a pantheist to evoke such a meaning. Other Wordsworthian texts, such as "Lines, Written above Tintern Abbey" or "The Prelude" do enable the reader to participate in pantheistic attitudes.

Brooks's interpretation, as Hirsch admits even while rejecting it, does greater justice to the negative emphasis of the text. Yet we must not forget that this, too, is Brooks's particular experience with the text. He infuses a quality, especially indicated through his repeated use of "horrible," that other readers may not elicit from the text. For example, I tend rather to feel, not horror, but an almost stunned realization of the brute fact of lifelessness. If we free ourselves from the obsession with a single correct reading, whether of the autonomous "poem itself" or of the author's meaning, we can recognize that such differences between what readers make of a text can validly exist. And extrinsic evidence can help us to differentiate the author's probably intended "meaning" from the meanings nevertheless validly derived from the text by contemporary or later readers.

The Blake and Wordsworth poems illustrate the problem of readers' engagement with works of an earlier period. A. E. Housman's "1887," written on the occasion of Queen Victoria's fiftieth year as monarch, demonstrates that problems of interpretation and the author's intention can arise even in relation to contemporary readers.

1887

From Clee to heaven the beacon burns,
 The shires have seen it plain,
From north and south the sign returns
 And beacons burn again.

Look left, look right, the hills are bright,
 The dales are light between,
Because 'tis fifty years to-night
 That God has saved the Queen.

Now, when the flame they watch not towers
 About the soil they trod,
Lads, we'll remember friends of ours
 Who shared the work with God.

To skies that knit their heart strings right,
 To fields that bred them brave,
The saviours come not home to-night:
 Themselves they could not save.

It dawns in Asia, tombstones show
  And Shropshire names are read;
And the Nile spills his overflow
  Beside the Severn's dead.

We pledge in peace by farm and town
  The Queen they served in war,
And fire the beacons up and down
  The land they perished for.

'God save the Queen' we living sing,
  From height to height 'tis heard;
And with the rest your voices ring,
  Lads of the Fifty-third.

Oh, God will save her, fear you not:
  Be you the men you've been,
Get you the sons your fathers got,
  And God will save the Queen.[12]

On its publication, Frank Harris read the poem as a fully ironic attack on unthinking loyalty to the monarchy. He complimented Housman on its "splendid mockery" of snobbish patriotism. To Harris's astonishment, Housman replied, "I never intended to poke fun, as you call it, at patriotism. . . . I meant it sincerely: if Englishmen breed as good men as their fathers, then God will save their Queen."[13]

Here it seems that we have an unequivocal statement of the author's intention. Yet even this has been questioned by some scholars, who ask whether Housman might not have permitted his dislike of Harris to dictate a contradictory reply. But even if Housman's statement is to be taken at face value, the need to avoid the intentional fallacy remains. No matter what the poet's intention, the fact is that the text permits of being validly read in several different voices. Central to any reading are the variations played on the stock phrase, "God save the Queen"—"God has saved the Queen," "Who shared the work with God"; "Themselves they could not save"; "Oh, God will save her, fear you not"; "And God will save the Queen." The diversity in interpretation depends in large part on how these phrases are integrated with the rest of the text:

1) These words can be read simply as statements of fact or belief: the resulting poem is an expression of fervent and unquestioning patriotic feeling.

2) The variations on "God save the Queen" can be read as question-

119

ing the adulation of the power of the divine over human affairs; thus the poem as a whole may express patriotic admiration for the brave and loyal men who actually did the great work attributed to God.

3) The variations can also be felt as ironic questionings of the whole state of mind represented by the phrase, "God save the Queen": this negative attitude can also be transmitted to the responses to the entire text, infusing it with "the bitter sarcasm" Frank Harris sensed. Thus the last stanza could be read in a tone of voice implying "If you breed sons like the self-sacrificial fools you have been, we can go on trusting that the queen will, indeed, be saved, but not by God, who will nevertheless be given credit for it.

Each may argue for his particular interpretation, and point to syntactic elements that support it.[14] Each selects out a particular set of assumptions. Clearly, readers bringing different attitudes and expectations to Housman's text validly make different poems out of this same total pattern of words. We shall require extrinsic evidence to decide which of these readings is *probably* closest to the author's intention. But we cannot legislate that as the only possible valid reading.

T. S. Eliot's *The Waste Land* provides another illustration of a particularly "open" text. In the edition that reproduces the original manuscript, Eliot is quoted as saying: "Various critics have done me the honour to interpret the poem in terms of criticism of the contemporary world, have considered it, indeed, as an important bit of social criticism. To me it was only the relief of my personal and wholly insignificant grouse against life; it is just a piece of rhythmical grumbling."[15] It is possible to read the text entirely in the personal terms Eliot affirms as a symbolic expression of an intensely felt sense of personal frustration and emptiness. Yet this does not require us to reject the readings that imposed a public context, so to speak, and that evoked a poem giving symbolic form to a widely diffused dissatisfaction with the dehumanizing tendencies of modern life.*

*Since these pages were written, James E. Miller, Jr., has published *T. S. Eliot's Personal Waste Land* (University Park: Pennsylvania State University Press, 1977) which cogently develops the case for multiple interpretations—the author's *and* others'. He reminds us that Eliot had supported this view in his own later writings:

In one sense, but a very limited sense, he [the poet] knows better what his poems "mean" than anyone else; he may know the history of their composition, the material which has gone in and come out in an unrecognizable form, and he knows what he was trying to do and what he was meaning to mean.

The Quest for "the Poem Itself"

The problem of how the text comes into being should be differentiated from the problem of how it functions in relation to readers. The first, the process of creation at a particular time in a particular culture and by a particular personality, will explain the reasons why the verbal pattern crystallized as it did. We often seek to recapture the point of view of the author and his time, yet we cannot assume that this is necessarily the ideal reading. If the text was produced in a complex society, whether Elizabethan or Victorian or twentieth-century England, say, the various problems concerning heterogeneity of interpretation mentioned above would already operate even at the time of publication or dissemination of the work. The readers of the First Folio brought many linguistic variables and many worlds to it.

Moreover, in a time such as the twentieth century, part of the cultural equipment of a reader would usually be an awareness that he was reading a work produced in another era. This is very different from the reading of a text by a contemporary of the author's. We have agreed that the reader might also as a scholar seek to participate in the mental attitudes and life of an earlier age. However, as Santayana said of the twentieth-century man who had reproduced an eighteenth-century home perfect in every detail, there still remained one anachronism—himself.[16] We shall later deal with this double vision, one might term it, of the reader aware not only that the text was produced by another person, but often aware also that through the text he comes into relationship with another age and another culture.

The "life" of a work is surely not "its own," as Wellek and Warren contend, but a function of the changing life-material, so to speak, which readers in different ages have brought to the text. Both the continuity and the changes manifested in the different readings grow out of this relationship between readers and the text. "Continuity" in the life of a literary work depends not only on the continuing existence and potentialities of the text but also on continuity in the history of its generations of readers, in their basic human experiences

---

But what a poem means is as much what it means to others as what it means to the author; and indeed, in the course of time a poet may become merely a reader in respect to his own works, forgetting his original meaning, or without forgetting, merely changing. (*The Use of Poetry and the Use of Criticism* [New York: Barnes & Noble, 1933], pp. 129–30)

and concerns, that sometimes even transcend cultural boundaries. Its "life" derives from the stream of readers who incorporate the text into the changing matrix of their lives. Each carves out of this experience something that, say, he recognizes as the *Iliad*. But this differs in some ways from the *Iliad* of his contemporaries and of past readers. The account of these shifts in interpretation, the movement from one kind of reading to another, constitutes the "development" of which Wellek and Warren speak. Their metaphor, implicit and explicit, of growth of an entity or organism confuses the issue.

The solution to the problem of the "identity" of the *Iliad* of the ancient Greeks and the *Iliad* of our time is probably, first, to abjure any such terms as "identity" and, second, to recognize that we have only the various evocations from the text *to compare with one another* in relation to that text. Readers bringing to the text different personalities, different syntactical and semantic habits, different values and knowledge, different cultures, will under its guidance and control fashion different syntheses, live through different "works." As every reading is an event in time and place, involving a particular reader and a particular text, a history of the sequence of such events involving a particular text is possible. Thus one would seek to establish the similarities, the repetitions, the variations and differences in what constituted the *Iliad* in the readings of each epoch over the centuries. The study of, as the French phrase it, *"la fortune"* of particular works in succeeding periods tends to become, of course, a history of the different kinds of habits, sensitivities, and values brought to the text by readers, beginning with the author himself.

Ludwig Wittgenstein's approach to the problem of meaning in his *Philosophical Investigations* has application here.[17] He suggests the notion of families of usage: a general concept such as "a game," for example, cannot be defined in any set of abstract traits to be found in all the situations to which the term is applied. Rather there is a linkage and partial overlapping of the various uses of the term, so that we can think rather of "a family" of situations to which "game" applies. In the same way, there is a family resemblance among the various readings of the text called the *Iliad*, but it is arbitrary to assume that the title stands for a single ideal or complete interpretation to which the individual readings are only approximations.

The successive readings of a text by an individual reader (even the author himself) will also usually differ, since the first organized experience will influence the expectations and sensitivities which the reader brings to the second reading, and so on. Also, the changes in the reader's other experiences in life and in literature will affect the new relationship with the text. The assumption that successive evocations from a text will necessarily have a cumulative, "funded," effect is unwarranted, however, if by funding is meant a simple addition of elements from one reading to the other. Again, one must have recourse to the historical reading events, which *may* be cumulative in that sense, but which also may not be. The reader's memory of the preceding reading may be more or less clear, his own intellectual and emotional state, his own preoccupations, may lead to greater or less attention to certain details in one reading than in another, or may make more or less readily available certain synthesizing insights or ideas. In other words, over the course of ages or over the course of an individual's biography, the "life" of the work resides in the history of individual reading-events, lived-through experiences, which may have a continuity, but which may also be discontinuous with only a varying "family" resemblance.

Caught between insistence on the identity of the work and recognition of change, Wellek and Warren use another argument in the effort to avoid the horns of their dilemma. Like Hirsch, they invoke the concept of adequacy of interpretation. Rejecting his fixation on the author, they nevertheless introduce absolutistic overtones by situating the basis for judgment entirely within "the subject" itself: "It will always be possible to determine which point of view grasps the subject most thoroughly and deeply. A hierarchy of viewpoints, a criticism of the grasp of norms, is implied in the concept of the adequacy of interpretation. All relativism is ultimately defeated by the recognition that 'the absolute is in the relative, though not finally and fully in it' " (p. 156). Our earlier discussions of specific poems have demonstrated, however, that the very sound concept of adequacy of interpretation does not inevitably entail a *single* universally accepted set of criteria by which viewpoints can be hierarchically rated. "Thoroughly and deeply," in the statement above, suggest two valid axes of concern for a system of evaluation of interpretations. Even these criteria might be implemented differently by different evaluators, however (i.e., tests of thoroughness or depth might differ). And there are other bases for rating adequacy of interpretation which would lead to a different hierarchical ordering.

The unrealistic notion of "the poem itself" as a continuing autonomous object does not serve. Universal criteria of adequacy cannot be extrapolated from the text itself, but require also a fulcrum or outside point of view from which to judge the adequacy to the text of the work that the reader organizes in response to it. Thus the readings of the same text—a Shakespeare play, for instance, or Milton's *Paradise Lost*—by various established critics could be ranked in different ways (in a different "hierarchy") according to different criteria of what constitutes an adequate interpretation of a text. The criterion of degree of complexity, for example, which has especially been applied by the contextualists to evaluation of texts, is at present also often applied to the evaluation of readings. See, for example, the influence of Empson and the New Critics on standards of what constitutes good interpretation. Thus we cannot avoid admitting that the actuality encompasses the possibility of a diversity of evocations from a text *and* a diversity of criteria of adequacy of interpretation.

To seekers after absolute standards, this represents a frighteningly relativistic view of the literary situation. Yet there is no need to fear the "anarchy and chaos" of *de gustibus non disputandum*. The concept of adequacy of reading (or interpretation) is not rejected when we recognize that there may be diverse or alternative sets of criteria of adequacy. Nothing prevents our evaluating the adequacy of any particular reading of a particular text: *Clarification or specification of the criteria being applied is needed to obviate confusion.* Such evaluation becomes easier, of course, when various interpretations are involved. If what one reader has made of a text is being compared with another's reading of it, the standards of adequacy by which they are being compared can be and should be made explicit.

Thus, I am ready to accept Hirsch's criteria of validity as *one* possible basis for evaluating a reading. As a student of comparative literature, I frequently read to discover the probable meaning of a text for the author and his contemporaries. My reading, then, should be judged in terms of the extent to which I have been able to limit myself to the horizon of the author and his age.

I am even ready to say that in most readings we seek the belief that a process of communication is going on, that one is participating in something that reflects the author's intention. And especially if our experience has been vivid or stirring, we may wish to ascertain what manner of temperament, life-situation, social or intellectual or philosophic environment, gave rise to this work. Especially if it is a text of the past, we may wish to discover to what degree our experience differs from that of the author's contemporaries. All of the approaches of the literary historian become potentially relevant—textual study, semantic history, literary, biographical, and other types of history. All of these may aid the reader to limit himself to the horizon of the author and his time.

Such acceptance of the traditional approach to the work as primarily the expression of a particular person, time and place, however, should first of all be qualified by an awareness of, and vigilant guarding against, the dangers of the absolutistic concern with the author's "meaning." We need to recognize the uncertainty of being able to duplicate the author's mentality or that of his contemporaries. Hence the danger of either unconsciously or, like Hirsch, consciously substituting knowledge *about* the author and his times in place of an actual aesthetic engagement with the text. The text thus becomes a document in the author's biography, a weak one at that, requiring support from more direct biographic and historical sources.

First and foremost, the priority of the lived-through relationship with the text should be maintained. Anything, any knowledge, that may help us to such participation is to be valued. With that clearly in mind, we can welcome any "background knowledge" that may enhance our ability to validly organize the experience generated by the text. Hence we can reject the notion of the intentional fallacy to the extent that knowledge of the author's intentions may alert us to textual clues that might have been overlooked.

To object to the monolithic views of Hirsch is not to reject the author but to recognize the complexity of the relationship between reader and author. Hirsch would lead us to make of the poem merely the starting point for a scholarly investigation. Rather, we need to keep our priorities clear. Whatever knowledge or insight we might gain by nonaesthetic means will be valued if it enhances the work-as-experienced. Anything else can be valued as biography, as literary history, as social documentation; but these will not be confused with or substituted for the literary experience.

Interest in the author's intention is not the only justification for reading a text. As in the cases of Blake's or Wordsworth's poems discussed above, other criteria of adequacy may be acceptable. A reader of the twentieth century may bring to these poems or to a Shakespeare play, be it *Hamlet* or *Coriolanus*, a "world" that enables him to evoke an experience whose intensity, complexity, subtlety, and human range can be judged to be an acceptable reading of the text, that is, to activate the actual words of the text and not to impose meanings for which the text offers no valid basis. Here, the criteria of adequacy are implicit in such words as intensity, complexity, subtlety, human range. Again, I am aware that such a reading may not meet the criterion limiting us to what we know of Elizabethan attitudes or beliefs, yet by the second yardstick the twentieth-century reading may rate higher. Often, but not necessarily always, the two sets of criteria may be satisfied by the same reading.

Just as we reject the absolutism that accepts only the author's reading, however, so we must avoid the provincialism or dogmatism that would legislate that a twentieth-century reading of Shakespeare would necessarily be more adequate than an Elizabethan. We can merely elucidate the criteria that are guiding us and explain why according to them a particular reading does, or does not, do full justice to the text, or can be preferred to another reading, even to the hypothetical intention of the author. If I am interested, for example, in discovering what Housman's own reading of "1887" might have been, I must apply the usual criteria for scholarly and historical evidence. The accounts of Housman's interest in the Jubilee celebration cited above tend to support the view that he had serious patriotic intentions in writing "1887," and cast doubt on the suggestion that his letter to Harris was obfuscatory. Yet we may believe that the text also supported Harris's—and, undoubtedly, others'—alternative readings of it as a satiric attack on imperialism.

Applying the criterion of literary complexity to the readings suggested above, I find that the satiric readings (2 and 3) provide a much more subtle, finely modulated experience, requiring a sensitive perception of many fine nuances of tone. I recognize also that these satisfy my own point of view about the self-complacency of British imperialists. Of the two alternative possible satiric readings, I again find the predilections I bring to the text leading me to prefer reading 3. In this, the common man is honored for patiently and efficiently doing his duty as he sees it, while political or even divine powers are seen as given the credit and the glory. I sense, too, an overtone of reproach that he lets himself be used in this way for questionable ends. If I compare these satiric readings with the author's supposed intention, I can only become more acutely aware of how much my own structure of ideas and expectations colors my reading and of how much my point of view may differ from Housman's.

Similar reasoning applies to the alternative readings (see above) supported by the text of Dickinson's "I heard a Fly buzz." (A recent work[18] cites a number of critics who are as divided in their readings of this text as my students.) To decide which would have probably been Dickinson's own reading would require extrinsic aids drawn from her other texts, her letters, and other biographical sources. She might have stated her intentions, and we should still have to return to the text to decide whether those intentions were fulfilled. Her other texts might be interpreted to discover her typical attitudes. Yet even this cannot be definitive, since other criteria, purely intellectual or aesthetic, might still lead us to wonder whether in this instance the poet had sought to express an atypical mood. It is argued, for example, that Dickinson, with the New England housewife's traditional zeal for cleanliness, would naturally feel only disgust for the fly. This seems to me to make for a much more coarse-grained work, emotionally and technically, less worthy of her talent than the alternative reading discussed earlier.

In the above discussion of "A slumber did my spirit seal," the criterion of the primacy of the text led me to reject the interpretation based on extrinsic biographical sources. The text did not support the hypothetical interpretation derived from knowledge about Wordsworth's philosophical attitudes.

The quotation from Empson's comments on the line from Shakespeare's Sonnet 73 ("Bare ruin'd choirs where late the sweet birds sang" [Chap. 4]) can also serve to illustrate the point about alternative criteria of validity. Empson's remark that the association with young choir boys was appropriate to Shakespeare's presumed homosexual relationship to the "you" of the sonnet reflects a reading of the text as a biographical document. Nothing in the text of that sonnet requires such a reading. Empson actually excused his reference to the ruined monasteries as "historical background." This suggests a reading of the text as a document in which the imagery is analyzed for clues to the author's awareness of contemporary historical events.

The scholarly standards on which such biographical and historical interpretations are based differ from the criteria to be applied to an aesthetic reading of the text. In this, the persona evoked from the text is dissociated from the historical person who wrote the words. The ideas and feelings implicit in the words of Sonnet 73 can be experienced as an utterance that someone who feels himself or herself aging might address to a loved one. The validity of any such interpretation would be judged on the basis of literary criteria: its organizing principle should include responses to the total text, and should synthesize sensuous imagery, emotional overtones, and structuring ideas. The same criteria would apply to the reading of this text as part of a sonnet sequence embodying a narrative; in that context, these lines might be interpreted differently.

Those who bring a particular systematic ideology to the text especially need to weigh the effect on their criteria of validity. For example, early Christian exegetes read the Old Testament with the underlying assumption that the only acceptable interpretations were ones that made every part of the Old Testament a prefiguring of the New Testament. Only interpretations that, say, make Adam a foreshadowing of Jesus would be acceptable. A Jewish theologian who might argue that his interpretation did greater justice to the text would make little impression: the essential differences would reside in their standards of validity of interpretation. Historians and readers who approach the Old Testament as literature would have still other criteria of validity by which to evaluate the theologians' various interpretations, as well as their own. Those who apply a Freudian or a Marxist ideology to their readings are also usually introducing very special criteria of validity of interpretation.

It is sometimes maintained that readers tend to agree on the work and to differ only on matters of detail.* This impression—which is by no means generally supported by the evidence—is largely due to the fact that discussion of a text tends to be carried on among people sharing a common cultural climate. Within the setting of a particular time, culture, and social milieu, a group of readers or critics can bring a sufficiently similar experience to the text to be able to arrive at fairly homogeneous readings. And when they have in common a set of criteria of what constitutes a sound reading, they can then rank the various interpretations and agree on some "hierarchy of viewpoints." Despite the inevitable uniqueness of each life, readers under such circumstances may have acquired the language under similar conditions, had a similar literary training, read the same books, participated in the same social milieu, and acquired similar ethical and

---

*See Wayne C. Booth, "Preserving the Exemplar," *Critical Inquiry* 3, 3 (1977), 412. Unanimous amusement at Mr. Collins's proposal to Elizabeth Bennet requires that Austen's readers share certain cultural assumptions, e.g., that marriage proposals should be couched in romantic terms.

aesthetic values. Such a body of readers may thus be able to communicate easily with one another about their still, to some extent, diverse individual responses to a text. They may also be able to come to a common judgment about which reading seems most satisfactory. But always this judgment will be in terms of particular linguistic, semantic, metaphysical factors appropriate to a particular time and place *and* a particular—more or less coherent—set of criteria for an adequate reading.

Actually, since the discussion of a reading of a particular work tends to be carried on among people within a particular cultural context, the text as "control" or "norm" usually seems to them to be paramount. The readers point toward the set of symbols as they seek to compare what the words called forth for them. The adequacy or inadequacy of a reading can be demonstrated by indicating the parts of the text which have been ignored, or which have not been woven into the rest of the semantic structure built on the text. The readers sharing a similar "background" take for granted their commonly held assumptions. Yet, as we have seen, even within the same general cultural situation, differences in what the reader brings to the text and differences in criteria of adequacy will make possible different though equally "acceptable" readings.

In the aesthetic orientation, the reader probably selects, out of many potential systems of limitations, an arc within which he seeks to synthesize all of the aspects of reference and feeling that the text evokes in him. He brings to this also a particular set of criteria for evaluating the soundness of his own performance. The more self-aware the reader, the more he will feel it necessary to critically scrutinize his own evocation of "the poem" as a transaction between himself and the text.

To speak of the text as a constraint rather than a norm or "system of norms" suggests a relationship rather than a fixed standard. Instead of functioning as a rigid mould, the text is seen to serve as a pattern which the reader must to some extent create even as he is guided by it. The text presents limits or controls; the personality and culture brought by the reader constitute another type of limitation on the resultant synthesis, the lived-through work of art. The reader's attention constantly vibrates between the pole of the text and the pole of his own responses to it. The transactional view of the "mode of existence" of the literary work thus liberates us from absolutist rejection of the reader, preserves the importance of the text, and permits a dynamic view of the text as an opportunity for ever new individual readings, yet readings that can be responsibly self-aware and disciplined.

7

INTERPRETATION,

EVALUATION,

CRITICISM

*W*ALTER Pater, a century ago, asserted the priority of the experience, the evocation: "To know one's own impression as it really is, to discriminate it, to realise it distinctly," he declared to be "the first step."

What is this song or picture . . . to *me?* What effect does it really produce on me? Does it give me pleasure? and if so, what sort or degree of pleasure? How is my nature modified by its presence, and under its influence? The answers to these questions are the original facts with which the aesthetic critic has to do; and, as in the study of light, of morals, of number, one must realise such primary data for one's self, or not at all.[1]

This statement holds not only for the particular kind of critic Pater called "aesthetic," more usually labeled "impressionist," but for all critics. Moreover, Pater's first step for the critic is the first step required of him simply as a reader. Much, much else can flow from the literary experience, many further benefits may be derived from reflection and criticism. But the intrinsic value of a literary work of art resides in the reader's living through the transaction with the text.

Transactional theory differs in important respects from the impressionist point of view, however. Pater has been invoked here partly in order to make this clear, since mention of the importance of the reader almost invariably elicits the fallacious inference that the old impression is being revived. This is emphatically not the case. Pater still holds to the old dualistic assumptions. Thus he tacitly suggests a certain passivity on the part of the reader, and he seeks in the clarification of his impression what he calls "the formula" of the "object," the work. Also, Pater is considered the type of the excessively subjective impressionist critic. The most frequently cited example of this is his rhapsody on the Mona Lisa.[2] He charms us away from the painting and creates a work of art in its own right. Yeats even excerpted this passage from the essay, arranged it as free verse, and made it the opening item in his *Oxford Book of Modern Verse*. Although much in Pater's writings avoids such extremes, his impressionist theory remains vulnerable, and his imitators made the text mainly a point of departure for the critic's "self-expression." The transactional conception of the literary experience entails a different view of criticism, rejecting both the formalist's so-called objectivity based on an hypostatized work and the impressionist's subjectivity.

With these qualifications, we can accord full importance to Pater's first step for the reader and critic. The reader's primary goal as he meets the text is to have as full an aesthetic experience as possible, given his own capacities and the sensibilities, preoccupations and memories he brings to the transaction. Critics tend to concentrate on the admittedly important question of how texts differ in their ability to generate such intensity and complexity. But the reader needs to slough off the old self-image as passively receiving the electric shocks of the verbal stimuli. Then the quality of the work-as-experienced is seen as a function also of his close attention to the qualitative nuances produced by his own handling of his responses.

True, the ephemeral personal evocation which is the literary work cannot be held static for later inspection. It cannot be shared directly with anyone else; it cannot be directly evaluated by others. Its ineffable and inward character undeniably presents problems. Yes, in talking about the literary work we must have recourse to intro-spection and memory—anathema though they be to those who simplistically seek the objectivity of the scientist. We must face these difficulties, not wishfully deny their existence.

Chapter 4 sketched some of the major processes involved in evok-ing the work from the text. Virginia Woolf in "How Should One Read a Book?" declares that "to receive impressions with the utmost un-derstanding is only half the process . . . we must make of these fleeting shapes one that is hard and lasting." She sees this as happen-ing without conscious effort, when she adds, "But not directly."

Wait for the dust of reading to settle; for the conflict and questioning to die down; . . . Then suddenly without our willing it, for it is thus that Nature undertakes these transitions, the book will return, but differently. It will float to the top of the mind as a whole. And the book as a whole is different from the book received currently in separate phrases. Details now fit them-selves into their places. We see the shape from start to finish; it is a barn, a pig-sty, or a cathedral. Now then we can compare book with book as we compare building with building.[3]

Not everyone would agree that the shaping process is always com-pletely unconscious or subliminal, or that it always occurs some time after the reading has ended. Woolf may be somewhat idiosyncratic in this. We have seen that the organizing process goes on during the reading, that tentative structures are created and modified as new elements enter the focus of attention. The essential point, however, is her emphasis on the reader's crystallizing a sense of the experi-enced work as a whole, as a structure that, despite its ethereal nature, can be an object of thought. This may not be quite so ephem-eral as some tend to fear. Psychologists, we know, have taught themselves and their clients to recall dreams, that form of imagina-tive experience which offers various analogies with the literary expe-rience. (The two should not be confused with one another, however. The literary work, as the Freudians tend to forget, is always an-chored in the text.)

Sometimes the backward glance simply registers a sense of having organized and completed a sequence of experiences, of having reached a conclusion. Sometimes one is drawn into reflecting on what has been evoked, in the effort to realize it more keenly, to arrive at a tighter organization, a firmer knitting-together of elements. For instance, one may search for a more satisfactory underlying connec-tion among the various speeches or actions of a character in a novel or play. Such looking backward is especially apparent in the reading of particularly "open" texts—plays, for example, or much contemporary poetry, or the types of narratives that abjure the explicit clues offered by the omniscient narrator. I have already mentioned the openness of the multiple-point-of-view or stream-of-consciousness novels and the so-called anti-novels. But we have seen that the reading of traditional, less obtrusively open, texts also engenders such retrospective glances and such a crystallization of structure. In the chapter on the reading process, this was referred to in general terms as the effort at a resolution of questions or a closure of various strands of thought and feeling. Because of differences both in texts and in readers, there is undoubtedly great variation in the timing of the point at which one may say that a sense of the work as a whole, as Woolf describes it, has crystallized.

The evocation of even the simplest work is tremendously subtle and complex, with its blending and balancing of overtones, attitudes, feelings, and ideas. Whether unconsciously produced, as with Woolf, or consciously willed, the aim is to clarify, to "fix" (as a painter "fixes" the colors of his painting) the work-as-evoked, to sense its movement and pace and structure, to register the personalities encountered or empathized with, to hold on to the special quality and texture of the experience.

Maud Bodkin explains precisely what she has been analyzing in her discussion of *Hamlet*. She has not, she says, been speaking of the character of Hamlet as though he were an actual man; nor has she been analyzing "the intention in the mind of Shakespeare." "Our analysis," she says, "is of the experience communicated to ourselves when we live in the art of the play attending with all the resources of our own minds to the words and structure of the drama that Shakespeare has given us."[4] Reflection on the literary experience becomes a reexperiencing, a reenacting, of the work-as-evoked, and an ordering and elaborating of our responses to it.

The chemist or the biologist "interprets" natural phenomena. He explains them through some formula (e.g., H_2O) or some set of descriptive terms (e.g., the traits of mammals). No one confuses these descriptions with the complex actuality of the phenomena thus interpreted. The scientist recognizes that his explanation of the phenomenon or his description of the species is an abstraction from the actuality. He knows that different formulae, different traits, might be yielded by the same phenomena, through setting up different codes of analysis (e.g., Newtonian or Einsteinian physics, Euclidean or non-Euclidean geometry). Such abstractions serve the scientist's purposes; he is not called upon to find formulae that will reproduce the qualitative "feel" of the actual phenomena he is describing. Given the assumptions of his particular science, he need only supply the operational means for testing his interpretation.

An inherent part of literary interpretation, in contrast, must be an indication of the quality and character of what the reader sees as the work of art. Since he cannot externalize the lyric or the story or the play, he too, must of necessity select out, abstract, from the complexities of the world he has conjured up by means of the text. Literary interpretation thus paradoxically involves an effort to indicate the sensed, felt, thought, nature of the evocation while at the same time applying some frame of reference or method of abstracting in order to characterize it. The reader interprets the evoked work within the context of the total literary transaction.

The reader or critic is faced essentially with a problem in communication—to make clear *what* is being interpreted as well as to comment on it. The qualitative character of the experience, the assumptions and ideas that entered into our shaping of it *and* our responses to the evocation, all demand attention. Of course, this process of reporting on the aesthetic event does not occur in a vacuum but is deeply conditioned by the social context. Whether there will be any such discussion, what form it will take, what aspects will be articulated, what assumptions or interpretive systems will be brought to bear, vary widely, as the history of such activities in, for example, English-speaking societies, demonstrates. Recall Gibbon's delight at discovering that one might pay attention to, and discuss, the feelings that a work aroused within him. Self-evident is the tremendous importance of prevailing educational modes in general and, in particular, the ways in which individuals are led to participate in literary works.

Some few, in order to achieve as direct a transfer of experience as possible, attempt to use artistic means, words or some other medium, to parallel the feelings, the tensions, the moods, of the work. Note, for example, the illustrations for *The Divine Comedy* or Debussy's "L'Après Midi d'un Faune" or, again, Pater's encomium on the Mona Lisa. Evidently we are being asked to engage in another aesthetic transaction deemed analogous to the one the interpreter has lived through. This usually simply compounds the original problem and draws the attention away from the original transaction or work of art, which then serves mainly as a stimulus for a new creative enterprise. Moreover, probably no work of art can suffice as interpretation of another work. To do full justice to the literary transaction, we want not only to depict the work as we envision it but also to characterize it in terms of the second stream of responses that contributed so much to its texture and import. Hence in most instances the reader or critic resorts to words as the medium of interpretation.

A great many abstractive approaches are available. We may characterize the work in terms of our emotional responses—the most overt being laughter or tears. We may report the sequence of ideas and attitudes of the persona, in, for example, a paraphrase of a sonnet. We may describe the personae and characters evoked in a novel not only through noting significant details of appearance and various actions and speeches but also through stating the psychological assumptions by means of which we linked them together and were enabled to see a coherent personality. We may summarize the episodes in a novel or play and identify the settings and the situations or complications. We may focus on the structure of the evocation—such as the flashback rethinking of "The Lottery" or the anticlimax of "I heard a Fly buzz" mentioned earlier. We may make explicit the bonding of idea, emotion, and event, whether through seeing them as causally connected—an action or episode, for example, felt to be a consequence of earlier ones—or through some other organizing principle such as a theme or an underlying philosophic attitude. We may emphasize the symbolic context by means of which we organized our responses to a text, as in the readings of "The Sick Rose" quoted above. And we shall probably be looking at our evocation through the prism of some literary concepts, such as lyric, drama, novel, sonnet, pastoral elegy, satire, or tragedy. The more sophisticated the reader, the better equipped he is to accept or reject such habitual patterns and to see their limitations or interdependence.

Any one of these methods obviously presents a very partial abstraction from the resonant complexity of the lived-through poem or novel or play. The act of interpretation requires a wide range of such angles of vision, and it can avoid the dessicating effect of excessive abstraction by incorporating as much as possible the personal matrix within which the work crystallized. Hence my insistence that much greater concern than is usual should be accorded the "first step," the registering or savoring of the literary transaction. Whatever the reader may later add to that original creative activity is also rooted in his own responses during the reading event. His primary subject matter is the web of feelings, sensations, images, ideas, that he weaves between himself and the text.

Some may claim that this sounds too mentalistic or psychologistic. The transactional rebuttal is that always the text is the external pole of the process. Always we can turn from any aspect of our evocation to seek what in the text gave rise to it. The text as a set of verbal symbols becomes, we have said, not only the stimulus but also the public control by which we check the relevance of what we have conceived. The "close reading" of the New Critics centered on the text. *The transactional view also assumes close attention to the words of the text. But it assumes an equal closeness of attention to what that particular juxtaposition of words stirs up within each reader.* We cannot look simply at the text and predict what a reader will make of it; but he and we can turn to the text to judge whether his reported evocation, that is, his interpretation, either ignores elements in the text or projects on it experiences for which there is no defensible basis in the text. As we have seen in earlier chapters, the question of validity of interpretation always involves both elements. This in no way constitutes a denial of the difficulties that flow from the ineffable nature of the literary work of art.

The list of kinds of interpretative activities the reader may engage in as he attempts to describe his evocation obviously is a list also of some of the activities that critics engage in—whether paraphrase, qualitative expression, statement of psychological or philosophic linkages, or theme. The inference is likely to be that this merely demonstrates that the critic must begin by being a reader. Paradoxically, the contrary is also true: the reader must be a critic. Various aspects of what is usually considered criticism have their roots in the reading process itself, not only in the evocative and interpretative aspects but also in what I have called the second stream of response. For example, the shaping of a sense of the work demands a kind of embryonic critical testing of tentative organization against the text itself. As he engages with the text, the reader, we have seen, sets up hypothetical frameworks, entertains expectations as to what will follow, and uses these as guidelines for selecting out from alternative responses. As the text presents new elements, he may find it necessary to revise earlier syntheses or to develop new structuring principles. Thus an element of self-criticism vis-à-vis the text—a concern with validity of interpretation—enters into the very evocation of the work.

Moreover, we have seen that there is an accompanying stream of responses to the evolving work, to what the text "stands for." Much of this remains unarticulated and may be characterized by such terms as a sense of pleasure or disquiet, pleasant or unpleasant feelings of tension, a shocked reaction or a flash of illumination at ideas or images that contradict prior assumptions. Sometimes the responses are fully articulated and self-conscious. All of these cumulatively affect the texture of the experience, and it is through screening out and organizing aspects of both the evocation and the secondary responses that the critic builds his later activities—whether interpretation of the work, evaluation of it, or the effort to place it in broader personal, social, and intellectual contexts.

Given this fact that every reader is to some degree an embryonic critic, and every critic one who carries further the inherent activities of the reader, the distinction between ordinary reader and critic is a vague and wavering one. Samuel Johnson's contrast between the judgment of the critic and the "common sense" of the ordinary reader places the emphasis on the common reader. The common or ordinary or general reader as I see him or her is one who chooses to devote part of life's short span to the kind of experience called literary—to aesthetic reading—doing this not as a professional but for personal satisfactions. The adoption of the aesthetic stance toward a text is the essential criterion: the question of the quality or "level" of the reading is a separate question, depending both on the text and the reader. Hence general readers would include the reader of a comic book as well as the reader of Kafka's *The Penal Colony.*

Recent critical and literary theory is replete with references to "the informed reader," "the competent reader," "the ideal reader." All suggest a certain distinction from, if not downright condescension toward, the ordinary reader. This reflects the elitist view of literature and criticism that in recent decades has tended to dominate academic and literary circles. We need not here repeat the various explanations of the forces in our society and intellectual environment that contributed to the alienation of many writers and led to their acceptance of a gulf between themselves and their readers.[5] In transactional terms, the consequence has been the production of many texts with a paucity of clues for the reader, a recourse to personal or esoteric metaphor and symbol, and an absence of transitions and direct comment. This enhanced the role of the critic; the authors themselves seemed to give him pride of place, calling on him to serve as mediator between their texts and ordinary readers. T. S. Eliot's footnotes appended to *The Waste Land* (for whatever reason)[6] seemed actually to invite the kind of critical-scholarly treatment usually accorded, say, Milton's "Lycidas." James Joyce cooperated with friends who wrote explanations and explications of the complicated schemas that had guided his writing of *Ulysses* and *Finnegans Wake*.[7] The obscurity that may have been, for artists like Joyce and Eliot, the price of innovation often became for their imitators its essence. They were inspired to create texts of extreme complexity, ignoring, or even consciously increasing, the problems of the reader. If their texts did gain limited audiences, it was usually through the interventions of critics. Saul Bellow, in his 1976 Nobel Prize lecture, was impelled to make this "separation between great writers and the general public" the starting point of his lecture. "They developed a marked contempt for the average reader and the bourgeois mass."[8]

The New Critics had set themselves the seemingly modest task of explication of texts. The task of criticism, it was said, is "to put the reader in possession of the work of art."[9] That they produced brilliant, but often sterile, criticism has become something of a commonplace. The complaint focuses largely on their lack of historical and biographical interest and their isolation of art from social and political concerns. My particular complaint has been that their faulty theory of the nature of the poem often led them, like the predecessors they condemned and the successors who condemn them, to neglect the living work of art as they concentrated on an allegedly impersonal analysis of form and technique. They did perform an important service in insisting that the text was not simply a biographical or historical document. It was often hard to understand, however, why they explicated one text rather than another, except that it offered greater opportunity for intricate analysis. In creating the image of the impersonal critic, they neglected to recognize themselves and others as first of all individual and, even at their most impersonal, still highly personal readers.

Under the hegemony of the New Criticism and parallel movements of "objective" literary analysis, such as those applying the frameworks of Freudian symbolism, Jungian mythology, Marxian determinism, or, more recently, structuralism, our century has been praised as primarily "an age of criticism." Precisely those who had acquired enough education to be respectful of the critics often seemed also the most insecure in relation to literary texts. Lacking confidence, or lacking interest, in their own direct responses and thus cutting themselves off from their own aesthetic roots, they turned for guidance to explications and criticisms and often devoted more attention to these than to the texts themselves. Literature became almost a spectator sport for many readers satisfied to passively watch the critics at their elite literary games.*

Complementary to this situation is the mass-production of popular texts which make few demands on their readers and whose readers make few demands on the texts or on themselves. Paradoxically, it is probably among these readers that the freest, most honest, and most personal literary transactions occur. If readers are indeed to be helped to be "in possession of the literary work of art," the real problem is the maintenance of that spontaneity and self-respect while at the same time fostering the capacity to undertake rewarding relationships with increasingly demanding texts.

Concern for an increasingly literate and sophisticated reading public might seem to counter my championing the ordinary or common reader's spontaneous transaction with the text. Have I fulfilled the prediction of anarchic egalitarianism? It seems to me that these positions can be reconciled, and that indeed the first—a rise in the level of the readership—will be actively furthered by a greater respect for the common reader.

The solution, as I see it, lies in rejecting the preoccupation with some illusory unspecifiable absolute or "correct" reading or ideal reader. Let us look at the reality of the literary enterprise, of "literature" as a certain kind of activity of human beings in our culture. Instead of a contrast or break between the ordinary reader and the knowledgeable critic, we need to stress the basic affinity of all readers of literary works of art. The general reader needs to honor his own relationship with the text.

The analogy between aesthetic reading and the musical performance may again help us. There can be many performances, of course, of, say, a Mozart concerto. Some may be halting, mechanical,

---

*Ruth Mathewson, in the *New Leader*, 6 Dec. 1976 (p. 11), warns of "the likelihood that we are developing a new 'literati' who depend utterly on reviews for information, for a kind of knowledgeability and—with fiction and poetry—for a merely vicarious experience of a writer's power." And, one might add, illusory, since for fiction and poetry "vicarious" and "experience" are self-contradictory.

or sentimental; others may be technically perfect, brilliant, exalting. Should our admiration for the latter lead us to denigrate the humbler efforts? Do we not recognize that much as I may enjoy the virtuoso's performance, there is value for me in my efforts to perform that concerto to the best of my ability? And should we all stop singing if we are not Sutherlands or Carusoes?

Am I saying that any reader and any reading is as "good" as any other? Perhaps we should recall the popular paraphrase of Touchstone's words about his Audrey—A poor thing, sir, but mine own. And perhaps the reader should not be so ready to accept someone else's judgment about his own performance. "Poor" for whom and under what circumstances? The common reader may have concerns other than the criteria by which his performance is dismissed as "poor." In terms of the capacity to exercise one's own powers of creativity, his personal reading of a text may have satisfactions and meaningfulness that do not contradict the values of the virtuoso-critic's performance.

Like all analogies, this requires certain delimitations, which, however, strengthen my point concerning the autonomy of the reader's performance of a text: the master pianist's rendition of the score can be experienced by others; his interpretation can be communicated by means of his instrument.* The virtuoso "ideal" critic-reader can give us only the verbal abstractions of his interpretation; his evocation remains ineffable. All the more reason, then, for the ordinary reader's refusing to abdicate his own role as a creator, or evoker, of a work from the text. Here we return to the transactional reality: no one else, no matter how much more competent, more informed, nearer the ideal (whatever that might be), can read (perform) the poem or the story or the play for us.

The amateur violinist who imagines himself a Menuhin is fatuous, of course. And the ordinary reader who thinks his interpretation of *The Tempest* as "good" as G. W. Knight's is probably equally fatuous. Yet there is a sense in which his reading is indeed as "good": drawing on the reservoir of his own past life and reading, he has lived through the experience himself, he has struggled to organize it, felt it on his

---

*Like the reader's interpretation, the pianist's is an interpretation of his inner reading or evocation of the score. What he produces by means of a piano may fall far short of what he has evoked in his "inner ear." Still, concertgoers are less parasitic than the reader of critical expositions, since they can adopt the aesthetic stance and participate more directly in the musician's performance.

own pulses. It is now part of the life experience with which he encounters the future.

The critic or academician is understandably shocked by this. Feeling primarily responsible to the text, he points to all the riches of the work that are being ignored. It is better, no one will deny, to do justice to the subtleties of *The Tempest*. My concern is simply with the social and intellectual atmosphere that sets up "good literature" as almost by definition works accessible only to the elitist critic or literary historian, and that leads the average reader to assume that he simply is not capable of participating in them. Our whole literary culture tends to produce this defeatist attitude. Critics, professional and academic, have reinforced it.

In a study of the intellectual, social, and literary factors that contributed to the break between writers and the public in the preceding century, I discerned the crystallization of attitudes that underlie much of the current alienation of writers. The solution, as I saw it, is the education of a reading public that would appreciate aesthetic values and accord the serious artist freedom and support. But the artist also has a responsibility. The creation of such a nurturing reading public would be fostered by the elimination of the contempt for the general public that Saul Bellow lamented as characteristic of contemporary authors. Their mediators with the public, the literary community of critics, scholars, and teachers, have unfortunately tended to reflect and reinforce those negative attitudes.

Moreover, do not critics and literary scholars tend to represent a rather narrow spectrum of response? Readers may bring to the text experiences, awarenesses, and needs that have been ignored in traditional criticism. Women, for example, are finding their own voices as writers and critics, as are the ethnic minorities and special cultural groups. Workers—not as a homogenized proletariat but as people making a special contribution to society on farms and in the cities— are themselves becoming articulate and self-aware. Some of these groups have felt the dominant literary ethos to be so alien to them that they have reacted with the absurd claim that, say, only women could speak about women in literature, or only blacks understand the works written by blacks. This, of course, negates the capacity of the literary work of art to enable the reader to transcend personal limitations, whether of temperament, sex, race or culture. The aim should be to widen the range of critical voices—not to reject the contributions of the professional students of literature but to strengthen the affinities between them and ordinary readers.

At this time, precisely when we have been passing through a period of literary elitism on the one hand, and on the other are witnessing the emergence of forces that threaten and even degrade the general level of literacy and taste, the continuity between common reader and critic needs to be affirmed. Despite the differences between the readings of great or technically complex works and the readings of popular "trashy" works, they share some common attributes: the aesthetic stance, the living-through, under guidance of the text, of feelings, ideas, actions, conflicts, and resolutions beyond the scope of the reader's own world. It is possible to discriminate between the oversimplified view of human beings and society, the stereotyped situations and solutions, the philistine value systems, the worn diction, of a popular romance and the fact that it nevertheless belongs in the category, though on a low level, of literary work of art. A sense of the potentialities that link all such readers together can surely have an effect on writers and critics of even the highest caliber. The capacity to participate in verbally complex texts is not widely fostered in our educational system, and desirable habits of reflection, interpretation, and evaluation are not widespread. These are goals that should engender powerful reforms in language training and literary education. But none of these are attainable if good literary works of art are envisioned as the province of only a small, highly trained elite. Once the literary work is seen as part of the fabric of individual lives, the gap may be at least narrowed, without relinquishing recognition of standards of excellence.

The reader needs to realize fully, to honor, what he is living through in his evocation of the work. This can spark a sense of engaging, in no matter how amateur a fashion, in the same kind of creative enterprise as the expert, the critic. In the light of some illusory unspecifiable absolute or ideal reading, all readings are failures. The emphasis should be rather on a creative transaction, a coming-together of a human being (with all that implies of past experience and present preoccupations) and a text (with all that implies of potentialities for participation). From this standpoint, the reader can think realistically about the strengths and weaknesses he brings to that particular text. In this resides the germ of that concern about the relationship between reader and text which we academicians label a concern for validity of interpretation.*

Scientists have developed highly controlled techniques of research to prevent potential personal bias or distortion. Even so, they recognize that the observer is part of the observation, the instrument part of the findings.[10] Statisticans speak of a "coefficient of error." The same principle, it seems to me, applies to the problem of the validity of literary interpretation, except that, given the nature of the aesthetic stance, the personal factor is to be seen as the source of a positive as well as a negative coefficient.

Looking at his students' interpretations of poems with an underlying concern for correctness or validity of interpretation, I. A. Richards categorized the "difficulties of criticism" and emphasized the potential weaknesses of readers: failure to make out the plain sense, poor sensuous apprehension, erratic evocation of imagery, susceptibility to mnemonic irrelevances, stock responses, overfacility or inhibition of emotion, irrelevant adherence to doctrines or beliefs, rigid technical presuppositions and critical preconceptions.[11] This negative emphasis should not, however, be interpreted, as the formalists tended to do, as justifying an effort to denigrate or eliminate the personal factor in valid interpretation. Parallel to each of these categories, the reader can be seen as the source of a positive as well as a negative coefficient. For example, Richards speaks of "mnemonic irrelevances": "misleading effects of the reader's being reminded of some personal scene or adventure, erratic associations, the interference of emotional reverberations from a past which may have nothing to do with the poem." Such memories may indeed lead to a faulty reading and should be discounted, ignored, cleared away. But we must keep in mind that it is our memories, our mnemonic *relevances*, that make it possible for us to have a literary experience at all. The work-as-experienced becomes the object of reflection, for a perhaps more satisfactory sorting out of the relevant from the irrelevant.

Each reader brings to the transaction not only a specific past life and literary history, not only a repertory of internalized "codes," but also a very active present, with all its preoccupations, anxieties, questions and aspirations. These have played a role in achieving both

*The general question of validity of interpretation has already been treated in chap. 6 where the conditions for consensus were shown to involve a cultural community with shared assumptions and criteria.

the work-as-evoked and his interpretation of it. As he thinks back, keeping the text and his own responses in focus makes possible a multifaceted kind of clarification. On the one hand, he senses the codes under whose sway he has been living during the reading. On the other hand, he can be made aware of the needs, the assumptions, the sensitivities, and blind spots that he had brought to the transaction. The satisfaction that he felt may have come precisely from the fact that he had been freed for a time from the limitations of his own codes. "Sublimation" is the term most often invoked when we have imaginatively shared in actions forbidden or frowned upon in our own culture. But the displacement from the accustomed is more general than simply the release of repressed emotions or impulses. It ranges over the potentialities of human temperaments, over scales of values, over attitudes toward physical phenomena, in short, over the whole gamut of assumptions that constitute the different temperaments, situations, societies, and cultures that can be experienced aesthetically through verbal texts.[12]

Hence interpretation should be paralleled by an effort to see the implications of one's second stream of accompanying responses. Understanding, say, *King Lear* or *Pride and Prejudice* or *Waiting for Godot* should have as its corollary the reader's establishing his own points of reference. The sense of personal identity, as George Herbert Mead and his successors have made clear, comes largely from self-definition as against the "other," the external world of people and things. Literary texts provide us with a widely broadened "other" through which to define ourselves and our world. Reflection on our meshing with the text can foster the process of self-definition in a variety of ways.

Actually, readers (at least, those who have not been trained to ignore their responses) often pay attention first of all to the feelings and ideas accompanying the emerging work. The most subtle and seemingly objective cogitation on the nature of a tragedy also draws on this concurrent dialogue with the text. Especially when the new experience challenges the reader's assumptions and understandings, he may be stimulated to clarify his own values, his own prior sense of the world and its possibilities.

What within myself, the reader may ask, what temperamental leanings, what view of the world, what standards, made it less or more easy for me to animate the world symbolized by the text? What hitherto-untapped potentialities for feeling, thought, and perhaps action, have I discovered through this experience? The possibilities are infinite: the insights derived from contrasts with my own temperament and my own environment; the empathy with violence, the sadistic impulse, that may now be faced and perhaps controlled; the compassion for others formerly felt to be alien; the opportunity for what C. S. Peirce called "ideal experimentation," that is, the trying-out of alternative modes of behavior in imagined situations. The reader, reflecting on the world of the poem or play or novel as he conceived it and on his responses to that world, can achieve a certain self-awareness, a certain perspective on his own preoccupations, his own system of values.

Learning what others have made of a text can greatly increase such insight into one's own relationship with it. A reader who has been moved or disturbed by a text often manifests an urge to talk about it, to clarify and crystallize his sense of the work. He likes to hear others' views. Through such interchange he can discover how people bringing different temperaments, different literary and life experiences, to the text have engaged in very different transactions with it.

We are used to thinking of the text as the medium of communication between author and reader (though, as our discussion in chapter 5 reminded us, this is by no means an automatic process). Perhaps we should consider the text as an even more general medium of communication *among readers*. As we exchange experiences, we point to those elements of the text that best illustrate or support our interpretations. We may help one another to attend to words, phrases, images, scenes, that we have overlooked or slighted. We may be led to reread the text and revise our own interpretation. Sometimes we may be strengthened in our own sense of having "done justice to" the text, without denying its potentialities for other interpretations. Sometimes the give-and-take may lead to a general increase in insight and even to a consensus.* Sometimes, of course, interchange

*Unfortunately, I have found that those who have been most extensively "trained" in literature—such as graduate and undergraduate English majors—are often most reluctant to yield to the need to share experiences. They have become insecure, fearful that a spontaneous response will "give them away," reveal their failure to make the "correct," or at least sufficiently sophisticated, interpretation. Obviously, a theory of literature implies a theory of literary education; in an earlier work, *Literature as Exploration*, I suggested some of the ways in which classrooms could provide an environment favorable to uninhibited interchange, as the starting point for growth in critical power.

Anthropologists would probably also remind us that our culture, in contrast to, for example, Mediterranean cultures, discourages expression of emotion and, to a certain reveals that we belong to different subcultures, whether social or literary. Our conceptions of the nature of art, our habits of approach to the text or ways of handling our responses to it may be so much at variance that we can find no common fulcrum for discussion. This, too, can lead to very basic self-awareness if it brings out into the open those often tacit underlying assumptions about the literary transaction. Take for example the difference between the Freudian approach to the literary evocation, very much as though it were a dream to be analyzed, and the approach that deals mainly with the manifest literary content.

Outstanding among the other readers from whom we may gain such perspective are the critics. Having rejected the critic-as-surrogate-reader, I am now ready to welcome him as a fellow reader who earns my interest through his special strengths in carrying out the processes I have outlined as essential to the literary transaction. Undoubtedly, he will possess a high degree of sensitivity to verbal nuances and will have devoted much energy to acquiring a capacity for intellectual and emotional self-awareness and self-criticism. Other valued attributes are a deeply humane personality and broad literary experience. (I link these, because I believe that it takes much more than a knowledge of the tradition of the pastoral elegy to do justice to "Lycidas.") Possession of knowledge or insight—historical, philosophical, psychological, political, for example—may yield special angles of vision or powerful organizing frameworks. The critic may be considered a professional because, while retaining the ordinary reader's capacity for reading for pleasure, he not only systematically tries to become a better reader but also seeks to develop the ability to communicate his experience to others. He will be aided in this by a fuller recognition of the transactional nature of reading events.

No more than any other reader, however, can the critic read the text for us. Nor should we turn to him as an authority decreeing what we should live through in the reading. To learn the critic's interpretation before our own encounter with a text often inhibits a spontane-

---

extent, emotional self-awareness. Thus the recent emergence of a variety of organized efforts "to help people get in touch with their emotions" is seen as part of "the counterculture." Although I am concerned with intellectual as well as emotional self-awareness, this cultural situation undoubtedly complicates the problem of tapping the personal resources latent in literary transactions. Again, this could lead us into discussion of possible educational solutions.

ously personal reading. Expectations have been aroused; we "know what to look for." The critic had to achieve his organizing principle through the active process sketched in chapter 4. When the reader passively receives it from him, the whole creative process is short-circuited. The reading becomes largely a matter of confirming the critic's experience rather than a fresh personal evocation and interpretation. Perhaps the critic himself may have to take responsibility for limiting the influence of his own interpretation through at least introducing reminders of its personal matrix.

Coming to the critic after one's own transaction with the text, one can be helped to realize more keenly the character of that experience. Like other readers, critics may reveal the text's potentialities for responses different—perhaps more sensitive and more complex—from our own. The critic may have developed a fuller and more articulate awareness of the literary, ethical, social, or philosophic concepts that he brings to the literary transaction, and may thus provide us with a basis for uncovering the assumptions underlying our own responses. In this way, critics may function not as stultifying models to be echoed but as teachers, stimulating us to grow in our own capacities to participate creatively and self-critically in literary transactions. Nothing in such a relationship would hinder the critic from fulfilling Matthew Arnold's injunction to disinterestedly transmit the best that has been known and thought in the world, thus aiding us to place our literary encounters in a broader and more humane context.

Superseded then is the image of the critic presenting "the work" as a self-contained object which he is with almost scientific assurance describing for us.* Instead, he comes to us as a fellow reader who has gone through the arduous process of creating a literary work from a text, with all the implied personal involvement, trial-and-error or-

---

*Ironically, the midcentury preoccupation with criticism spawned what ultimately was a *reductio ad absurdum* of the claim for the objective explication of the hypostatized work. Publishers began to produce collections of critical articles on a single author or work for use mainly in school and college classes. The implication is that these articles present different approaches to the same objective work. What often actually emerges is evidence of the evocation of different works from the same text.

F. C. Crews's satire on these collections, *The Pooh Perplex* (New York: E. P. Dutton, 1963), with its clever parodies of different critical "approaches"—e.g., the formalist, the Freudian, the Marxian, the historical—to A. A. Milne's *Winnie the Pooh*, provoked much amusement but was interpreted mainly as revealing the narrowness and pomposity of the different schools rather than as evidence of the transactional nature of reading.

dering of responses, frustrations, and fulfillments. Criticisms addressed to the general reader should reflect more of the dynamics of a reading, reporting it as an event in time, in a particular personal or environing context. Moving in this direction, some critics today do articulate the attitudes and experiences they bring to the text. Or at least they alert us to assumptions or systematic approaches that enter into their critical activities. In a sense, this requires that the critic help us both to participate in the particular work he has evoked from the text, and also to understand his reflections on his concurrent responses to that work.

But, it will be asked, how, in this day of thousands of publications and many different reading publics, shall we know what texts to select? Here, the critic, I have suggested, offers us more than we need—indeed, perhaps the richer the fare he offers the more overwhelming he becomes as a guide. We need, instead, someone who will point out enough so that we can judge what works seem worthy of our time and attention. This suggests the important role that the reviewer can play. Again, we need to know his scope, his assumptions about the nature and function of literary works and the criteria he brings to the text. If we find him congenial and respect his taste, we can accept his recommendations.

Unfortunately, many who play the role of reviewer in newspapers and magazines feel impelled to do more than this, and take on also the functions of the critic, usually without the needed period of reflection and self-criticism. We sometimes protect ourselves by disregarding their efforts to convey the work they have evoked or their specific judgments on it, but it is unfortunate that often we must approach a text with expectations and tentative interpretations that actual intercourse with the text requires us to throw off, precisely because we are individual readers. Perhaps the solution would be for a critic to publish a list of the works that he has read and has found worthy of attention, with the understanding that his critical review or critical essay will appear after a suitable interval, during which readers will have done their own reading! If this is utopian, we must at least hope for an increasingly independent body of readers, who take the critic not as model but as a fellow reader, with whom to agree or disagree, or whose angle of vision may in some instances seem remote from their own.

Much reflection on the literary transaction, we have seen, is validly involved with laying bare the assumptions about human beings and society and the hierarchy of values that govern the world derived from the text—*Coriolanus*, say, or *Man's Fate*. Too often at present one must engage in a similar analysis of the critic's implicit assumptions. Critical discourses addressed to the general reader would be more meaningful if the critic were more articulate about the structures of ideas or values that he brings to the text. It seems legitimate to ask of the critic a high degree of the kind of self-awareness and self-criticism that we have urged on any reader. Since comparison with other readers can be enlightening to each of us, we can expect the critic to provide an especially clear sounding board against which to clarify our own assumptions and values.

The reasons for seeking out literary criticism undoubtedly vary with each individual and each circumstance. The most fruitful approach, it has been suggested, is to turn to the critic much as we might turn to a friend for conversation about our shared encounter with a text. We place our own reading in the context of that of another whose sensitivity and attitudes we respect. Undoubtedly, we may enjoy the personality of the critic, the way his words convey the movement of his mind. But mainly we are interested in what he has made of the text we share with him. We are grateful for the more sophisticated framework of ideas, the greater conversance with other texts, the widened horizons, he offers us.

Seldom does the reader approach a piece of criticism interested primarily in discovering the particular personality pattern or unadmitted yearnings of the critic. Search for subconscious motivations seems irrelevant. A critic's literary responses and values may have certain subconscious sources, but we are concerned with what he has built on them, what superstructure of literary and social concepts he has brought to bear. Of course, we may have studies of critics, well-justified analyses of a Matthew Arnold or an Edmund Wilson. Then the subject-critic's text receives the kind of study usually accorded texts of literary works of art. But for the general reader, criticism primarily offers the opportunity to look at the work as evoked by another personality and to see what frames of reference, what interpretive and evaluative criteria the critic has applied, what assumptions about art, human beings, and society he brings to the text. This, in turn, assumes that the critic has reflected on his reading self-critically, and that he is able to help us participate in his experience.

The preceding pages, distinguishing between evocation and interpretation, rest on the assumption of a responsibility toward the text. In the recent reaction away from the-work-as-supposed-object, some have swung to the opposite extreme and are satisfied simply to concentrate on the reader's response. The main concern is to discover the psychological patterns or complexes of each reader. Such questions have great interest, of course. Over the years I have repeatedly pointed out that a reader's characteristic responses may reveal much about him. Literary transactions can free him to give utterance to underlying biases and obsessive attitudes. In pointing to the value of interchange among readers as a way of increasing self-understanding, I was assuming that often such personal differences would reveal themselves.

Still, aggressively subjective approaches can easily ignore what makes the transaction a specifically literary one, that is, the two-way transactional relationship of reader and text. Instead, the reader is encouraged to attend to the memories and free associations that may have been stirred up. His responses become a secondary text studied as symptomatic of underlying drives and fantasies. Thus the text may be reduced to the function of a Rorschach inkblot. However, the neutral inkblot upon which the viewer projects an interpretation seems a much more scientific aid to psychological study. The text—created by a particular individual utilizing the socially produced medium of language—introduces externally generated patterns into the amalgam. The transactional view, while insisting on the importance of the reader's contribution, does not discount the text and accepts a concern for validity of interpretation. Misinterpretations may thus provide clues to the reader's preoccupations, but responses may also be a function of characteristics of the text, viewed in the light of the peculiarly complex nature of the literary encounter.

It is not my purpose here to evaluate the many possible psychological frameworks that might be used to interpret readers' responses.*

---

*Those interested in insight into specific readers' personality patterns tend to approach the recorded responses with particular assumptions about human development and a system of patterns—defense mechanisms, fantasy, Oedipal syndrome, inferiority complex, compensation—into which to fit the observed responses. In a research or teaching situation, there is the possibility of a certain circularity resulting from indoctrination of subjects or students with the very hypothetical psychological concepts that should be being tested. I am not here referring to the general concepts of depth psychology, with their postulations of unconscious or subconscious activities, but rather to the particular repertory of psychological mechanisms such as the Freudians and other schools have produced and whose usefulness as tentative hypotheses seems often nullified by the dogmatic, Procrustes-like, reductionist use of them.

Nor should this be considered opposition to bibliotherapy, the use of literary texts by trained people in psychological counseling and treatment. On the contrary, reports of success in the use of literary works in psychological therapy have in some instances been offered as empirical verifications of my earlier published views on the personal, experiential nature of the literary transaction.[13] My point is simply that the use of literary works for the purpose of studying personality or for therapeutic purposes presents many methodological hazards. And it should be clearly differentiated from literary interpretation and criticism.

Virginia Woolf speaks of perceiving the literary work "as a barn, a pig-sty, or a cathedral." This evaluative aspect of the reader's activities, up to this point in our discussion, has largely been taken for granted. Yet it is an inherent and continuing element in the reading event, intermingled with the evocatory and interpretive processes. The kinds of reflection that differentiate between the value systems of the evoked work and those of the reader, leading to what we have called self-awareness, have often, of course, an evaluative aspect. Not putting down the text is itself a minimal act of evaluation. The simple "I liked it" or "I disliked it" sums up cumulative responses to the emerging work. Sometimes our reaction is so decided that it expresses itself at once as a rejection of the pig-sty or a feeling of awe at the grandeur of the cathedral. The evaluation may take the form of deciding whether the experience was worth the time and effort expended. Usually the judgment involves some comparison (even though often implicit) with other literary transactions. Sometimes we find ourselves comparing the potentialities of this text with other texts by the same author, sometimes with other texts of the same genre, sometimes with the whole body of remembered readings.

In such weighings, we are applying some standards or criteria—vague, amorphous, inconsistent, implicit though they may be. As members of a particular culture and of a particular subculture or social group, we have absorbed concepts governing the nature of the literary arts, the satisfactions to be sought, the conventions to be observed, the qualities to be admired. Not only the family but also the schools, the radio and television, the newspapers and magazines propagate many of the value concepts that each reader brings to the text. He will share many assumptions about the nature and satisfactions of literature with the culture of his own society—note the differences in reading and reading habits from one century to another within even the same language, for example, English literature or differences between cultures, such as in the conceptions of values to be sought in poetry.

Yet within any one culture, we know that there are often many subcultures, groups with very different yardsticks of literary value. And within such groupings we again encounter the fact of the uniqueness of the individual reader. Especially in our heterogeneous society, we must include within our purview the sharing of standards derived from a common western culture along with the wide range of diversifications due to the multiplicity of interacting social groups and varieties of educational and vocational training. In the last analysis, it is always individual readers evaluating their own personal transactions with the text; we must recognize the uniqueness that derives from the individual's particular selecting-out of elements from the cultural milieu, and the special value-demands due to the unique moment in the reader's life in which the literary transaction takes place.

As with the evocatory and interpretive aspect of the reading process, reflection can lead to clarification, and to confirmation or revision, of those primary evaluative responses. Even more perhaps than in the area of interpretation, evaluation offers no simple or static absolutes. It is hardly necessary to cite the changing fortunes of even those texts we today consider the great masterpieces or the differing valuations placed on particular contemporary texts. The theory of the transactional nature of the reading event has been charged with leading inevitably to *de gustibus non disputandum,* to evaluative chaos. The logic of evaluation refutes this and provides a basis for literary judgment.

The first question—and the one usually ignored—is: What, in fact, is being evaluated? In general, the fixation has been on the worth or greatness *of the text,* presumably in isolation. Literary judgments—on, say, "Byzantium" or *Middlemarch*—are actually judgments on the potentialities of those texts to enable readers to evoke an aesthetic transaction. Those who think in terms of the excellence of the text usually do not specify the nature of the reader or audience. *They nevertheless always assume a reader.* Sometimes the critic asserts a valuation that can be placed upon the text only by those readers with great literary sophistication and special "background" knowledge. (Of course, implicit is the assumption that the critic is such a reader.)

But is it not theoretically valid to posit another criterion? Tolstoy's *What Is Art?*[14] throws this into relief since he is ready to reject any text—even Shakespeare's!—that cannot be expected to stimulate a lively emotional response in the ordinary human being, to arouse in him a sense of his common humanity with all others. Tolstoy applies also particular religious and moral criteria, but his basic view of what constitutes a work of art rests on this capacity of the text to evoke or communicate emotion to the ordinary reader. Is this any less narrow than the criterion that focuses almost entirely on the traits of a text regardless of its accessibility to readers?

What is lacking in each instance, of course, is explicit recognition of the concept of the work as residing in the literary transaction. Once understood, assessment of an actual transaction is possible, according to a variety of criteria. The standard we have mainly treated thus far has concerned validity of interpretation, that is, faithfulness to the text. But why cannot we judge the quality *of the transaction* as an aesthetic event, so to speak? Suppose we apply the criterion of the fullness and intensity of the reader's sense of his evocation, testing it not only by the fidelity to cues offered by the text but also by the complexity of the strands of awareness woven into a coherent structure? (Others would undoubtedly suggest other tests of aesthetic quality of experience.) One can envisage the possibility of a reader carrying out a more complete organization of finely sensed and deeply felt experiences from an encounter with *David Copperfield* than with *The Brothers Karamazov*, though the potentialities of the latter *text* would generally be considered greater.

Concern with the quality of the literary transaction should not, however, be vulgarized into an assumption that "poorer" or "easier" texts are being prescribed for the general reader. It is possible that despite the reader's not assimilating some of the elements of *The Brothers Karamazov*, he might still be stirred to organize a more sensitive, more firmly structured evocation from that text than from one to which he could "do greater justice."

The logician would point out that the statement "This poem is good, or great" is, to put it simply, incomplete, since the nature or criterion of the goodness or greatness is not specified. "Good in what respects, according to what standards?" must be specified. And because "poem" implies a reading of a text, the further questions should be answered: "For whom and under what circumstances?"

The monolithic notion of a "good" or "great" work—or a "poor" work—masks a network of evaluative criteria. An interpretation of a literary work, we have recalled, is an abstraction, a framework of ideas derived from the living complexity of the actual literary evocation. Literary judgments, too, are the result of particular abstract criteria being applied to selected aspects of the existential multiplicity of the evoked work.

Another point should be cleared up: the transactional approach does not permit honorific use of the terms "literary work of art" or "literature." We all have heard, "It's interesting, but is it art? or literature?" The transactional view accepts into the aesthetic realm *all* readings in which the reader attends to the lived-through experience engendered by the text. We can thus leave open the evaluative question of whether the transaction has produced a poor or a good literary work of art. We can apply our criteria of what constitutes a good work of art, whatever they may be. In other words, we can have recourse to our usual criteria, but always knowing that they are being applied to a lived-through experience. If the transaction has afforded few or low-degree or no positive answers to these demands, we may say that the work was poor or even worthless. We may turn to the text, to see what may have given rise to these negative values. Or others may demonstrate that we have failed to do justice to the text. But it had first of all to be approached with the aesthetic stance, that is, as a work of art, for us to come to this evaluation.

Walter Pater in his essay on "Style"[15] posited specifically "literary" qualities as the primary basis for evaluation. But he was then faced with the further problem: given works that met his stylistic or formal criteria equally well, how evaluate them further? In a hurried finale, Pater found it necessary to introduce additional yardsticks of value, such as ethical, political, or psychological considerations. In fact, in his practical criticism he often recognized that the literary work of art *as a work of art* encompasses not only the formal or technical or stylistic but also the other values. Especially when one sees that the literary work of art is indeed an event in time, it seems essential to free ourselves from the formalist fallacy. "Literary judgment" or "literary evaluation" is more accurately viewed as the umbrella term under which all the various and varied scales or categories of criteria—from the technical to the moral and political and personal—are subsumed.

It is necessary to speak of *categories* of criteria; any one of these categories represents a wide range of differing standards. Under the category of formal values, for example, note the differences among contemporary readers in their valuation of complexity and subtlety as against simplicity and ordered structure. Pater suggested a category that may be termed "scope"—how much of the stuff of life a work encompasses. Under that category, we may agree that *War and Peace* ranks higher than *Pride and Prejudice*. But note in this category current disagreements about how much of the minutiae of human physiology is acceptable in fictional treatments of sexual relationships. As for the ethical, religious, or political categories, it seems superfluous to illustrate the differing value systems of readers under any one of such headings.

The general reader, and *a fortiori* the critic, needs to recognize that many strands enter into literary judgment, and that varying valuations of the same work may result both from the application of different categories of criteria *and* from the differing hierarchies of values within any one category. Thus someone who places more emphasis on the category of form than of scope, and who under the category of form gives priority to clarity of structure will probably be less appreciative of *War and Peace* than of *Pride and Prejudice*. Someone who emphasizes scope and who has perhaps a more "romantic" view of form would undoubtedly reverse that judgment.

The person reflecting on "Crossing the Bar" may value its enabling him to organize his feelings about death. He may give little thought to the technical, formal or sensuous aspects, to which he may nevertheless have responded during the transaction. We may say that he is applying only a particular yardstick, a religious, or perhaps eschatological, criterion. Someone else may place the poem high on a technical or formal scale but rate it low so far as sophistication of thought and feeling is concerned. Those who insist on the formal or technical as the only legitimate artistic criterion simply disregard the other yardsticks or, more usually, unconsciously smuggle in their own moral and social assumptions under the rubric of art for art's sake.

Actually, the art-for-art's-sake position is in one sense supported by the transactional nature of the literary work. The lived-through event has a certain autonomy of time and circumstance. The experience can be judged independently in terms of its own dynamics, its coherence, its subtlety, its intensity, its ordering of sensation, thought, feeling, its opening up of new vistas. It can be evaluated as an aesthetic event.[16] Yet in the life of the reader, the aesthetic experience, though distinguishable, is not separable from the ongoing life out of which he comes to the text, and to which he must return. The literary transaction, like the act of literary creation, has social origins and social effects and hence can be evaluated by other categories of criteria.

Naïve readers—indeed, not-so-naïve-readers—may tend most readily to articulate judgments in categories closely linked to their own life concerns. If these predominate to the degree that they block out considerations of form and style and structure, we may censure them as treating the text simply as a moral or political document. Yet, as Pater discovered, the critic who claims to evaluate the work only in terms of the so-called formal aspects is equally false to the work of art. To be enchanted by the technical virtuosity displayed in a text should not preclude judgment on its lack of scope or its embodiment of a system of values repugnant to one's own ideals. *Per contra*, we often find it necessary to differentiate between the admirable social or ethical values affirmed by a text and its trite ideas, crude style, or confused structure. These various categories of value are simply frames of reference for looking at the organic totality of the literary transaction. Obviously, we seek a text that we can rate high in many categories.

Much of this evaluative activity occurs as the work is being evoked and interpreted, and while we test the validity of that interpretation. Hence self-awareness, making articulate the assumptions and attitudes lived through, which I stressed earlier, becomes even more important as the process of evaluation takes over. The blandness and quiet dogmatism of much literary discussion might disappear with such articulateness of criteria. This candor might also rescue the good and great works of the past and the present from their aura of unassailability and thrust them into the purview of ordinary readers.

Literary transactions are woven into the fabric of individual lives. Personal meaningfulness should be recognized as at least *one* of the possible criteria to be applied by a reader assessing the reading-event. Of course, powerful personal reverberations and moments of intensity or illumination may be the result of the coming-together of the reader and the text at an especially propitious moment. The reader, it can be said, provides at that point in his life or in that social situation, a particularly receptive context, a kind of amplifier, for what he derives from the text. We should of course recognize the extent of the reader's projective contribution. Nevertheless, we should honor the intensity or fullness of consummation of the experience.

This view creates problems because of the range of reading events it encompasses. Few would object to the suggestion that a mature person will have a richer literary experience with the text of *King Lear* than he would have had as a teen-ager. But how about instances in which the reader projects much more into the transaction than the text would ordinarily justify? Bereavement may bring a reader to a text in an emotional state of readiness that enables it to help him focus, organize, give vent to, intense feeling. One often hears with great embarrassment the reading of stereotyped texts on the death of a loved one. Such a reading can be diagnosed as sentimental, as a manifestation of emotion excessive in relation to the cues offered by the text. But one must admit that components of this transaction may be paralleled by someone else's reading of Donne's "Death, be not proud." For the latter also entails the reader's personal need to face "death's dominion" and provides a verbal means of handling and dominating emotion. We may judge one text superior in its potentialities for inducing thought and feeling, but we cannot deny that they have in common a similar relationship to readers.

We are ready to be amused at the Babbit or Monsieur Jourdain who declares, "I don't know anything about art (or music, or poetry) but I know what I like when I see it (or hear it or read it)." Despite their ignorance of the importance of understanding stylistic traditions and craftsmanship, that naïve statement registers a fact: people do have evaluative responses to whatever they make of an aesthetic stimulus. We can regret that such readers come to texts ill prepared to make much of them or to handle their own responses self-critically. But the criterion of personal acceptance or rejection, of personal pleasure or indifference, deserves recognition as relevant even when other more sophisticated criteria are applied. Too much of the reading of critics and students seems to thrust this consideration aside; it is hard at times, in reading twentieth-century analyses of the themes and symbols and technical strategies of a work, to discover whether the critic had even a glimmering of personal pleasure in the literary transaction, or a sense of personal significance.

Those who deplore "naïve" or "unsophisticated" or "personal" responses sometimes seem especially blind to the human values of literary experience. This is understandable, given the cliché-ridden texts that elicit popular enthusiasm. The verbal banality seems indi-

158

visible from emotional and intellectual banality. Yet the texts may nevertheless give rise to a personally meaningful transaction, in which the aesthetic stance is adopted and gives some rewards, even though these might rate low according to generalized literary criteria. One is often amazed that sophisticated writers of the past whom we admire found satisfaction in mediocre contemporary works. For them, as often for ourselves and our contemporaries, the criterion of personal meaningfulness was evidently operating. Perhaps we dismiss too scornfully works of the past that were important to human beings at a particular time and place and are so no longer. This in no way rules out the criterion that some of Shakespeare's texts meet so magnificently—the capacity to transcend cultural differences and to appeal to many different generations of readers.

The notion of the continuity of different kinds or levels of literary experience applies also to the single individual's readings. Both Coleridge and Poe, for somewhat different reasons, declared that there can be no long poem.[17] Their statements reflected the belief that the highest form of poetry resides in the intensity of thought, feeling, and attention associated with lyric poetry. Thus Poe could claim that *Paradise Lost* consisted of sequences of poetry and nonpoetry, as the reader's powers faltered and revived, but that if he started at another point in the text, the very passages that had been nonpoetry would come alive and the former poetic sections would grow inert. This places an even more extreme emphasis on the reader's contribution than I should venture to subscribe to.

Even though we may not accept high lyric intensity as the sine qua non of poetry, we should honor Poe's concern about the reader's powers of attention and his capacity to persist on a high plane of aesthetic awareness. Few can assimilate a steady diet of masterpieces. Even the most highbrow of readers may indulge in a detective story, which, with its minimal emotional appeals, its presentation of a simple problem, its stress on (of course, misleading) clues, makes slight demands on him. Yet within the detective novel as a genre, the very breadth of its reading public makes for a rise toward a higher level of literary merit. Perhaps because the cinema has not yet become a fully recognized art form, its public approaches more nearly to the kind of democratic cross section that is suggested above for literature: poets, novelists, and academics are willing to admit being "film buffs." The experimental or "serious" films can be seen to influence the commercial films made for a broad public. Perhaps the last author to enjoy such a cross-section public was Charles Dickens, whose works, as a contemporary reviewer noted, were read by the master and mistress in the drawing room, the children in the school-room, and the maid in the attic!

Recognition of each reading as a personal event does not necessitate disregard for the more usual criteria of evaluation, predicated on some kind of consensus. As I have suggested earlier, as soon as one looks for such a consensus, one finds not one but divergent publics, each achieving its own consensus through commonly held criteria. Some judgments rely on evidence in the text of appeals to the common human experiences—of birth, death, family, ordinary social relationships. Others depend on the reactions of a highly selected group of verbally sophisticated readers. Still others are based on the persistence through time and changing generations of perhaps a limited group of readers for a text. The more generalized criteria, almost by definition, make little allowance for personal idiosyncrasy or situations. Yet it should be possible to say that a particular poem or story has particular value for oneself, to see for what reasons, in oneself and in the text, this is so, and still understand that by general literary criteria the text would be accounted mediocre. Reflection on such a reading can lead to self-understanding in the same way as reflection on one's responses to a more generally valued text.

Another consideration: the reader undertakes to see the work as a whole, yet in actual literary transactions it may sometimes be some minor part that had intensely personal reverberations. A poem may live in the memory through only one phrase that suddenly embodies for us the "joy" and the "juice" of life. Some scene, some brief dialogue, some episode may spark an insight into one's own or another's nature, or unleash a new way of understanding, a new sense of possibilities. Such moments of intensity may constitute for us the merit of the work, overshadowing any evaluation based on the probable general consensus concerning the worth of the whole work.

The academic critical culture persists in ignoring, or at best laments, the mass and "middlebrow" literary institutions in our society. The transactional formulation offers a theoretical bridge between the two literary cultures that now exist side by side. The bridge, as I see it, need not facilitate Gresham's law of the bad driving out the good. Rather, awareness of the continuities in basic literary processes and concerns, from the humbler echelons of the literary enterprise upward, could affect criticism and education and lead to a rise in the general level of aesthetic literacy.

If today there is a great gap between "good" works and popular works, is that not to some extent because so-called good literature has too often not been subjected to criteria based on actual personal and social life needs? Always there looms the supposedly crushing riposte: Shall we consider *Uncle Tom's Cabin* a great work because of its acknowledged impact on people's ideas and emotions? Actually that question assumes a different position from the one I am suggesting. Unlike Tolstoy, I am not contending that personal or social meaningfulness be the sole or major criterion. It should simply be accepted as one standard of judgment, among others. Since the text never exists *in vacuo*, it can be evaluated in relationship, actual or potential, to particular readers at particular points in time and space. Then "good" and "great" will have many dimensions.

Such an effort to consider texts always in relation to specific readers and in specific cultural situations, and to honor the role of literary experience in the context of individual lives, has powerful educational implications, which cannot be elaborated here. At least this can be indicated: a primary concern throughout would be the development of the individual's capacity to adopt and to maintain the aesthetic stance, to live fully and personally in the literary transaction. From this could flow growth in all the kinds of resources needed for transactions with increasingly demanding and increasingly rewarding texts. And from this would flow, also, a humanistic concern for the relation of the individual literary event to the continuing life of the reader in all its facets—aesthetic, moral, economic, or social.

Evocation, interpretation, evaluation—thus far, it has been possible to discuss these basic activities as they engage the whole spectrum of readers. The critic was distinguished from his fellow readers simply by his greater proficiency and professionalism. It is essential, however, to differentiate specifically literary criticism from the many other kinds of professional activities related to texts. Crucial to this is, again, the basic distinction between aesthetic and efferent stances. Precisely because of the ineffable, elusive nature of the literary evocation, the critic must guard against a distortion or slippage of focus.

The text of a literary work of art, it must again be reiterated, can also be read efferently. And like any other human activity, the production and reading of texts can be studied in their social contexts from a variety of angles by practitioners of disciplines such as history, sociology, economics, or anthropology. The text can be analyzed as a document to be correlated with other evidence concerning the structure and development of the language. It can be studied as a document in the author's biography, for the light it sheds on his earlier experiences, his temperament, his knowledge, his reading. It can provide evidence concerning the society in which it was produced.

All this, so well known, is recalled because the tendency has been to lump together indiscriminately under the term literary criticism many such efferent treatments of literary texts. When, however, these other interests become ends in themselves, or predominate, the student or scholar is functioning, not as a literary critic, but as a linguist, a biographer, a historian, a psychologist, a literary theorist, a stylist, or whatever title his technical or scholarly specialization confers. This should in no way be considered a denigration of such interests. Nevertheless, failure to discriminate in this way has blurred understanding of the special personal nature of the transaction that generates a literary work of art.

The term "literary critic" should be reserved for one whose primary subject is his aesthetic transaction with the text; he reflects on the work of art that he has evoked. Earlier pages have suggested some of the kinds of intellectual frameworks that might help to shape interpretation and evaluation. Yet such mainly efferent concerns may tempt interest away from the inwardly focused, lived-through experience which constitutes the essential work of art. The literary critic draws on the results of efferent analysis or study in order to illuminate, to reinforce or enrich, to place in context, that aesthetic event. *In the basic paradigm for literary criticism, then, the movement is from an intensely realized aesthetic transaction with a text to reflection on semantic or technical or other details in order to return to, and correlate them with, that particular personally apprehended aesthetic reading.*

The critic is often led to ask, How did the specific elements of the text lead me to create that particular experiential work? How did a text like Faulkner's *Absalom, Absalom!* help me to construct a different persona from each of the narrators of that multiple-point-of-view novel? Or what aspects of the text explain my sensing a voice, a style, that seems unique to that author?

Such questions, which prompt analysis of theme or style or technique, can foster confusion of stance. I am not referring here to the kind of heightened awareness of word or phrase or recurrent effect that happens during the reading-event. I refer rather to the efferent reading or "study" of the text that takes the form of isolating certain kinds of textual details.

In earlier chapters, it was repeatedly necessary to differentiate between efferent and aesthetic implications of traditional rhetorical and literary terms and concepts. Recall also (chap. 4) how Empson's discussions of "ambiguities" were seen sometimes to become efferent speculations on alternative meanings without sufficient referral to their relation to the total aesthetic work.

As with any attempt to carry out a systematic investigation, such study requires a hypothesis as to what elements are potentially important. Are they repetitive or cumulative? One may count their incidence and look for patterns of recurrence. Obviously, such questions require an impersonal scrutiny of the text. Hence, sometimes such investigations have recourse to such new technologies as the computer and to new statistical techniques, for example, multivariate analysis. Efferent classification and analysis of the elements of the text can yield much interesting data. But it can lead to neglect of the work, the actual aesthetic event in time. The frame so absorbs the attention that the absence of the picture it should enhance goes unnoticed.

What can we derive from such analyses in themselves? They undoubtedly reveal something about the linguistic habits internalized by the author. As a linguistic document, the text can throw light on how the author's language system resembles or differs from that of other texts, of his own time or of other periods. Nothing, of course, prevents our defining "style" as whatever an efferent analysis reveals. We can set computers to work determining whether a specific text is, say, by Shakespeare or by Marlowe. But how, then, should we *characterize* the styles? By such things as percentages of abstract words? The question still remains: What qualitative importance, if any, do these particular quantitative differences have for the work-as-evoked by specific readers?[18] Moreover, study of readers' responses may reveal that a majority noticed certain syntactic or semantic elements, but this simply tells us something about that group of readers. It cannot provide a recipe for a uniform aesthetic reading by all potential readers.

Studies of Shakespeare's imagery may further illustrate how textual analysis either can be utilized for purely efferent purposes or can serve literary criticism as I have defined it. Caroline Spurgeon's pioneering work on Shakespeare's imagery,[19] because of her dual aims, illustrates both tendencies. Given the paucity of biographical knowledge about Shakespeare, she hoped that by classifying and counting recurrent images in his plays she would gain clues as to his experiences, his likes and dislikes, and perhaps his personality. This was a straightforwardly efferent, inductive piece of fact-gathering and reasoning from the evidence. (Actually, her biographical inferences are disappointing, even if one discounts the problem of the dramatic usage of the imagery.) The second part of her book, entitled, "The Function of the Imagery as Background and Undertone in Shakespeare's Art," in contrast, merits inclusion under the category of literary criticism. Here she seeks to relate the dominant imagery—for example, the recurrent images of flashing lights in *Romeo and Juliet* or the images of bodily pain in *King Lear*—to the effect of the play as a whole.

Wolfgang Clemen's *The Development of Shakespeare's Imagery*[20] reinforces my point even more clearly. He gives due credit to Spurgeon's work, but seeks to dissociate himself from the trend toward "classifying and cataloguing." A "rigid schematic system of classification," he claims, "destroys a living feeling both for the unity and for the many-hued iridescent richness of the poetical work." Although he phrases his views largely in terms of the author's choices in shaping the text, Clemen repeatedly scrutinizes the imagery through the eyes of the "audience." Writing about the tragedies, he says,

The imagery, especially in the first few acts, often implants certain expectations in the minds of the audience, it puts riddles, as it were, and hence arises a dramatic tension which is not without influence on the imagination and attitude of the audience. For the dramatist the imagery becomes a subtle way of influencing and leading the audience through the play without their knowing. The various trends, chains and patterns of imagery combine to form, as it were, a second network of action running below the actual plot and interconnecting with it in several ways. (p. 223)

A less passive—a transactional—phrasing would be: while the reader is attending primarily to the dramatic actions signaled by the words of the play, he is also aware of intermingled feelings and attitudes triggered by the images he evokes.

Clemen's opposition between "the living feeling" for the play and the urge for "classifying and cataloguing" its components tacitly contrasts aesthetic and efferent stances toward the work.

The principal source of error in the statistical method of approach is that a set of statistics gives us the illusion that all the phenomena encompassed by it are equal among themselves. In reality, however, this is only seldom the case. If, for example, we state that in a certain play there are three sea-images as opposed to eight garden-metaphors, the statistical statement itself is still of very little help and may indeed be misleading. The three sea-images may be comprehensive, they may stand at important points and may have a far greater significance for the drama than the eight metaphors from the garden. (p. 8)

Perhaps Clemen does not quite do justice to Spurgeon's point that the recurrence of certain images or types of image may have a cumulative effect. But surely Clemen is correct in judging the crucial factor to be the reader's aesthetic assimilation of an image in its context. Far from a computerlike uniformity, the reader's response is regulated, we have seen, not only by the incidence of elements in the text but also by what he brings to it. Personal attitudes, social and literary expectations, tentative organizing frameworks, reactions to the emerging evocation, guide the reader's attention and influence the varying impact of the textual stimuli. Clemen seeks to communicate his aesthetic synthesis, his reading of a play, and to show how in specific instances imagery contributed to this evocation.

In the light of this theoretical position, much literary analysis remains incomplete or irrelevant as literary criticism. The parallel, and at times seemingly opposing, trends of the American New Criticism, the exploiters of one or another myth typology, the Russian formalists, or the more recently emerged French structuralists, seem from the transactional angle of vision to be manifestations of a similar yearning for the "objectivity," precision, or system of the scientist. And the science that has especially provided the model or, to use the fashionable terminology, paradigm, has been linguistics. The American (or Bloomfieldian) linguists offered their assumption of a structure prior to, or discernible apart from, meaning. The Saussurians provided their view of an ideal *langue* free of the chance particularities of *parole*. Their method of study approached language as a system of relationships that could be disengaged from the seeming disorder of actual phenomena. This method could be applied to all kinds of conventional systems—as Claude Lévi-Strauss applied it to culture or Roman Jakobson and the French structuralists applied it to the literary work of art.

Roman Jakobson, developing the Saussurian approach, has contributed many of the linguistic concepts that have inspired the methodology of workers in other fields. Moreover, perhaps because of his early participation in the Russian formalist movement, he has made some of the most interesting applications of linguistic concepts to the analysis of poetry. His brilliant contributions and immense influence make it all the more important to underline the absence in his work of a clear demarcation between the text viewed efferently and the poem evoked aesthetically. The statement on "Linguistics and Poetics,"[21] which Jakobson presented at the famous 1958 Indiana conference on style in language, "delineates in concentrated form Jakobson's theory of poetry as it has evolved in his researches over the last forty years."[22] In that paper (in which he demonstrates the breadth and subtlety of his linguistic system), he makes poetics a subdivision of linguistics and reiterates his view of poeticity as the use of words for their own sake. His reference to "the poetic function" and his adoption to certain Husserlian or phenomenological formulae do not seem to have modified his preoccupation with the systematic analysis of linguistic devices in the text. Nor does he anywhere, it seems, adequately meet René Wellek's rebuttal at that conference: that "literary analysis begins where linguistic analysis ends" (p. 417), and that "there is no collection of neutral, value-proof traits that can be analyzed by a science of stylistics. A work of literature is, by its very nature, a totality of values which do not merely adhere to a structure but constitute its very nature" (p. 419). Ironically, despite Wellek's insight into the flaws in Jakobson's position, he shares, as we have seen, Jakobson's concentration on the text as in some way embodying "the poem itself," neglecting the fact that values imply always a human valuing—not simply for the sake of the words themselves but of what the words call forth in author or reader.

A recent example of Jakobson's method is his analysis (with Lawrence G. Jones) of Shakespeare's Sonnet 129, "Th'expence of spirit in a waste of shame."[23] Applying the principle of "binary" correspondences and oppositions, they analyze "Constituents: Rimes, Strophes, Lines." Chapter headings include "Pervasive Features," "Odd Against Even," "Outer Against Inner," "Anterior Against Posterior," "Couplet Against Quatrains," "Center Against Marginals." The analysis yields numerous syntactic, semantic, and phonemic correspondences and oppositions, symmetries and asymmetries, recurrences and permutations. The elaborateness and subtlety with which the codified patterns are worked out is most impressive; the regularities and the deviations take on a deterministic weight, and one recalls Jakobson's remark, "This cannot be accidental."

This study certainly offers systematic proof of Shakespeare's phenomenally sensitive ear and mastery of resources of the language. But an efferent description and labeling of the elements of the text does not help us to understand the process by which this great text came into being, and the poetic function of many of the coded elements remains to be hypothetically glimpsed by an aesthetic reading that may even be hindered by the magnification as under a microscope of the phonetic, syntactic, even semantic, correspondences and oppositions.

Jakobson (one knows from other evidence) is a sophisticated evoker of poems, but this study fails to communicate much about his reading of the text. A pedestrian paraphrase, stressing Elizabethan punning usage of the words "shame" and "spirit," is mistitled "Interpretation." A final section rejects various readings by others, but it is not clear that all of the detailed analysis was needed to sustain these rejections, which, it is claimed, are "corroborated by a structural analysis of [the] text and poetic texture in all its interlaced facets." But only occasionally is there a suggestion of the relationship between a particular "binary" pattern and the "poetic texture." How the numerous details noted would contribute to, or function in, an evocatory synthesis, is not made clear. The text, not the work, has been analyzed. This is a subtle piece of linguistic analysis, but it falls short of fulfilling our demands for literary criticism. That would start with awareness of a qualitative event ("the poetic texture") and would seek to discover which of the efferently noted rhythmic, phonemic, semantic details might have contributed to it, and in what way.

The fact of "selective attention" must again be recalled. The reader who has adopted the aesthetic stance will not pay equal attention to the effect on him of all the complex stimuli offered by the text. Some will color the whole experience, some will have sharp impact, others will be glossed over or remain on the outer fringes of consciousness. To speak of some of the patterns perhaps acting subliminally is only another way of saying that whatever the efferent methods of analysis achieve, they cannot be used to predict or prescribe—but must rather be interpreted in the light of—the actual lived-through literary transaction.*

Perhaps Jakobson's analyses suggest some of the kinds of limitations or control the text *potentially* offers, for example, syntactic patterns, phonemic and morphological occurrences and recurrences—but this does not contradict the semantic options and coexistent openness of the text as individual readers actively synthesize their responses within those limitations. Again, the difference in emphasis becomes apparent: one can, with Whorf and others, emphasize the extent to which the language by its very structure of categories limits the thinker, or one can (as I do) recall Boas's pointing out that any language is capable of generating the terms to cover new ideas, when that need occurs.[24] Just as a language system provides both flexibility and limitation, so the text which offers the blueprint for a literary work of art offers both openness and control.

The French structuralists,[25] emerging in the sixties and only recently becoming known in this country, have carried the analogy with a linguistic system to an extreme. The springs of "la nouvelle critique" (not related to the American "New Criticism") are found in the work of the anthropologist, Claude Lévi-Strauss, who, drawing inspiration from Saussurian linguistics, applied the concept of pure relational forms to the study of culture. This movement seems to me to offer the most explicit instances of the substitution of efferent analysis in place of the aesthetic evocation. The French structuralists talk much about the reader, about the text, and about *écriture*, the act of creation of the text; they accept the view that the reader is an inevitable participant, that we cannot assume that only the author's intention governs interpretation. It might seem that here will be found reinforcement for the transactional theory.

Unfortunately, we are again in the presence of the flight from the work of art as a lived-through event, with only lip service given to reading as a total personal transaction with the text. The controlling impetus is the search for a method of systematic description of a

---

*In a review in the 28 May 1970 *Times Literary Supplement*, I. A. Richards starts by announcing Jakobson's study as the revolutionary opening of a new era, but ends with a list of possible bad effects of this approach, and contends that "probably only some, not all, of the features consciously discerned and included in the *account* will be actually operative in shaping the *response*."

hidden underlying structure: the text is there to be "translated" or "transcoded." The reader, it is true, is free to bring anything that he wishes to the reading; he is not limited by past interpretations. But his responsibility seems to be primarily toward the application of one or another code—linguistic, semantic, Marxian, psychoanalytic or psychological, or sociological. The basic model is the linguist's uncovering of an underlying pattern.

Roland Barthes takes positions that particularly might seem supportive of transactional theory. He nevertheless can serve to illustrate the complaint that the structuralists lead us away from the concept of the work of art qua art residing in the transaction between reader and text. One sympathizes with Barthes's effort in *On Racine* to free French criticism from the academic historical tradition, and with his assertion in *S/Z*, that he evaluates a text according to whether he would desire "to put [it] forth as a force in this world of mine" (p. 4). But in this commentary on Balzac's story, *Sarrasine*, Barthes begins by contrasting the "readerly" (*lisible*) and the "writerly" (*scriptible*) and soon reveals his bias.

Why is the writerly our value? Because the goal of literary work (of literature as work) is to make the reader no longer a consumer, but a producer of the text. Our literature is characterized by the pitiless divorce which the literary institution maintains between the producer of the text and its user, between its owner and its customer, between its author and its reader. This reader is thereby plunged into a kind of idleness—he is intransitive; he is, in short, *serious*: instead of functioning himself, instead of gaining access to the magic of the signifier, to the pleasure of writing, he is left with no more than the poor freedom either to accept or reject the text: reading is nothing more than a *referendum*. Opposite the writerly text, then, is its countervalue, its negative, reactive value: what can be read, but not written: the *readerly*. We call any readerly text a classic text. (P. 4)

What starts out as an affirmation of the importance of the reader ends as a distinction between two kinds of texts. Barthes imputes to the text the quality of being either writerly *or* readerly, instead of seeing these as attitudes of the reader toward any text, classic or modern. It is not the classic *text* that makes the reader passive or "intransitive." (In fact, we have seen that he can never be completely passive and still derive any meaning from a text.) What is involved in Barthes's "readerly" is the traditional notion that the reader must find in the text the particular work or interpretation that some authority, tradition, teacher or critic, decrees is acceptable. Michel Butor's work

169

evidently represents for Barthes quintessentially writerly texts, but a text of Racine's, as Barthes's own practice shows, is also pluralistic. The relatively greater openness of many "modern" texts was noted in chapter 5, but this, it was seen, does not constitute a difference in kind, only of degree. Although some texts provide more clues for the reader, all require activity, a two-way transaction.

In the method of his actual approach to the text, Barthes clearly leaves behind the image of the reader as "producer." He sets up a process of analysis which rejects the "naturalness" of ordinary or habitual reading: "[The text] will ceaselessly be broken, interrupted without any regard for its natural divisions (syntactical, rhetorical, anecdotic); inventory, explanation, and digression may deter any observation of suspense, may even separate verb and complement, noun and attribute; the work of commentary, once it is separated from any ideology of totality, consists precisely in *manhandling* the text, *interrupting* it" (p. 15). The arbitrarily chosen units are commented on in terms of five "codes" or "voices" which he terms, sometimes rather idiosyncratically: hermeneutic, semantic, proairetic, cultural, and symbolic. "The five codes create a kind of network, a *topos* through which the entire text passes (or rather, in passing, becomes a text" (p. 20). By refusing "to structure each code, or the five codes among themselves," Barthes assumes that he provides a demonstration of the plurality or multivalence of the text. He claims that he thus provides "the semantic substance of several kinds of criticism (psychological, psychoanalytical, thematic, historical, structural) . . . which is the hearing of one of the voices of the text" (pp. 14–15).

Barthes refuses to present *an* interpretation, but he fails to admit that the various digressions, analyses of implications, discussions of what is going on in the story (suggestion of "an enigma," the building of suspense, or such things as the implications of the equivalence of sexual, economic, and literary elements, indeed, the sexual analogy with reading), or expressions of contempt for the outmoded "stereotypes" in Balzac's work, do at times imply not only a particular reader approaching the text efferently, but also one who again and again falls back on his own personal sense of the work.

Often in brilliantly striking and quixotic terms, Barthes sets forth ideas that are entirely congenial to my transactional theory: that the reader always approaches the text with a set of culturally acquired assumptions, values and ideas, and particular literary attitudes; that any text embodies semantic, literary and cultural elements or "codes"; that any text is susceptible to multiple readings. And he raises interesting semiotic questions, especially about narrative. What is lacking throughout is sufficient recognition of the essential dynamic interplay of particular reader and particular text. Any reading—no matter how rigidly classic and "readerly," any text—no matter whether potentially a work of art or not—requires some degree of "writerly" activities from a reader.

Moreover, Barthes's analysis takes for granted that a literary *work of art* is involved. He does not distinguish in his commentaries those "writerly" activities that might explain the evocation from this text of a work of art, and those that simply efferently present knowledge to be retained according to one or another analytic system. For the French structuralists, two kinds of confusion result: a conflation, so to speak, of the creative activities of the author and the reader, and failure to distinguish between the creative and efferent activities of the reader-critic. The underlying fallacy in this is the merging of efferent activities and comments about the text with the special experience-oriented aesthetic process that evokes a poem or story or play.

Structuralist analysis thus strikes one mainly as an efferent breaking-up of the text into atomistic segments classified by one or another system or code, or by such concepts drawn from linguistics as the synchronic versus the diachronic axes of interpretation. The mosaic is then rearranged and interpreted to the satisfaction of the critic-reader, guided by the assumptions of his code, for example, Freudian or Marxian. The efferent analysis, on the basis of which an "interpretation" is erected, may have its uses and its "validity" in terms of the particular codes adopted but still remains an activity that may or may not be relevant to the empirical aesthetic transaction between any living reader and that text—and that includes the structuralist critic-reader as well! The ultimate result of this ignoring of the literary work of art as a personal, transactional event in time is perhaps what some structuralists term "the destruction" or "deconstruction" of the text. In other words, they concentrate on the openness of the text as a *vide*, an abstract form, a vessel, into which meaning derived from one or another code or metalanguage is to be poured.

This contrast between the structuralist and transactional approaches reflects a much more basic contrast in the whole conception of the human being. In the structuralist analysis, not only is the text translated into a network of codes but the reader also dissolves into such a locus of intersecting systems. An important study points out this "aspect of Structuralism as a movement—its militant anti-humanism, as found both in Marxists (Althusser) and in anti-Marxists (Foucault) alike—[which] must be understood conceptually as a refusal of the older categories of human nature and of the notion that man (or human consciousness) is an intelligible entity or field of study in himself."[26]

If this were merely a rejection of the old notion of the ego as an isolable entity interacting with an external world, there would be no disagreement with the transactional view presented at the very outset of this discussion. Even the view of "the subject" or conscious-ness as a locus of relationships does not offer a problem for one who espouses transactional or ecological naturalism. Insistence on the transactional relationship between organism and environment, on each being a function of the other, carries with it the recognition that "the mind"—the world of "information processing"—is not limited by the skin. The implication to be rejected, however, is that the indi-vidual consciousness is somehow a kind of construction, something to be seen as merely a collection or intersection of patterned forces, social and natural.

To affirm that the individual consciousness embodies forces that transcend the biological organism, that there is no sharp division between the subjective consciousness and its object does not require dispensing with the vital, dynamic, active, empirical self. The Ames experiments described earlier dramatize the degree to which our perceptions are shaped by past experience and may mislead us. But those same experiments demonstrate that we can learn to see new clues and to impose new patterns of interpretation. Recall the Jame-sian view of the selective attention, the Deweyan reminder that the organism plays an active and selective role in the transactional re-sponse to environment. As important as the interdependence of the self and the world is the potentiality of choice among alternatives, the capacity to revise and reshape our perceptions and our actions.

Thus the transactional view, freeing us from the old separation between the human creature and the world, reveals the individual consciousness as a continuing self-ordering, self-creating process, shaped by and shaping a network of interrelationships with its envi-roning social and natural matrix. Out of such transactions flowers the author's text, an utterance awaiting the readers whose participation will consummate the speech act. By means of texts, we say, the individual may share in the funded knowledge and wisdom of our culture. For the individual reader, each text is a new situation, a new challenge. The literary work of art, we have seen, is an important kind of transaction with the environment precisely because it permits such self-aware acts of consciousness.

The reader, bringing his own particular temperament and fund of past transactions to the text, lives through a process of handling new situations, new attitudes, new personalities, new conflicts in values. These he can reject, revise, or assimilate into the resources with which he engages his world. The structuralists, the formalists, and others are entitled to choose whatever type of descriptive system they wish to use, and to focus on any level of analysis, but the essence of a work of art is precisely that a consciousness is living through a synthesizing evocation from a text which involves many—one is tempted to say all—levels of the organism. We should recognize that *any* attempt at efferently analyzing or describing this event singles out some aspects for attention and is not to be confused with, or substituted for, that particular moment of relatedness-between-the-organism-and-the-environment which we call a literary work of art.

Literary criticism calls for keen awareness of shifts in stance: the value of efferent generalizations or information would thus depend on their relevance to, their providing a context for, even an organizing framework for, the lived-through work, the total personal impact and human import of the literary transaction. Because the aesthetic stance has been taken for granted and neglected, I have insisted on the contrast between literary criticism and other modes of reading. In chapter 2 the contrast between the efferent and aesthetic stances was also at first formulated in the most extreme terms. As in the earlier discussion, it is now possible to recognize that my formulation of the paradigm for literary criticism represents a continuum: Most literary criticism will mingle reports of the aesthetic evocation with efferent analysis.

Such shuttling between the two modes is especially appropriate to critical studies of the author's creative process. Perhaps because many critics are, as it is claimed, *poètes manqués*, they often identify with the author behind the text and try to sense his problems, the alternatives open, and the forces guiding his choices. The critic seeks

173

all kinds of clues to the author's possible intention and scrutinizes the literary and biographical pressures at work. Sometimes the study of revisions or different versions of the text reveals the creative tensions that had to be resolved. The discussion of the author's intentions in chapter 6 reminded us, however, that the critic needs to test such clues on his own pulses, in the light of a scrupulous aesthetic reading of the text. This insures respect for the author's final text.

Perhaps the process envisaged in preceding pages should be termed "transactional criticism," to differentiate it both from so-called "objective" criticism and from self-exploiting narcissistic impressionism or subjectivism. The reader-critic savors as fully as possible his personal evocation during the lived-through transaction with the text. This is "the literary work of art." This is his subject. He must keep his sense of it as vividly and fully in mind as possible, as he goes on to ponder his response to it. He achieves a certain objectivity through reflective self-awareness, through understanding that the work envisaged is a product of the reverberations between what he has brought to the text and what the text offers. He seeks to understand how his own sense of life, his own values, coincide with, or differ from, the world that he has participated in through the transaction with the text. This kind of objectivity screens out the irrelevantly personal but, far from scientific impersonality, affirms the inexorably personal component. With the aesthetic transaction as his fulcrum, the reader-critic can range as far as he wishes, bringing to bear ever wider and richer circles of literary, social, ethical, and philosophical contexts.

The transactional concept can only reinforce interest in the dynamics of the relationship between the author, the text, the reader, and their cultural environments. Elsewhere, I have made a case for literary activities as an especially fertile matrix for study of social and historical processes.[27] Literary history, instead of being often a rather miscellaneous chronology, can provide data for study of the crystallization of convention, the rhythms of innovation and change, the interlocking tendrils of intellectual, institutional, and economic factors. Such study is actually part of the domain of, say, history or sociology or anthropology, and the practitioners of such disciplines become literary critics only through interest in specific encounters with specific texts. No matter how impersonal and objective, no matter how descriptive and technical, historical or critical interests may seem, the raw data, so to speak, must be individual personal encounters with texts. We peel off layer after layer of concerns brought to bear—social, biographical, historical, linguistic, textual—and at the center we find the inescapable transactional events between readers and texts.

The linked images of the author, the text, and the reader opened our discussion. The primary task has been to illuminate the reader's evocation of the literary work, to understand more fully the reader's role in that meeting of personalities and societies across time and space made possible by the author's text. Walt Whitman, that grandly individualistic yet profoundly social author, saw that his vision of a great literature for a truly democratic society required a vision, too, of the reader:

Books are to be call'd for, and supplied, on the assumption that the process of reading is not a half-sleep, but, in highest sense, an exercise, a gymnast's struggle; that the reader is to do something for himself, must be on the alert, must himself or herself construct indeed the poem, argument, history, metaphysical essay—the text furnishing the hints, the clue, the start or frame-work. Not the book needs so much to be the complete thing, but the reader of the book does. That were to make a nation of supple and athletic minds, well-train'd, intuitive, used to depend on themselves, and not on a few coteries of writers.[28]

Notes / Index

NOTES

1. THE INVISIBLE READER

1. Ralph Ellison, *Invisible Man* (New York: Random House, 1947), p. 3.
2. Émile Zola, *Mes Haines* (Paris: Charpentier, 1869), p. 229.
3. John Stuart Mill, "Thoughts on Poetry and Its Varieties," *Dissertations and Discussions* (London: John W. Parker, 1859), I, 71.
4. Louise Rosenblatt. *L'Idée de l'art pour l'art* (1931; rpt. New York: AMS Press, 1977), pp. 295 ff.
5. Anatole France, *La Vie Littéraire* (Paris: Calmann Levy, 1889), p. iii.
6. *Practical Criticism* (New York: Harcourt Brace, 1929).
7. Cf. Walter Sutton, *Modern American Criticism* (Englewood Cliffs, N.J.: Prentice Hall, Inc.), p. 98 ff.;
W. K. Wimsatt, *The Verbal Icon* (Lexington: University of Kentucky Press, 1954), pp. xvii, 32, and passim.
8. *Journal*, ed. D. M. Low (London: Chatto and Windus, 1929), p. 155, Item for 31 Oct. 1762.

2. THE POEM AS EVENT

1. Robert Frost, *Complete Poems* (New York: Henry Holt, 1949), p. 555.
2. Note that the following discussion draws on study of hundreds of such "protocols" responding to this and many other texts.
3. Wallace Stevens, *Collected Poems* (New York: Knopf, 1964), p. 358.
4. Aaron Copland, *Music and Imagination* (Cambridge, Mass.: Harvard University Press, 1953), p. 51. Cf. Roger Sessions, *The Musical Experience* (Princeton University Press, [1958]), pp. 82–83.
5. John Fowles, "Notes on an Unfinished Novel," in Thomas McCormack, ed., *Afterwords* (New York: Harper & Row, 1969), p. 170.
6. T. S. Eliot, *The Frontiers of Criticism* (Minneapolis: The Gideon D. Seymour Memorial Lecture Series [April 1956]), pp. 15–16, reprinted in *On Poetry and Poets* (New York: Noonday Press, 1961).
7. John Dewey and Arthur F. Bentley, *Knowing and the Known* (Boston: Beacon Press, 1949), p. 69 ff. and passim; A. F. Bentley, "Kennetic Inquiry," *Science*, 112 (29 Dec. 1950), 775–83, reprinted in *Inquiry into Inquiries*, ed. Sidney Ratner (Boston: Beacon Press, 1954), pp. 337–54; Sidney Ratner et al., eds., *John Dewey and Arthur F. Bentley: A Philosophical Correspondence, 1932–1951* (New Brunswick, N.J.: Rutgers University Press, 1964).
8. Arthur F. Bentley, "The Fiction of 'Retinal Image,' " in *Inquiry into Inquiries*, ed. Sidney Ratner (Boston: Beacon Press, 1954), p. 285.

9. John Dewey, "The Reflex Arc Concept in Psychology," *Psychological Review*, 3 (July 1896), 357–70, reprinted as "The Unit of Behavior," in *Philosophy and Civilization* (New York: Capricorn, 1963); quotation from "Conduct and Experience," ibid., p. 255.

10. Jean Piaget, *Structuralism*, tr. and ed. Chaninah Maschler (New York: Basic Books, 1970), pp. 71, 140, 142. See also, Jean Piaget, *Genetic Epistemology*, tr. Eleanor Duckworth (New York: Columbia University Press, 1970), pp. 16 ff.

11. Adelbert Ames, Jr., *The Nature of Our Perceptions, Prehensions and Behavior: An Interpretative Manual for the Demonstrations in the Psychology Research Center, Princeton University* (Princeton University Press, 1955) and "Reconsideration of the Origin and Nature of Perception," in Sidney Ratner, ed., *Vision and Action* (New Brunswick, N.J.: Rutgers University Press, 1953); Franklin P. Kilpatrick, ed., *Human Behavior from the Transactional Point of View* (Hanover, N.H.: Institute for Associated Research, 1952); Hadley Cantril and William K. Livingston, "The Concept of Transaction in Psychology and Neurology," *Journal of Individual Psychology*, 19 (May 1963), 3–16; Hadley Cantril, ed., *The Morning Notes of Adelbert Ames, Jr.* (New Brunswick, N.J.: Rutgers University Press, 1960); William H. Ittleson and Samuel B. Kutash, *Perceptual Change in Psychopathology* (New Brunswick, N.J.: Rutgers University Press, 1961). See also Gregory Bateson, *Steps to an Ecology of Mind* (New York: Ballantine Books, 1972), p. 463 and passim.

12. John R. Searle, *Speech Acts* (Cambridge University press, 1969).

13. Searle, p. 17.

14. C. E. Shannon and W. Weaver, *The Mathematical Theory of Communication* (Urbana: University of Illinois Press, 1949). See also, Colin Cherry, *On Human Communication* (New York: Wiley, 1957), p. 169.

15. Franz Boas, "Anthropology," *Encyclopaedia of the Social Sciences*, Vol. I (New York: Macmillan, 1937); Dell Hymes, ed., *Language in Culture and Society* (New York: Harper, 1964); Edward Sapir, *Selected Writings in Language, Culture, and Personality*, ed. David Mandelbaum, (Berkeley: University of California Press, 1949); Benjamin Lee Whorf, *Language, Thought, and Reality*, ed. John B. Carroll (Cambridge, Mass.: M.I.T. Press, 1956); J. Ruesch and G. Bateson, *Communication: The Social Matrix of Psychiatry* (New York: Norton, 1951); George A. Miller, *Language and Communication* (New York: McGraw Hill, 1951); James J. Jenkins, "Mediated Associations, Paradigms and Situations," in *Conference on Verbal Learning and Verbal Behavior*, ed. Charles N. Cofer and Barbara S. Musgrave (New York: McGraw Hill, 1963); Thomas A. Sebeok, Alfred S. Hayes, Mary Catherine Bateson, *Approaches to Semiotics* (The Hague: Mouton, 1964); D. S. Steinberg and L. A. Jakobovits, *Semantics* (Cambridge University Press, 1971); G. A. Miller and P. N. Johnson-Laird, *Language and Perception* (Cambridge, Mass.: Harvard University Press, 1976); J. Fodor, T. Bever and M. Garrett, *Psychology of Language* (New York: McGraw-Hill, 1974); Jack Kaminsky, *Language and Ontology* (Carbondale: Southern Illinois University Press, 1962), chap. 13.

3. EFFERENT AND AESTHETIC READING

1. Frank Smith, ed., *Psycholinguistics and Reading* (New York: Holt, Rinehart and Winston, 1973), pp. 8, 28, 70 ff.
2. John Keats, *The Poetical Works*, ed., H. W. Garrod (Oxford: Clarendon Press, 1958), p. 483.
3. S. T. Coleridge, *Biographia Literaria*, ed. J. Shawcross (London: Oxford University Press, 1907), II, 6.
4. Walter Pater, *The Renaissance* (London: Macmillan Co., 1920), p. 144.
5. Arthur Schopenhauer, *The World as Will and Idea*, tr. R. B. Haldane and J. Kemp (London: Routledge, 1957); Eliseo Vivas, *Creation and Discovery* (Chicago: Henry Regnery Co., 1965), p. 263; Edward Bullough, *Aesthetics*, ed. Elizabeth M. Wilkinson (Stanford, Calif.: Stanford University Press, 1957), p. 95; John Dewey, *Art as Experience* (New York: Minton, Balch, & Co., 1934), pp. 252–53; Immanuel Kant, *Critique of Aesthetic Judgment*, tr. James Creed Meredith (Oxford: Clarendon Press, 1911), Introduction.
6. In 1926, "the importation of [Brancusi's] sculptures was held up by the United States customs who regarded them not as works of art, which may enter free of duty, but as manufactured metal implements, and stamped them 'block matter—subject to tax.' " After two years of litigation, the case was resolved in the artist's favor. David Lewis, *Constantin Brancusi* (London: Academy Editions, 1974), p. 13; the most complete account of the case is in Carola Giedion-Welcker, *Constantin Brancusi*, tr. M. Jolas and A. Leroy (New York: George Braziller, 1959), pp. 212–19.
7. *Biographia*, II, 6.
8. Wallace Stevens, *The Man with the Blue Guitar* (New York: Knopf, 1952), p. 28.
9. (New York: Harcourt Brace, 1949), pp. 15 ff.
10. P. W. Bridgman, *The Logic of Modern Physics* (New York: Macmillan, 1927), p. 5; P. W. Bridgman, "Operational Analysis," in *Reflections of a Physicist*, p. 5 and passim. Cf. Philipp Frank, *Modern Science and Its Philosophy* (Cambridge, Mass.: Harvard University Press, 1959), p. 44; Alfred J. Ayer, ed., *Logical Positivism* (Glencoe, Ill.: Free Press, 1959); Alfred J. Ayer, *Language, Truth, and Logic*, 2d ed. (London: Gollancz, 1946); B. F. Skinner, *Verbal Behavior* (New York: Appleton-Century-Crofts, 1957). See review by Noam Chomsky, *Language*, 35 (1959), 26–58, reprinted in J. A. Fodor and J. A. Katz, eds., *The Structure of Language* (Englewood Cliffs, N. J.: Prentice-Hall, 1964), pp. 547 ff.
11. Ferdinand de Saussure, *Cours de linguistique générale*, ed. C. Bally and A. Sechehaye (Paris: Payot, 1916), Introduction, chap. 4; and Tullio de Mauro, Introduction to 1976 edition, p. v. Cf. Leonard Bloomfield, *Language* (New York: Holt, Rinehart & Winston, 1933).
12. Noam Chomsky, *Aspects of the Theory of Syntax* (Cambridge, Mass.: M.I.T. Press, 1965); Noam Chomsky, *Language and Mind* (New York: Harcourt, Brace & World, 1968); John Lyons, ed., *New Horizons in Linguis-*

tics (London, Penguin Books, 1970); Jerrold J. Katz, *The Philosophy of Language* (New York: Harper & Row, 1966).

13. Eric Wanner, "Do We Understand Sentences from the Outside-In or from the Inside-Out?" *Daedalus*, 102 (Summer 1973), 164. See also Ragnar Rommetveit, *Words, Meanings, and Messages* (New York: Academic Press, 1968), p. 29 and passim; George A. Miller, E. Galanter, and K. H. Pribram, *Plans and the Structure of Behavior* (New York: Holt, Rinehart & Winston, 1960).

14. Charles E. Osgood, George J. Suci, and Percy H. Tannenbaum, *The Measurement of Meaning* (Urbana: University of Illinois Press, 1957).

15. Rommetveit, p. 167; see also H. Werner and B. Kaplan, *Symbol Formation* (New York: Wiley, 1963).

16. L. S. Vygotsky, *Thought and Language*, ed. and tr. Eugenia Hanfmann and Gertrude Vakar (Cambridge, Mass.: M.I.T. Press, 1962), pp. 8, 40, 124 ff.; Jean Piaget, *The Language and Thought of the Child*, tr. Marjorie Gabar (New York: Humanities Press [1926]).

17. William James, *The Principles of Psychology* (New York: Henry Holt, 1890), I, 284–86; *Radical Empiricism* (New York: Longmans Green, 1912), pp. 10, 11, 145. See also, Dewey, "Reflex Arc" (supra fn. 9, chap. 2) and Bentley, *Inquiry*, p. 242; David J. Mostofsky, ed., *Attention: Contemporary Theory and Analysis* (New York: Appleton-Century-Crofts, 1971), pp. 62–63, 72–74; and Eleanor and James Gibson, "The Senses as Information-seeking Systems," *Times Literary Supplement*, 23 June 1971, p. 711; Jerome Bruner, *On Knowing: Essays for the Left Hand* (Cambridge, Mass.: Harvard University Press, 1962), p. 6: "Selectivity is the rule and a nervous system, in Lord Adrian's phrase, is as much an editorial hierarchy as it is a system for carrying signals."

18. W. K. Wimsatt, Jr., "The Affective Fallacy," *The Verbal Icon* (New York: Noonday Press, 1958), p. 21.

19. W. H. Auden, "In Memory of W. B. Yeats," *Collected Poems* (New York: Random House, 1945), p. 48.

4. EVOKING A POEM

1. S. T. Coleridge, *Biographia Literaria*, ed. J. Shawcross (London: Oxford University Press, 1907), I, 202. See also, *Miscellaneous Criticism*, ed. Thomas M. Raysor (London: Constable and Co., 1936), pp. 42–43.

2. See, e.g., Rudolf Arnheim et al., *Poets at Work* (New York: Harcourt Brace, 1948); Virginia Woolf, *A Writer's Diary*, ed. Leonard Woolf (New York: Harcourt, Brace Jovanovich, 1954), and Virginia Woolf, *The Pargiters*, ed. and with an Introduction by Mitchell A. Leaska (New York Public Library and Readex Books, 1977), a study of "the artist at work."

3. George A. Miller, E. Galanter, and K. H. Pribram, *Plans and the Structure of Behavior* (New York: Henry Holt, 1960).

4. *Miscellaneous Criticism*, p. 89; *Shakespearean Criticism*, ed. Thomas Middleton Raysor (London: Constable and Co., 1930), I, 233; II, 170–71.

5. See Louise M. Rosenblatt, *Literature as Exploration,* 3d ed. (New York: Noble and Noble, 1976; now distributed by the Modern Language Association), chap. 6.

6. William Empson, *Seven Types of Ambiguity* (London: Chatto & Windus, 1930), p. 3; *Shakespeare's Songs and Poems,* ed. Edward Hubler (New York: McGraw-Hill, 1959).

7. Shirley Jackson, *The Lottery* (New York: Farrar, 1949), p. 1.

8. Kenneth S. Goodman, "Psycholinguistic Universals in the Reading Process," in Frank Smith, ed. *Psycholinguistics and Reading* (New York: Holt, Rinehart and Winston, 1973), pp. 23–27. Dr. Kenneth Goodman and Dr. Yetta Goodman have been leaders in developing methods of analysis of the nature of children's "miscues" as a means of helping each individually to develop strategies of handling responses to the printed word.

Recognizing that his discussion concentrates on efferent reading, Dr. Goodman notes briefly that "the reader needs strategies that adjust to very different constraints in literary materials," but does not develop this point. One important difference, of course, is that the substitution of efferently synonymous words would have to be treated very differently in aesthetic reading. The notion of "comprehension" changes.

9. *The Poems of Emily Dickinson,* ed. Thomas H. Johnson (Cambridge, Mass.: Harvard University Press, 1958), I, 358.

10. My findings concerning the importance of attitudes toward the fly are reinforced by an interchange in the *Explicator,* (Nov. 1961). Caroline Hogue indicates the lines of the continuing argument:

Here in this poem the central figure of the drama is expected to make a glorious exit. The build-up is just right for it, but at the moment of climax . . .—a blowfly.

How right is Mr. Gerhard Friedrich in his explication of April, 1955, (XIII, 35) to associate the fly with putrefaction and decay. And how wrong, I think, is Mr. John Ciardi in his of January, 1956 (XIV, 22), in calling the fly "the last kiss of the world," and speaking of it as one of the small creatures Emily Dickinson so delighted in. She could not possibly have entertained any such view of a blowfly. She was a practical housewife, and every housewife abhors a blowfly. It pollutes everything it touches. Its eggs are maggots. It is as carrion as a buzzard.

11. *Psychology,* I, 225, 276 ff.

12. A. C. Bradley, *Shakespearean Tragedy* (New York: Macmillan, 1952), p. 317.

5. THE TEXT: OPENNESS AND CONSTRAINT

1. Edward Sapir, *Language* (New York: Harcourt Brace, 1921), p. 41.

2. Morris Bishop, *New Yorker,* 26 Oct. 1946, p. 34.

3. Samuel A. Levine, *Clinical Heart Disease* (Philadelphia: W. B. Saunders Co., 1958), p. 103.

4. Colin Cherry, *On Human Communication* (New York: Wiley, 1957), pp. 273–76.

5. Jerry A. Fodor and Jerrold J. Katz, eds., *The Structure of Language* (Englewood Cliffs, N.J.: Prentice-Hall, 1964), pp. 483–89.

6. Charles C. Fries, *The Structure of English* (New York: Harcourt, Brace and World, 1952), p. 70.

7. Ronald Gross, "Found Poetry," in *Page 2*, ed. Francis Brown (New York: Holt, Rinehart and Winston), p. 157.

8. *Essays in Criticism*, 2d ser. (London: Macmillan, 1915), "Wordsworth," pp. 157–58; "The Study of Poetry," p. 17.

9. *Seven Types of Ambiguity* (London: Chatto and Windus, 1930), p. 103.

10. *Shakespeare's Sonnets*, ed. A. L. Rowse (New York: Harper and Row, 1964), p. 148.

11. Rowse, p. 149.

12. Kenneth S. Goodman, in Frank Smith, *Psycholinguistics and Reading* (New York: Holt, Rinehart and Winston, 1973), p. 25; Frank Smith states it even more directly: "1. Only a small part of the information necessary for reading comprehension comes from the printed page. 2. Comprehension must precede the identification of individual words. 3. Reading is not decoding to spoken language" (p. v).

13. *Encyclopedia of Poetry and Poetics*, ed. Alex Preminger (Princeton University Press, 1965), "Form," pp. 286–88, by G. N. G. Orsini; "Structure," pp. 812–13, by Martin Steinmann, Jr.

14. Clive Bell, *Art* (New York: Stokes, 1914).

15. *Biographia*, II, 10. See John Dewey, *Art as Experience* (New York: Minton Balch and Co., 1934), chap. 6, "Substance and Form"; A. C. Bradley, "Poetry for Poetry's Sake," in *Oxford Lectures on Poetry* (Oxford: Clarendon Press, 1909).

16. "In every novel the work is divided between the writer and the reader; but the writer makes the reader very much as he makes his characters. When he makes him ill, that is, makes him [in] different, he does no work; the writer does all. When he makes him well, that is, makes him interested, then the reader does quite half the labor." Henry James, *Views and Reviews*, "The Novels of George Eliot" (Boston: Ball, 1908), p. 18 (originally published in *Atlantic Monthly* [Aug. 1866]).

17. Alain Robbe-Grillet, *For a New Novel*, tr. R. Howard (New York: Grove Press, 1966).

18. I. A. Richards, *Philosophy of Rhetoric* (New York: Oxford University, 1936), pp. 89–112; *Princeton Encyclopedia*, "Metaphor"; René Wellek and Austin Warren, *Theory of Literature* (New York: Harcourt Brace, 1949), chap. 15; Philip Wheelwright, *The Burning Fountain* (Bloomington: Indiana University Press, 1954); Max Black, "Metaphor" *Proceedings of the Aristotelian Society*, NS 55 (1955), reprinted in *Models and Metaphors* (Ithaca, N.Y.: Cornell University Press, 1962). (Current work on the respective contributions of the two sides of the brain may have relevance for my position here.)

19. *Principles of Literary Criticism* (London: Kegan Paul, Trench,

Trubner, 1934), p. 240; see also, W. B. Stanford, *Greek Metaphor* (Oxford: Blackwell, 1936), p. 101.

20. Ragnar Rommetveit, *Words, Meanings, and Messages* (New York: Academic Press, 1968) pp. 30, 80–81. Cf. Dan Sperber, *Rethinking Symbolism*, tr. Alice L. Morton (Cambridge University Press, 1975), which came to my attention after the above pages were written.

21. *Practical Criticism*, p. 216.

22. Laurence Perrine, "The Importance of Tone in the Interpretation of Literature," *College English* (Feb. 1963), 395.

23. William Blake, *Poems*, ed. W. H. Stevenson (London: Longman, 1971), pp. 216–17.

24. E.g., Mark Schorer, *William Blake: The Politics of Vision* (New York: Henry Holt, 1946), p. 242; Kathleen Raine, *Blake and Tradition* (Princeton University Press, 1968), I, 200.

25. Fredson Bowers, "Textual Criticism and the Literary Critic," in *Bibliography, Text, and Editing* (Charlottesville: University Press of Virginia, 1975), pp. 320–21.

6. THE QUEST FOR "THE POEM ITSELF"

1. T. S. Eliot, *Selected Essays*, new ed. (Harcourt, Brace, 1950), p. 11.

2. Eliot, pp. 124–25.

3. René Wellek and Austin Warren, *Theory of Literature*, 3d ed. (New York: Harcourt Brace and World, 1956), p. 146. All further references to this work appear in the text.

4. Roman Ingarden, *The Literary Work of Art*, tr. George G. Grabowicz (Chicago, Ill.: Northwestern University Press, 1973); "Phenomenological Aesthetics," *Journal of Aesthetics and Art Criticism*, 33, No. 3 (Spring 1975), 260, a paper presented at Amsterdam in 1969 and first published in Polish in 1970.

5. (New Haven, Conn.: Yale University Press, 1967), p. 1. All further references to this work appear in the text.

6. In W. K. Wimsatt, Jr., *The Verbal Icon* (New York: Noonday Press, 1958), pp. 5–18.

7. Banesh Hoffmann, *Albert Einstein* (New York: Viking, 1972); Marston Morse, "Mathematics, the Arts, and Freedom," *Thought*, 34 (Spring 1959); Norwood Russell Hanson, *Patterns of Discovery* (Cambridge University Press, 1958); Henri Poincaré, *The Foundations of Science*, tr. G. B. Halstead (New York: Science Press, 1913), chap. 9, "Science and Hypothesis"; Anthony Storr, *The Dynamics of Creation* (New York: Athenaeum, 1972), p. 67; Thomas S. Kuhn, *The Structure of Scientific Revolutions*, 2d ed. (University of Chicago Press, 1970); Stephen E. Toulmin, *Human Understanding* (Princeton University Press, 1972).

8. Gottlob Frege, "Ueber Sinn und Bedeutung: A Translation by Max Black," *Philosophical Review*, 57, No. 3 (May 1948), 215 ff.

9. *Essays in Criticism*, 2, No. 1 (Jan. 1952): "The Critical Forum," " 'In-

tention' and Blake's *Jerusalem*," pp. 105–14 (John Wain, pp. 105–6, 110–11; F. W. Bateson, pp. 106–10, 113–14; W. W. Robson, pp. 111–13); F. W. Bateson, *English Poetry* (London: Longmans, 1950), p. 7.

10. See Kathleen Raine, *Blake and Tradition* (Princeton University Press), I, 274–77; Mona Wilson, *The Life of William Blake* (New York: Cooper Square Publishers, 1969), pp. 159 ff.; David Erdman, *Prophet Against Empire* (Princeton University Press, 1954), pp. vii, viii, 367–68.

11. The quotations are cited as from Brooks's "Irony as a Principle of Structure," in M. D. Zabel, ed., *Literary Opinion in America*, 2d ed. (New York: Harper, 1951), p. 736; and from Bateson, *English Poetry*, pp. 33, 80–81.

12. *Complete Poems*, ed. Basil Davenport (New York: Holt, Rinehart and Winston, 1965), p. 9.

13. Frank Harris, *Contemporary Portraits* (New York: Macauley Co., 1927), p. 280.

14. Cf. Charles C. Walcutt, "Housman and the Empire: An Analysis of '1887,' " *College English*, 5, No. 3 (Feb. 1944), 255–58; W. L. Werner, "Housman's '1887'—No Satire," *College English*, 6, No. 3 (Dec. 1944), 165–66; T. S. K. Scott-Craig, Charles C. Walcutt, and Cleanth Brooks in *Explicator* 2 (Mar. 1944) 34–35; Cleanth Brooks, "Alfred Edward Housman," *Anniversary Lectures* (Washington, D.C.: Library of Congress 1959), pp. 48–51.

15. *The Waste Land: A Facsimile and Transcript of the Original Drafts*, ed. Valerie Eliot (New York: Harcourt Brace Jovanovich, 1971).

16. *Reason in Art*, Vol. IV of *The Life of Reason* (New York: Scribner's, 1906), p. 128.

17. Ludwig Wittgenstein, *Philosophical Investigations*, tr. G. E. M. Anscombe (New York: Macmillan, 1953), pp. 31 ff.

18. Clark Griffith, *The Long Shadow: Emily Dickinson's Tragic Poetry* (Princeton University Press, 1964), pp. 135–37.

7. INTERPRETATION, EVALUATION, CRITICISM

1. *The Renaissance*, New Library Edition (London, 1910), p. viii.

2. Pater, pp. 124–25.

3. *The Second Common Reader* (Harcourt Brace, 1932), pp. 290–91.

4. Maud Bodkin, *Archetypal Patterns in Poetry* (New York: Vintage Books, 1958), p. 323.

5. See Rosenblatt, *L'Idée de l'art pour l'art*.

6. *On Poetry and Poets* (New York: Noonday Press, 1961), pp. 121, 127.

7. E.g., Valéry Larbaud, "James Joyce," *Nouvelle Revue Française*, 18 (1922), 385–405; Stuart Gilbert, *James Joyce's Ulysses* (London: Faber and Faber, 1930); Samuel Beckett et al., *Our Exagmination Round His Factification for Incamination of Work in Progress* (London: Faber and Faber, 1929). See Richard Ellman, *James Joyce* (New York: Oxford University Press, 1959), chap. 32 passim and pp. 715–16, 730.

A half century later, *Ulysses* can still be characterized by an admiring critic: "In the last analysis, however, the reading of *Ulysses* (and this holds good for *Finnegans Wake* as well) is not just the study of an artifact. It is a confrontation with the writer; a conflict of the reading public with Joyce's ego." Leo Knuth, "Joyce's Verbal Acupuncture," in *Ulysses/Fifty Years*, ed. T. F. Staley (Bloomington: Indiana University Press, 1974).

8. Saul Bellow, "The Nobel Lecture," *American Scholar* (Summer 1977), pp. 316–25.

9. Cleanth Brooks, "Foreword," in R. W. Stallman, *Critiques and Essays in Criticism* (New York: Ronald Press, 1959), p. xx.

10. Niels Bohr, "Discussion with Einstein on Epistemological Problems in Atomic Physics," in *Albert Einstein, Philosopher-Scientist*, ed. Paul A. Schilpp (New York: Harper, 1949), p. 210; Werner Heisenberg, "The Representation of Nature in Contemporary Physics," *Daedalus* (Summer 1958), pp. 95–108.

11. *Practical Criticism*, pp. 13–18.

12. Cf. *Literature as Exploration*, chap. 7 and pp. 292–98.

13. Jack L. Leedy, ed., *Poetry Therapy* (Philadelphia: J. B. Lippincott, 1969), pp. 88, 103; Caroline Shrodes, "Bibliotherapy: A Theoretical and Clinical Experimental Study," Diss. University of California 1949; but see Frederick Crews, *Out of My System: Psychoanalysis, Ideology, and Critical Method* (New York: Oxford University Press, 1975); Leon Edel, "Psychoanalysis and the 'Creative Arts,' " in Judd Marmor, ed., *Modern Psychoanalysis* (New York: Basic Books, 1968), pp. 626–41.

14. L. N. Tolstoy, *What Is Art?* tr. Aylmer Maude (London: Oxford University Press [1932]).

15. *Appreciations* (London: Macmillan, 1910), p. 38.

16. *L'Idée de l'art pour l'art*, "Conclusion" and passim; *Literature as Exploration*, pp. 24, 42–48.

17. *Biographia*, II, 11; Edgar Allan Poe, "The Poetic Principle," in *Works*, ed. E. C. Stedman and G. E. Woodberry (New York: Scribner's, 1914), VI, 3–4.

18. Meyer Schapiro, "Style," in *Anthropology Today*, ed. Sol Tax (University of Chicago Press, 1962), pp. 278–303; Dell E. Hymes, "Phonological Aspects of Style," in Thomas A. Sebeok, ed., *Style in Language* (New York: Wiley, 1960), pp. 115–16, 130:

Another limitation which, as far as I know, all stylistic approaches share is the making of untested assumptions about the psychology of poet or audience. Many of these assumptions are reasonable and intuitively correct to the student or practitioner of verbal art. But we do not in fact know that the use of a sound in one part of a poem has any effect on a reader in a subsequent part; we have no "just noticeable differences" for the prominence of sounds by repetition in a sonnet. Rather we analyze the poem, construct an interpretation, and postulate (or instruct) the reader's response.

19. *Shakespeare's Imagery and What It Tells Us* (Cambridge University Press, 1936).

20. (New York: Hill and Wang [1951]), p. 8. All further references to this work appear in the text.

21. Thomas A. Sebeok, ed., *Style in Language* (New York: Wiley, 1960), pp. 350–77.

22. Elmer Holenstein, *Roman Jakobson's Approach to Language*, tr. C. Schelbert and T. Schelbert (Bloomington: Indiana University Press, 1974), p. 86.

23. Roman Jakobson and Lawrence Jones, *Shakespeare's Verbal Art in "Th'expence of Spirit"* (The Hague: Mouton, 1970). I had the pleasure of hearing Professor Jakobson discuss this in his Gauss Seminar lectures at Princeton University in 1968.

24. Cf. Eric H. Lenneberg, *Biological Foundations of Language* (New York: Wiley, 1967), "Postscript to so-called language relativity," pp. 364–65.

25. Among those referred to under this rubric: Roland Barthes, Jacques Derrida, Michel Foucault, Jacques Lacan, Paul Ricoeur, Tzvetan Todorov. See Roland Barthes, *On Racine*, tr. Richard Howard (New York: Hill and Wang, 1964); *Writing Degree Zero and Elements of Semiology* (Boston: Beacon, 1970); *S/Z*, tr. Richard Miller (New York: Hill and Wang, 1974) (page references in the text are to this edition); Michel Foucault, *The Order of Things (Les Mots et les Choses)* (New York: Pantheon, 1971); Claude Lévi-Strauss, *Structural Anthropology*, tr. Claire Jacobson and Brooks Schoepf (New York: Basic Books, 1963); *The Raw and the Cooked* (New York: Harper and Row, 1969). Cf. Serge Dubrovsky, *The New Criticism in France*, tr. D. Coltman, with an Introduction by Edward Wasiolek (University of Chicago Press, 1973); Umberto Eco, *A Theory of Semiotics* (Bloomington: University of Indiana Press, 1976); Robert Scholes, *Structuralism in Literature* (New Haven, Conn.: Yale University Press, 1974), "Bibliographical Appendix."

26. Frederic Jameson, *The Prison-House of Language* (Princeton University Press, 1972), pp. 139–40.

27. *Literature as Exploration*, pp. 249–71.

28. "Democratic Vistas," in *Prose Works 1892*, ed. Floyd Stovall (New York: New York University Press, 1964), II, 424–25. See Louise M. Rosenblatt, "Whitman's *Democratic Vistas* and the New 'Ethnicity,' " *Yale Review*, 67, No. 2 (Winter 1978), 187–204.

INDEX

189

Index

Bodkin, Maud, 134
Bohr, Niels: "Discussion with Einstein," 187n10
Book of Isaiah, 35, 36, 45
Booth, Wayne C., 93n, 128n
Bowers, Fredson, 99–100
Bradley, A. C., 66
Brancusi, Constantin: his sculpture, *Bird in Space*, 31, 181
Bridgman, Percy W., 40, 72, 112
Brooks, Cleanth: on "A slumber did my spirit seal," 116–18
Bruner, Jerome: *On Knowing*, 182n17; mentioned, xiii
Burns, Robert: "O, my luve is like a red, red rose," 93–4
Butor, Michel: and Barthes, 169–70

Camus, Albert: *The Plague*, 38; *Man's Fate*, 150
Cantril, Hadley: on perception, xiii, 18
Carroll, Lewis: *Alice in Wonderland*, 79; "Jabberwocky," 80
Carson, Rachel: *Silent Spring*, 45
Characters: as evoked by readers from texts, 67–68, 127, 136
Chomsky, Noam: *Aspects of the Theory of Syntax*, 181n12; *Language and Mind*, 181n12; mentioned, 95
Cinema as art form: and diversified public, 159–60
Clemen, Wolfgang: *The Development of Shakespeare's Imagery*, 164; on audience, 164–65
Codes: linguistic, semantic, literary, social, cultural, visual, drawn on by reader, 91. *See also* Cues; Reading process
Coleridge, Samuel Taylor: on poetry and poets, 2, 4, 28, 158; on "suspension of disbelief," 32; on "Lyrical Ballads," 32, 39; on creative process, 50, 114; *Biographia Literaria*, 50
Communication: through reader's report on aesthetic event, 135; use of various media to create analogous experiences, 135–36; between author and reader, 146; among readers, 146–47
Concurrent streams of response: in reading process, 68–70
Conference on Methods in Philosophy and the Sciences, xiv
Contemplation as criterion of the aesthetic: views of various thinkers on, 30; differentiated from concept of aesthetic stance, 30. *See also* Aesthetic stance

Copland, Aaron: *Music and the Imagination*, 179n4
Critic: as reader, 137–38; relation to general readers, 138–43; as mediator between authors and public, 139; as fellow reader, 147–50; assumptions and personality patterns of, 149–50; essential requirements for literary, 162. *See also* Criticism
Criticism: rooted in reading process, 137; "age of," 139; basic paradigm for literary, 162; as continuum of aesthetic and efferent reading, 173; transactional, 174; mentioned passim
Cues: role in reading process, 51–52, 55–56, 64
Culture: interaction between reader and text from another culture, 121–30; readers in same, 128–30; readers in Anglo-American and Mediterranean cultures, 146–47n; values in different cultures, 152–53

Debussy, Claude: *L'Après Midi d'un Faune*, 135
Detective story: and reader's response, 159
Dewey, John: *Art as Experience*, xi; and phenomenology, xiv, 111n; on transaction, 16–18; and aesthetic experience, 37; humanistic view of the individual, 172; "The Reflex Arc Concept in Psychology," 180n9; *Philosophy and Civilization*, 180n9
Dickens, Charles: *David Copperfield*, 154; mentioned, 67
Dickinson, Emily: readings of her "I heard a Fly buzz," 63–65, 127, 136
Divine Comedy, The, 108, 135
Dostoyevsky, Fyodor: *The Brothers Karamazov*, 154
Doyle, Sir Arthur Conan: writings, 31
Donne, John: "Death, be not proud," 158
Dreiser, Theodore, 25

Eco, Umberto: *A Theory of Semiotics*, 188n25
Education: of readers, xi–xiii, 142–43, 146n; critic as teacher, 148
Efferent stance: defined, 25–27; mentioned passim. *See also* Aesthetic and efferent reading
Einstein, Albert: formula, $E=mc^2$, 73–74
Eiseley, Loren: *The Immense Journey*, 36
Eliot, George: *Middlemarch*, 153
Eliot, Thomas Stearns: on unified sensi-

Index

work, 121–22

Wellek, René: on fictionality and literature, 35; *Theory of Literature*, 35, 103; on autonomy of the literary work of art, 103–8; on the "life" of a literary work, 121; on Jakobson, 166

Wertheimer, Max: on productive thinking, xiii

Whitehead, Alfred North, xiv

Whitman, Walt: "O Captain! My Captain!" 74; on importance of the reader, 175

Whorf, Benjamin Lee: on limits of language, 168; *Language, Thought, and Reality*, 180n15

Wimsatt, W. K.: "The Intentional Fallacy," 109; *The Verbal Icon*, 179n7

Wittgenstein, Ludwig: works of, xiv; ordinary language approach of, 40; on families of usages, 122; *Philosophical Investigations*, 122

Women: as writers and critics, 142

Woolf, Virginia: on structuring one's sense of a book, 133–34, 152; "How Should One Read a Book?" 133

Wordsworth, William: on poetry and poets, 2, 4; on suspension of disbelief, 32; "Michael," 84; "A slumber did my spirit seal," 116–18, 127; "Lines, Written above Tintern Abbey," 117–18; "The Prelude," 118

Yeats, William Butler: "Byzantium," 23, 153; his poetry and readers, 44–45; Auden on, 44–45, 49; and Pater's Mona Lisa, 132